FAIR OR *FOUL*
THE COMPLETE GUIDE TO SOCCER OFFICIATING IN AMERICA

FOURTH EDITION

by

Paul E. Harris Jr.
&
Larry R. Harris

SOCCER FOR AMERICANS
Box 836
Manhattan Beach, California 90266

COVER BY JINGER HEFFNER

Library of Congress Catalog Number 83-61551

ISBN 0-916802-20-5

Printed in the U.S.A.

ACKNOWLEDGEMENTS

Dedicated to

The Referees... wherever they are.

With special thanks to:

The American Youth Soccer Organization

FIFA... For permission to present the laws

Ken Aston,
a man who comes along every generation or so.
Referee, lecturer, administrator, friend of all Referees,
but most of all, a wonderful human being.

Bill Mason,
who knows so much about the laws, he could have
written them himself. Bill was very helpful in the revision.

Bill Mason (left) and Ken Aston.

i

About the authors . . .

PAUL HARRIS – *"The majority of Referees lead lives of quiet desperation."*

Paul spends most of his time trying to create a better soccer world. His eleven books have been widely accepted, and in some cases even read by a few coaches who want to win games or players who want to do a bit more than stand on their left leg. And, one or two referees who want to survive have consulted his writings.

He bought a referee uniform and kept it in the closet for five years before he had the courage to whistle his first game. For five years he was National Director of Officiating for the American Youth Soccer Organization (AYSO), and has been in the middle for more than 1000 games with them. With AYSO, he began the Referee Camps, conceived the TRIO program for referee observation, and developed the PHield Test.

Still active as a referee, Paul has whistled club, high school, college, and professional soccer, including assignments as a Linesman in the NASL and ASL. As an evaluator, he has been asked to impose his opinions on referees in the NASL, ASL, and MISL. Paul has two ambitions relating to soccer: to score 100% on a referee test, and to convince one person that he is not related to Larry. (He is not.)

LARRY HARRIS – *"It's possible to do it by the book and get along. Just make sure it's the right book."*

Larry walked up to his co-author with an armload of conflicting rule interpretations in the Fall of 1971. Within three days, the idea for the book was born, and he went to work. A Human Factors Scientist, he has worked for and worried over consistent interpretation of the laws. He has taught in clinics and camps and served for a number of years as Commissioner of Certification in high school and college referee organizations. He has shown up for assignments in high school, college, club and professional competitions. Most of his games were completed.

Larry is the author of *FUTBOL MEANS SOCCER, Easy Steps to Understanding the Game,* and *SCORE, A Complete Training Course and Reference Manual for Baseball Score-keepers.* Both of these books are unique to their field.

He keeps in shape during the off-season by turning the pages of the law book, and umpiring high school and college baseball and softball. He has been known to run 30 or 40 feet to "sell" his calls. An avid roller skater, he competes in skating marathons and skates 20 miles to work. He is not Paul's father, son, brother, uncle, or cousin, but has admitted to all but one of those.

ii

INTRODUCTION TO THE FOURTH EDITION

Where have we been? It's been five years since the last *FAIR OR FOUL*. This is the same time frame which separated the first three editions combined! It's not that we aren't just as involved; perhaps it's taken us a little longer to evolve. We hope you are different, for change is constant. A new look at the game will serve you well as you progress. Our change has brought some hard thinking as to what is really important in Referee training.

As we see it, there are some things that have happened since our Third Edition:

1. The general standard of officiating is improving, with greater cooperation between Referee and Linesmen.

2. Better soccer at all levels is evolving, and the demands on the official are greater.

3. The Two Referee System, now gone from our colleges, is used only where money, referees, and training are in short supply.

4. The Modified Diagonal System (MOD) is struggling for acceptance, and the Diagonal System is becoming accepted in all areas of the country.

5. Referee assessment programs are emerging at each level of the game, though sensitive and non-threatening assessment is still a rarity.

6. Indoor soccer, a truly American sport, is presenting new and exciting challenges to the Referee.

7. Television in all its forms is with us, and players and referees alike are influenced by decisions viewed on the screen.

Happily, we find more correct information floating about at coaches' meetings, referee get-togethers, and on the sideline during games. We have entered a new era, where some basic correct decisions are being accepted, and sometimes even understood.

There are some excellent models for us to follow on the field, and they are visible everywhere. Some of the best refereeing is seen in volunteer youth programs, where the player comes first. Who could genuinely argue with the Referee who allowed a foul throw-in to be retaken, saying, "If he doesn't get it right now, he *never* will!" Naturally, we can't sanction such behavior of referees, but we must secretly applaud the understanding that so many of you have regarding what is really important. Nor can we criticize the Referee who allowed a kickoff when the ball traveled laterally on a kickoff. "Don't worry, I'll call what's important," was the ref's response to "Hey, ref, what about . . . "

We hope that each time you walk, not strut, on the field, you'll feel those goose bumps of excitement, and that your confidence and full control will emerge. We want each of you to continue to feel you're the best Referee for that game, and that you'll handle anything that comes your way. Be tough when you have to, intimidated by none. Be consistent without being predictable, knowing that total consistency is impossible. Be decisive, courageous, and honest. Above all, be human. Refereeing a soccer game in the best spirit may be one of the toughest tasks you'll ever face, and the most rewarding. We're with you.

REFEREEING... And the Need for a Universal Spirit

by Ken Aston

There were no Referees in the matches played during the first few years following the formation of The Football Association in England in 1863. The games were 'friendly' by definition and any matters in dispute were settled by the captains; the field of play was an arena for sport and sportsmen in every sense of the word. However, in 1871, the Football Association Challenge Cup Competition was started and the will to win became more intense. It was found necessary to appoint umpires, one to each half of the field, and a Referee stationed outside the field of play. The umpires were equipped with a handkerchief which could be waved to stop play. The umpires would then confer and having agreed, would award the appropriate punishment and restart the game. In cases of disagreement, they would refer the matter in dispute to the Referee, whose decision was final.

The advent of professionals in the game in the early 1890's increased not only the will to win but the need to win - if necessary at all costs - and in 1895 the Referee was moved into the field where he could more efficiently control not only the game but the players as well. The umpires were given flags, and ran up and down the touchlines the whole length of the field. Their duties were now restricted to signalling the ball in and out of play and giving an opinion when required by the Referee.

Match Control Develops

This system of match control continued virtually unchanged until 1934 when Sir Stanley Rous, at that time a Referee of International and Football League status, arrived to referee a match at Luton Town. The field was a sea of mud and it was raining heavily. Movement up and down the field, an essential for the current system of match control, was going to be very difficult if not impossible. As the world of football was to learn later when Sir Stanley became first Secretary of the F.A. and then President of F.I.F.A., he was a man of ideas and initiative. He sketched out a plan whereby his linesmen would each cover half of the field only and thus each be responsible for one set of forwards. They would always be on the spot for indications of Offside and for goal-line decisions. He as Referee would take care of mid-field, and not be obliged to run to the extremes of the field. On that day was born the Diagonal System of Control which, with amplifying notes and diagrams, was accepted by The International Board in 1936. It became universally practiced, and exists to this day.

Need for Consistent Interpretation

The game itself draws from a wide spectrum of races, climate, temperments and languages, and it is inevitable that some differences must arise between countries and teams in the playing of a body-contact game. Brought up in the soccer background of one particular country, Referees will naturally tend to interpret the laws as generally accepted by the players and media of that country. Complete uniformity - even within a country - will never by entirely achieved, since decisions depend on both opinion and the degree of courage a Referee has under the particular circumstances.

iv

In the 1950's and 1960's, there were fairly wide differences in interpretation of the Laws, especially between Europeans and South Americans. Shirt-tugging and unfair obstruction provoked European players, while the more physical game of the Europeans (and especially the tackle from behind) upset the South Americans.

Briefing sessions prior to recent World Cups have overcome these problems and have been responsible for a more uniform interpretation of the Laws. This began in the 1970 World Cup and was so successful that not one player was sent off during these games!

Pressures on Referees

Beyond a need for universal interpretation, there are numerous pressures that are brought on Referees. In some countries, Referees are directly under the control of the government. In others, television has brought pressures for flawless decisions, calls that are debated and replayed. Perhaps the greatest pressure of all, however, is that which springs from the steady breakdown of social discipline in general; the resistance to authority in all its forms, and the tendency of young players to adopt aggressive attitudes at the slightest provocation. It is the result of these problems that causes a steady 30% of Referees (of 380,000 throughout the world) to resign annually from the game; they are happy and able to control a game - but not the players taking part. There must be a return at all levels of the game to the standards of fair play and sportsmanship of the early days. This will not be achieved by legislation in any form, but by the spread of a new spirit in the game. Referees have an important role to play.

Ken Aston, considered to be the world's top expert on soccer officiating, is a close friend of American soccer. He has conducted a variety of clinics and Referee Camps, and thousands of referees have been inspired by his words. Mr. Aston has served as Chief Instructor for FIFA, has been Chairman of the Referee Committee for FIFA, and has served as President of the International Football Association Board. He has officiated the FA Cup Final and the final series of the World Cup. His travels have taken him to more than 50 countries.

*You're **how** old?*

TABLE OF CONTENTS

TABLE OF CONTENTS (Cont.)

TABLE OF CONTENTS (Cont.)

"It's you and I together."

I

I, You, the Referee

FACILITATOR

- Calls fouls commensurate with the level of play.

- Covers every inch of grass on the field if necessary.

- Is flexible.

- Prevents problems before they occur.

- Is respected by the coaches.

- Compliments and complements his Linesmen.

- Is aware of God.

- Communicates with wife.

- Quotes *Fair or Foul.*

IS REFEREEING FOR YOU?

Even as you read this, you may not be entirely convinced that refereeing is for you. If you have been recruited into a volunteer youth soccer organization, you will immediately know that there is more recognition elsewhere. Coaching, for instance, has its larger rewards of team parties, parental support, and player adulation. If you are entering through your experience in officiating another sport, you may find that soccer has its own peculiarities, lore, war stories, and challenges.

The first time you walk on the field, you have immediately become a member of a very large but exclusive club, a worldwide group that has nearly 400,000 members. When you become a Referee, you will never again see the game the same way. Immediately you will know more about the laws than many successful coaches. You will view law application in terms of dynamic play and the question of "Does it work?" will be changed to "Is it fair?". When you referee, you run the risk of being hooked. You will experience an exhiliration, a sense of well-being and self-confidence, a feeling that you are in control. It is a feeling that all is right with your world. In summary, it can change your life.

We must be totally honest with you about your task, for there are negative stories attached to soccer officiating. On any given day, at least one in twenty Referees, while officiating, wish they were elsewhere. They are unsure of themselves, and have been intimidated, abused, or maligned in any number of ways. Potential Referees on the sidelines view Referees in trouble and decide "It's not worth it." At season's end about one in five referees will not return. "It's a thankless job," are words often heard.

From the moment you begin, one of your tasks will be to improve the position of referees in the game. We want you to be among the four referees in five who continue from one season to the next. Here are some personal guidelines for your own advancement in the world of soccer officiating:

1. CHALLENGE YOURSELF. As you become comfortable in one level of competition, move up.

2. ASK FOR HELP. Request a game observation from an experienced fellow official.

3. LIMIT YOUR ACTIVITY. Two regular games in a day is maximum. If you whistle more, you will lose concentration and effectiveness.

4. RECOGNIZE YOUR FRAILTIES. Know you make mistakes, but forget them, and go on. Einstein said, "Only death can release you from making blunders."

5. SUPPORT OTHERS. You will see others in predicaments. Help them by making suggestions, if asked.

Above, all, take your job seriously, and keep improving.

 "Refereeing is Thinking."
Ken Aston

YOUR FITNESS FOR REFEREEING

It has been repeatedly observed that vast individual differences appear in Referee dress, attitude, experience, and ability. Conditioning and training present no exception. Some Referees train, almost religiously, for their task, yet others let the games provide the setting for their training.

If you are a fanatic for conditioning, don't try to outrun the ball, the players, or the play. Also, don't try to set a record by whistling nine games in a day, as one Referee did. Conversely, if you take conditioning lightly, you will probably not progress very far in refereeing. So . . . what is a realistic approach to the physical task that is before you?

In an earlier edition of this book we stated that condition was 50% of refereeing. We no longer believe that. At best, it is 25%, and maybe only 15%. The Referee who is confidently "in shape" will feel able to perform in the last minute as in the first. Other Referees will find that as the game clock runs down, so will the physical clock. The demands made upon the Referee are often greatest in the last minutes of the game, with frustrated players and desperate, fatigued, less-than-fully-coordinated moves by all.

Officials in various sports will find varying demands made upon them, depending on the game itself. The realities of your job will tell you that:

- You will spend a great deal of your time moving at medium speed, at a slow, easy, trot, at 60% efficiency.

- At least ten times in a game you must run full-speed, for 30 yeards or more, to view a quick attack on goal.

- Much of your effective running must be backwards, or sideways.

- You must have mobility to avoid players and the ball.

- Even the shortest game is stopped at least 50 times for throw-ins, goal-kicks, corner-kicks, free-kicks, goals, injuries, substitutions, etc. Don't let anyone tell you that soccer is continuous. When you do have these breaks in play, don't rush into your next position. Save your strength.

Lest you feel complacent, thinking that the job is not physically demanding, the following chart is offered:

	Referee	Linesmen
Two Referee System	7 – 8 miles	
Diagonal System	6 – 7 miles	2 – 3 miles
Modified Diagonal	5 – 6 miles	3 – 4 miles
One Referee System	8 – 10 miles	

These distances refer to the amount of "moving about" that an average Referee would do in a normal 90 minute game, and would, of course, be dependent on the size of the field.

HINTS

1. Before the game, run from one goal to the other as you inspect the nets. This effort will "warm you up" in cool weather and will impress both players and spectators with your enthusiasm and alertness.

2. A ball travels faster than any player or Referee can run. Keep up with the play, not with the ball.

3. Prior to the opening of a regular season, ask league officials for practice game assignments. This will aid in both mental and physical conditioning.

4. Through experience you will learn to avoid unnecessary running on the field, thus saving your energies for sudden breakaways on goal, when you must not be caught in the middle of the field.

5. Never smoke in view of spectators or players.

6. Never lean on a goal upright during a game stoppage.

7. Use the half time period for rest and for game discussion with your fellow officials.

Oto Maxmilian

Dante Maglio (right), a FIFA Referee, leaves the field, apparently more fatigued than the players. He is in top condition, and has given his all in this game.

EQUIPMENT

"When the occasion is worth dressing for, it's worth the best in dress."

The most obvious part of a Referee's equipment is his uniform, which shall consist of the following:

1. A long or short sleeved black shirt, with white collar and cuffs, with the crest of the Referee's association on the left side of the chest.

2. Black shorts, with length 4 to 5 inches above the knee.

3. Black stockings, with or without white at the top.

4. Black studded shoes, with black or shoe laces.

It is recommended that a transparent or black waterproof jacket be worn in rainy weather. A black visor/cap helps protect the Referee who wears glasses from the rain. It is also handy as a sun shade. When it is determined that one team's colors are in conflict with the standard black of the Referee, the Referee shall change to a shirt of contrasting color or pattern. A striped basketball shirt (as used by some soccer officials in the East) and the basic Referee shirt with the black and white reversed are two popular alternatives.

The Referee's equipment must also include a Referee data card (see Chapter IV) or a small pocket notebook and the following:

Whistles (2)	Coin
Watches (2) (one must have stop action)	Red and Yellow Cards (1 set)
Pencils (2)	

Many Referees have the following items in their equipment bag:

Glasses with yellow lenses	Increases contrast and visibility for games played at night, in rain, fog, or when very overcast.
Spare set of red and yellow cards	
Law Book	
Set of linesman's flags	
Shoe polish	
Spare pair of shoes	Screw-in cleats are best for a wet field.
Inflating pump and valve needle	
36" of a cloth tape measure	
Shoe laces – black and white	A spare pair. If you function as a linesman, you can change to match the Referee.
String/cord and a knife	For the emergency repair of nets.
Masking/Adhesive tape	To repair nets and to hold up ones stockings.
Captains' arm bands	
Screw-in cleat tool	
Band-aids and chapstick	
File for burrs on cleats, etc.	

A famous player once approached a Referee after a contro-
versial decision. "I've wanted to tell you for some time that
you are the second-best official in this league. The Referee's
curiosity got the best of him, and he asked the identity of
#1. The answer: "All of the others are tied for first."

Oto Maxmilian

"Toros, these new Referee   *"Why thank you, Emmett."*   *"No es para tanto"*
boots of yours are simply   *(BIG DEAL).*
smashing."

Oto Maxmilian

"Come, come, Gentlemen . . . can't you at least wait until the game has started?"

II

Before the Game

FIELD INSPECTION

The Referee is evaluated the moment he enters the field of play. His trademark is *not* his whistle, but the respect he commands for the unobtrusive and silent way he moves about the field, always with full authority.

When the Referee enters the field of play, his first job is to make a thorough inspection of the grounds. If field markings are poor or inadequate, this time before the game begins is to be used to correct these deficiencies. In particular, the penalty-spot should be stepped off to determine the condition of the spot and its exact location. If the spot is in a hole, it must be corrected by filling in the hole. Nets should be checked for holes or loose tie-downs, and corner and midfield flags inspected. This is to be followed by a general inspection of the field for dangerous water drains, holes, rocks, or other irregularities. If some conditions exist that cannot be corrected, a reminder of such conditions to captains and team managers is a courtesy, followed by a written report to the proper authorities.

If the Referee is working a game with another Referee or with two Linesmen, all of the above should be accomplished cooperatively and with a minimum of talk to players and managers. The Referee must be satisfied that the field is in playable condition before calling the captains to the center of the field.

A FIELD IS PLAYABLE WHEN:

1. The field is properly marked according to Law I, with nets and corner-flags secure.

2. A field is playable when the Referee can see both goals while standing in the center circle.

3. The ball, when dropped from the shoulder, will bounce. If wet areas exist, they should be few in number.

Would this goal pass field inspection?...   *This net wouldn't!*

STRETCHING, AND OTHER INJURY PREVENTION

Basic stretching will do wonders for you prior to game time, and serve to prevent the muscle pulls that can sideline you. Don't make the mistake young players do, of jumping right into the action. Rather, two minutes or less of gentle stretching will prepare you for the rigors of sprinting, turning, and stopping. The cooler the weather, the more care you should put into your physical game preparation.

For the Groin   Groin, Hamstring, and Back   Hamstring

Hold each stretch for 20-30 seconds. Build yourself up to game pace by jogging a bit just prior and after the stretch. Now you are ready for that 50 yard sprint to goal just after kickoff!

Other Common Injuries and Their Prevention

Ankle Sprains. Ankle sprains are usually caused by hazards on the field. Weak ankles will be weaker through ankle turns brought on by uneven surfaces. Three or four strips of 1½ inch tape applied to each ankle is the best prevention.

Blisters. A light pair of inner socks will prevent blisters brought on by too-tight or loose shoes. Tape will add protection to sensitive areas. Break in new shoes and socks in training, not in the game.

Sunburn. Some referees feel it is undignified or unprofessional to wear a hat while officiating. A visor or hat is sometimes almost a necessity, but the choice is yours. Sunscreen should prevent the burn.

The Heat. The tradition of the black and white uniform began in a country where heat is not a problem. The standard uniform requirement is braking down in warm weather climates, in favor of lighter colors. If you look sharp, light-colored jerseys with patch are acceptable. Do a maximum of two games in the heat, and take some fluid replacement. Fruit juice is recommended.

Other problems include knee injuries (soft, muddy fields), back strain (brought on by hard fields and weak abdominal areas) and injuries brought on by being struck by the ball (poor reading of the game, and being too close to play). Young and undertrained officials often experience the pain of shinsplints, probably from running too much on hard surfaces.

Game preparation and longevity in your refereeing career demands proper equipment, general good health, and the common sense that you must always use.

A RITUAL . . . THE MEETING IN THE MIDDLE

**The longer your pre-game instructions, the more
you are putting down all of the Referees who
preceded you.**

The meeting at midfield for instructions can be handled in a variety of ways, and is one of the more obvious ways of distinguishing yourself. Top officials find little need for words at this time, and by-pass this opportunity to impress team captains with their authority. On the other hand, Referees who prefer to give instructions to players before the game run the following risks:

1. During the game, they may have to follow through on promises or threats.

2. Coaches can become irritated by time-consumption when players are "warming down" and will resent this waste.

3. Players may ask too many questions, concerns that need long detailed answers for clarity.

4. The Referee may lose credibility when inattentive players must be silenced, or ignored.

5. Fellow officials, by having to listen and not participate, have secondary roles they don't deserve.

It is generally agreed that the Referee establishes little authority, exchanges even less worthwhile information, and impresses no one through pre-game oration.

Some experienced officials prefer to talk to teams individually by proceeding to the warm-up areas near goal. Inspection can take place, and more casual conversation can result. Players and coaches will disclose information which may help the Referee: "We use the offside trap a lot." or "We take free kicks very quickly to surprise the defense near-goal." and "We do a lot of subbing in the second half." This commonly shared information is never shared in the other team's presence. This relaxed atmosphere releases the coming tension of the match.

Instructions are nevertheless a matter of individual preference, and there may be some situations when a few words to the captain are in order.

If you carry important information about a team or situation into a game, and it will serve you to adjust your pre-game instructions accordingly, then do so. Above all, let your whistle in the game tell the players what they need to know, at a time when they've forgotten all your words of wisdom.

HINTS FOR REFEREES

1. Some Referees prefer to identify captains through the use of armbands, or identifying adhesives, to be worn on the upper arm, just below the shoulder. This is a purely optional procedure, as are all procedures in this chapter, with the exception of the tossing of the coin. Some captains consider this gesture as giving the captain a special mark of distinction, which is right. If, however, the captain refuses to wear the armband, the Referee shall not force him to do so.

2. The Referee should request that his neutral Linesmen be present during pre-game instructions, and they should be introduced to team captains.

3. Do not talk with one captain before the game until the opposing captain is present, for everything that is said must be heard by both parties.

4. A captain or coach may not eject a player from the field, but he is required to send the player off after the Referee has ejected him from the game.

5. The use of the yellow card for cautions and the red card for ejections is highly recommended. Never use a two-faced card.

6. Very few players or club officials are well-schooled in the laws of the game. Do not attempt to flaunt your own knowledge in order to correct this deficiency.

7. *All* players' equipment shall be examined before the game. Equipment such as headbands may be worn if the Referee feels they do not present a hazard to players. Necklaces, casts, rings, and wrist watches are usually not permitted. Armcasts are sometimes allowed by Referees (High School, Youth — NO), if they are wrapped in heavy sponge rubber or similar material.

8. . At the coin flip, it is considered courteous to ask the captain if there are any questions, but this is not required. Do not allow players to grill you on the laws of the game in order to test your knowledge.

9. In the event of disagreement between the teams, the Referee selects the game ball. It must pass his criteria for weight, size, composition, condition, and air pressure.

10. The coin toss shall be conducted at the conclusion of the pre-game instructions. The visiting team captain shall call the coin "heads" or "tails" while in the air, and if he wins he shall have the choice of direction or kick-off.

    If the coin is to be caught, the captain should be told that it will be re-tossed if it falls to the ground. This precludes any problems of the coin landing on edge in the grass.

    An acceptable gesture is to have the home team captain toss the coin. If this is done, use a 50-cent piece or silver dollar, due to its heavier weight. Let it land on the ground.

You can convey authority without being dictatorial.

-13-

"Alright, now that I know your name, what's your phone number?"

You have accepted an assignment, and someone calls with a more attractive one. What do you do?

Comment. Politely decline. If you take refereeing at all seriously, you may someday be given the position of making assignments. Do unto others. Your share of the good games will come to you, in time.

 "I used to think violence against Referees was deserved, until they went after me."

Eric Sellin
Author of *The Inner Game of Soccer*

DICTATOR

- Is inflexible and a sadist.

- Thinks it's his field.

- Wears multiple Referee badges.

- Tells players and coaches how lucky they are to have him.

- Makes player move the ball two feet to the left for a free-kick taken at midfield.

- Doesn't allow the coach to walk across the field anytime before kick-off.

- Overrides all of his Linesmen's calls.

- Is God.

- Beats his wife.

- Never heard of *Fair or Foul.*

"I think you were that far behind play, Mr. Linesman."

III

Mechanics

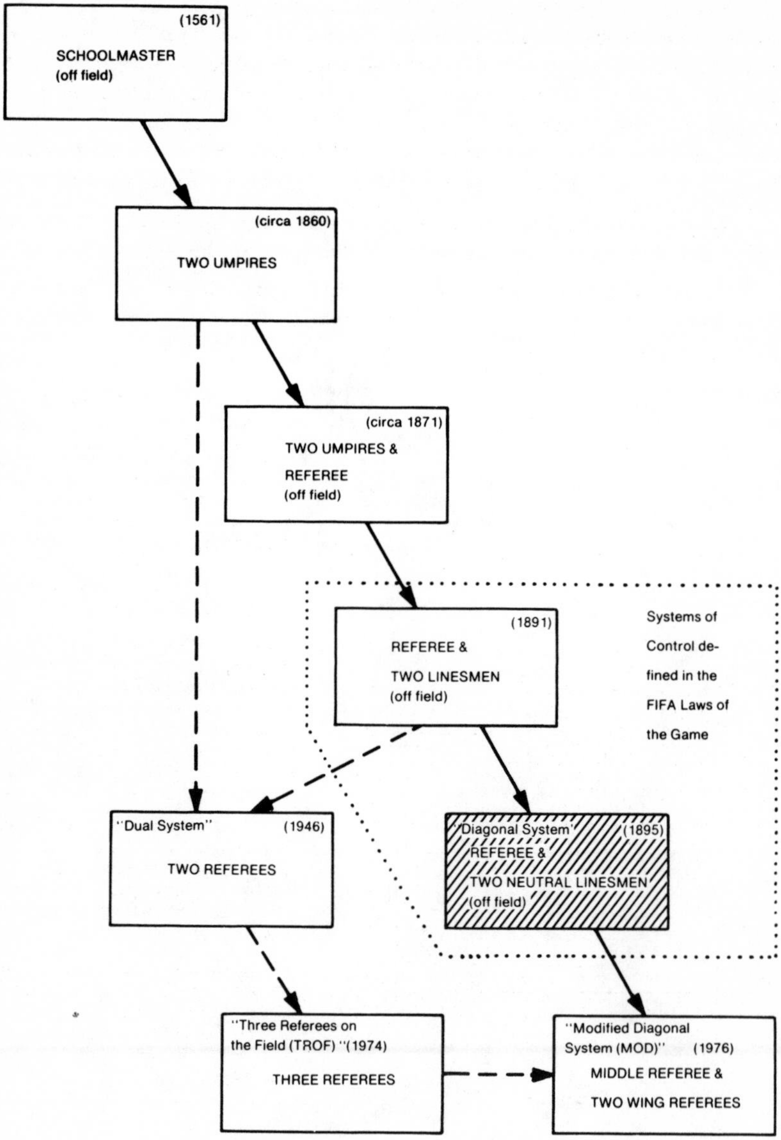
(1561)
SCHOOLMASTER
(off field)
(circa 1860)
TWO UMPIRES
(circa 1871)
TWO UMPIRES &
REFEREE
(off field)
(1891)
REFEREE &
TWO LINESMEN
(off field)
Systems of
Control de-
fined in the
FIFA Laws of
the Game
"Dual System" (1946)
TWO REFEREES
"Diagonal System" (1895)
REFEREE &
TWO NEUTRAL LINESMEN
(off field)
"Three Referees on
the Field (TROF)" (1974)
THREE REFEREES
"Modified Diagonal
System (MOD)" (1976)
MIDDLE REFEREE &
TWO WING REFEREES

Bill Mason

The Evolution of Soccer Officiating

THE DIAGONAL SYSTEM

Although the laws of the game neither prescribe a system of field control nor contain specific instructions on field positioning during a game, there is a system which has received worldwide approval. This method, called the *diagonal system,* makes the most effective use of the Referee and two neutral Linesmen, and is commonly used in club, professional, and international games. The key to efficient game control under the diagonal system is Linesman cooperation (Law VI). The Referee must know and respect his Linesmen, and Linesmen should respect and support the decisions of the Referee.

Referees should not necessarily keep to one diagonal on the field of play, and must adjust their positioning according to weather and grounds conditions.

The following diagrams will indicate the basic system of control, followed by referee positioning at various stages of play development. (Reprinted with permission of the Federation Internationale de Football Association.)

Diagram 1

The imaginary diagonal used by the Referee is the line A–B.

The opposite diagonal used by the Linesmen is adjusted to the position of the Referee; if the Referee is near A, Linesman L2 will be at a point between M and K. When the Referee is at B, Linesman L1 will be between E and F; this gives two officials control of the respective "danger zones", one at each side of the field.

Linesman L1 adopts the *Reds* as his side; Linesman L2 adopts the *Blues;* as *Red* forwards move toward Blue goal, Linesman L1 keeps in line with second last *Blue* defender so in actual practice he will rarely get into Red's half of the field. Similarly Linesman L2 keeps in line with second last *Red* defender, and will rarely get into Blue's half.

At corner-kicks or penalty-kicks the Linesman in that half where the corner-kick or penalty-kick occurs positions himself at N and the Referee takes position (see Diagram 4 – corner-kick; Diagram 9 – penalty-kick).

The diagonal system fails if Linesman L2 gets between G and H when Referee is at B, or when Linesman L1 is near C or D when the Referee is at A, because there are *two* officials at the same place. This should be avoided.

(N.B. – Some Referees prefer to use the opposite diagonal, viz., from F to M, in which case the Linesmen should adjust their work accordingly.)

Diagram 2

Diagram 2
START OF GAME

Position of Referee at Kick-off—R.
Position of Linesmen — L1 and L2:
in position with second last defender
Players — ○ and ⊗.
Diagonal followed by Referee A—B.
Referee moves to diagonal along line
←——→ according to direction of attack.
Ball —●.

Diagram 3
DEVELOPMENT OF ATTACK
(From Diagram 2)

Ball moves out to left wing, Referee (R) slightly off diagonal to be near play.

Linesman (L2) level with second last defender.

Two officials, therefore, up with play.

Linesman (L1) in position for clearance and possible counter-attack.

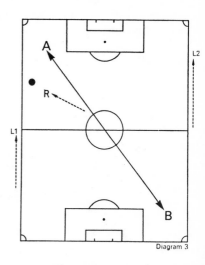

Diagram 3

Diagram 4

Diagram 4
CORNER-KICK

Positions of officials the same no matter at which corner-area the kick is taken.

Referee (R) along line shown.

Linesman (L2) — in accordance with the instructions from the Referee the Linesman (L2) shall be near the corner flag or on the goal-line near the corner flag, to observe whether the ball is properly played, whether the opposing players are at proper distance (10 yards), whether the ball is behind the goal-line, or whether incidents have happened possibly hidden from the Referee.

Linesman (L1) in position for clearance and possible counter-attack.

-20-

Diagram 5
THE COUNTER-ATTACK
(Following Diagram 4)

Referee (R) sprints to regain correct position on diagonal along path ------->.

(Note: The Referee who is physically fit is able to do this easily.)

Linesman (L2) hurries back to his correct position on the touch-line.

Linesman (L1) level with attack and in position to see infringements and indicate decisions until Referee regains his position.

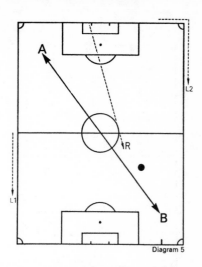

Diagram 5

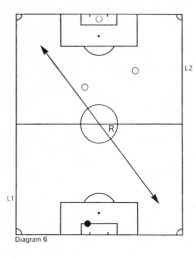

Diagram 6

Diagram 6
GOAL-KICK

Referee (R) in midfield adjacent to central point of diagonal.

Linesman (L1) exercising watch over goal-kick, positioned in line with the penalty-area.

Linesman (L2) in position in line with second last defender pending a possible attack by side taking goal-kick.

Diagram 7
FREE-KICK IN MIDFIELD

Players line up for kick ○ and ⊗. Referee (R) and Linesman (L2) in respective diagonal positions, level with players and able to judge accurately any questions of off-side or foul play. Linesman (L1) sees that kick is taken from correct position and also is in position for possible counter-attack.

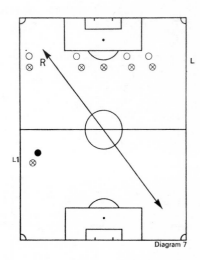

Diagram 7

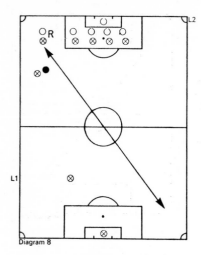

Diagram 8

Diagram 8
FREE-KICK NEAR GOAL
(Just outside penalty-area)

Players ⊗ and ◯ line up for free-kick.

Referee (R) takes up his position just off his diagonal so that he is placed accurately to judge off-side. Linesman (L2) is more advanced but can watch for off-side and fouls and also is in a good position to act as goal judge in the event of a direct shot being taken.

Diagram 9
PENALTY-KICK

Players ⊗ and ◯ with the exception of the goalkeeper and kicker are shown outside the penalty-area and at least 10 yards from the ball — goalkeeper on goal-line.

Referee (R) is in position to see that kick is properly taken and that no encroachment takes place.

Linesman (L2) watches goalkeeper to see that he does not advance illegally and also acts as goal judge

Linesman (L1) is in position should the goalkeeper save a goal and start a counter-attack.

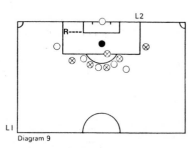

Diagram 9

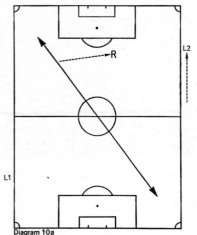

Diagram 10a

Diagram 10a
THROW-IN

Ball out of play and Linesman (L2) is in position with second last defender indicating position of throw and to which side.

Referee (R) crosses from diagonal to centre of field, in the same manner as a defence covering a throw-in.

Linesman (L1) in position in line with his second last defender for the possible counter-attack.

Diagram 10b
THROW-IN

Linesman (L1) is away from the throw-in but should be able to judge feet and probably to indicate which side is entitled to throw. He also maintains his position in line with second last defender in the event of a clearance.

Referee (R) can judge other throw-in infringements and veers slightly from his diagonal towards touch-line.

Linesman (L2) is in position with second last defender in his half of the field of play, and can see any infringement occurring before Referee can turn to follow play.

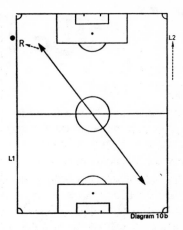

Diagram 10b

The Diagonal System is so named because of the relationship of the Referee to Linesmen, not so much because of the "diagonal" method of running. There are countless situations where running a "diagonal" will remove the Referee from the reality of play.

The USFA Cup Final was taken seriously in 1915, too. The officials were from Massachusetts, New York, and Pennsylvania. The stadium was Taylor Stadium in Bethlehem, PA. Notice that the Linesmen are carrying American flags!

-23-

LINESMEN

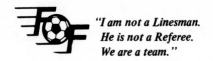

*"I am not a Linesman.
He is not a Referee.
We are a team."*

Signals

The basic signal is to raise the flag high and directly overhead. It is used for off-side, a foul throw, or encroachment. The Linesman stands rigidly straight, feet together, facing the field of play near where the incident occurred.

When Not Signaling

Proceed at all times with the flag unfurled at your side. The flag should always face the field. (This necessitates the changing of hands.) It should be pointed toward the ground.

Out of Bounds

If the ball is out-of-bounds and the Referee has not seen your flag, never put it down. This is a decision based on fact.

If the ball has obviously gone out of bounds, there is no reason to flag. Similarly, if one team has clearly last played the ball, the direction does not need to be pointed.

Throw-In

The Linesman usually watches for 'foot in the field' infractions (lower half of body) and Referee covers fouls originating from upper half). (Established in pre-game instructions.)

An infraction is indicated by holding the flag in the basic signal position. After acknowledged, give a signal indicating the type of throw-in violation (e.g., raising a foot or stepping into the field.)

After a throw-in decision, immediately move to the off-side position of your choice.

The Off-Side

To indicate - Give the basic signal. If the signal is not seen by the Referee, lower the flag quickly if the off-side has a minor impact upon the game or the direction of the play is reversed.

If the nature of the off-side is more severe, maintain it for a longer period of time.

If the off-side is whistled, stay exactly in line with the position from which the free-kick is to be taken and point with the flag to the area of the infraction (near, middle, or far side of the field).

The NASL variation is to keept the flag raised and to point to the offending *player* with your free hand.

If the ball went out-of-bounds on the Referee's diagonal, do not indicate the direction of the throw unless asked by the Referee. (A common signal is the Referee raising his head slightly.)

Methods of monitoring offside:

- Standard — Stay even with the second to last *defender*. (FIFA) This is the best method for new Linesmen. The main weaknesses are:

  1. Poor trail coverage, particularly when the defender lags.

  2. Defenders are harder to follow than attackers due to sudden shifting of positions.

- Option A — Stay even with the leading *attacker*.

- Option B — Stay even with the second to last *player*. (NASL)

The main drawback to the exclusive use of either Option A or B have to do with the Linesman getting into a position which results in his viewing play from a poor visual perspective.

Fair or Foul — Recommendations for experienced Linesmen are to stay even with the leading attacker in every case *except* when he has passed (gotten behind) the second to last defender. Whenever this occurs, you are to stay even with the second to last defender.

Wait a fraction of a second to determine the flight of the ball before calling the off-sides.

You may wish to move into the field a bit, if your visual perspective is poor.

Do not merely signal an off-side position each time it occurs. Signal only when the player is taking advantage of that position.

During Play

Follow every long ball to the goal-line or to the goalkeeper, no matter how futile this may appear.

Linesmen may occasionally go 10 to 15 yards into the other half of the field for superior positioning on infractions.

When the ball has not completely gone over the touch-line, the Linesman may indicate that the ball is still in play by pointing toward the field with his free hand.

Play On/Advantage

The safe sign (baseball) with the free hand is an indication of there being no foul. The advantage is indicated to the Referee with the free hand pointing in a straight ahead direction, parallel with the touch-line.

 "Lining is an art in itself and in my view a more difficult one than that of Refereeing."

Denis Howell
English Referee

Providing Assistance on Fouls

Questions asked before flagging.

- If I don't raise my flag, do I fail the Referee?
- If I do raise it, will I embarass him?

When indicating infractions, shake the flag and point at a 45 degree angle in the direction the kick should be taken. Indicate with the free arm, or by body movements, what type of infraction is being called. Then, having completed the signal, if the foul results in an IFK, give that signal.

If the Linesman flags an offense that was committed in the penalty-area he *does not* point to the penalty-mark but rather walks briskly to a position near the corner flag, all the while maintaining eye contact with the Referee.

If the Referee calls an infraction quite close to the penalty-area that the linesman feels does not warrant a penalty-kick, he stands at ease with the flag out of sight behind his back.

Free-Kick Close to the Goal

Linesman runs to the goal-line but only *after* the Referee has either moved into position for judging the off-side or has indicated goal coverage by a brief wave of his arm.

Scoring a Goal

If the Linesman feels the goal should not be awarded he looks at the Referee, keeps his flag down, and remains motionless. If he feels it is good, he runs towards the halfway line. If a goal is scored on a close situation (e.g., ball hits cross bar or Goalkeeper carries the ball completely within the goal), the Linesman should indicate that the ball has totally crossed the goal-line by standing on the goal-line and giving the basic signal. When the Referee acknowledges, then the Linesman points and runs toward the halfway line. This close situation, like the ball going out of bounds, is a decision of fact and should be treated accordingly. (This situation should be discussed in pre-game.)

- Verbal abuse is indicated by pointing to the player concerned with your free hand, then tapping the index finger on your lips.

Undetected Events

Signal for fouls that are observed by the Referee, but *only when the flag can be observed by him.*

- Report all incidents that are not observed by the Referee.

- Signal to the Referee in order to draw attention to the other Linesman's flag. This will usually happen during a temporary stoppage of play for "off-the-ball" situations, crowd control problems, subsitutions, or other disciplinary measures that must be handled by the Referee.

- To indicate the need to discuss a transgression which has escapted the Referee's attention on the field, hold the bottom of an unfurled flag parallel to the ground either waist high or overhead.

Providing Added Assistance

If a violation is *about* to occur, try to take care of it yourself, rather than placing the burden on the Referee. (e.g., prohibiting encroachment on all nearby corner-kicks/free-kicks and maintaining control through friendly warnings during play.) Let the players know that you are there. Don't be silent.

Never . . .

- Shout at the Referee.
- Leave your position behind the touch-line to retrieve a ball.
- Point to your watch to indicate the passage of time. Have a prearranged signal. One method is to point the flag toward the center of the field; another is to cover your Referee patch with your hand.
- Fail to immediately join the Referee at the conclusion of a period.
- Fail to support the Referee on all of his decisions, even if he overrules you.

Always . . .

- Attempt eye contact before making goal-line decisions.

NASL Photo Contest

Find the Referee. In times like this, the Referee needs all the help he can get.

LINESMEN'S GUIDE (DIAGONAL SYSTEM)

Occurrence	Lead Linesman	Trail Linesman
KICK-OFF	In line with the second-to-last defender. (FIFA) In between the halfway line and the second-to-last defender. (NASL) On the halfway line until the ball is played (ASL) *(Fair or Foul)*	In line with the second-to-last defender. (FIFA) On or 3 yards behind the halfway line. (NASL) On the halfway line (NASL) (ASL) *(Fair or Foul)*
GOAL-KICK To indicate: Move on the touch-line so as to be in line with the edge of the goal-area.	In line with the second-to-last defender. (FIFA) In line with the halfway line or the most advanced forward. *(Fair or Foul)*	1. In line with the edge of the goal-area for ball placement, then . . . 2. In line with edge of Penalty-area to see that the ball leaves the area, then . . . 3. Quickly getting in line with the second-to-last defender prior to the adoption of a position for correctly monitoring off-side. An infraction of (1) or (2) is indicated by the basic signal.
CORNER-KICK To indicate: Move rapidly around the corner flag on the goal-line.	If a near-side corner, he checks out the placement of the ball within the quarter circle, then... • He stands behind the flag (at or very near) - FIFA or • He goes ten yards in from the quarter-circle along the goal-line. (English F.A.) If defenders attempt to encraoch, call out "10 yards back" to the players. For any violation, he indicates it by using the basic signal.	At the halfway line in position for clearance and a counter-attack.
PENALTY-KICK If you flag for the foul, don't point direction. Move toward the corner-area.	Stands behind or very near the flag (FIFA) or on the goal-line at the intersection of the penalty-area line. (English F.A.) On the goal-line - 10 years from the goal post. (Ref is at the interstction of the goalline and the goal-area.) (NASL) He acts as goal judge and watches for GK foot movement. If the GK has moved, and gained an advantage from this move, this is indicated by giving the basic signal.	At the halfway line in position for clearance and a counter-attack. (FIFA) In line with the edge of the penalty-area to check for encroachment. *(Fair or Foul)* When there is encroachment, use the basic signal, the up-raised flag.
	The Linesman gives his signal for encroachment only when it would result in that kick having to be retaken.	

LINESMAN SIGNALS

Though players occasionally look to the Linesman for decisions, the signals from the Linesman are for the Referee. All of the signals are meant to assist the Referee.

Substitution

The flag is held in full view of the Referee to see. This same signal may be used when one Linesman needs to draw the attention of the Referee to the other Linesman.

Location of Offside

The accurate flag will indicate where the offside occurred. The offending players may appreciate this one, too.

Throw-In

All throw-ins should be signalled, no matter how obvious, unless the Referee has instructed otherwise. Note: Flag is not held across body. Hands are changed.

Offside

The flag is held upright, directly opposite the place on the field where the infraction occurred.

Corner-Kick

The flag is to be pointed to the quarter circle, while looking to the Referee in case of disagreement. As with the goal-kick, do not make decision on opposite (far) side unless asked to do so.

Goal-Kick

The flag is pointed to the corner of the goal area. As with the corner kick, do not make decision on opposite (far) side unless asked to do so.

Fouls

The flag is to be shaken vigorously. Be sure that your position is superior to that of the Referee and that the advantage has not been given. The closer the play is to the Linesman, the quicker should be the signal.

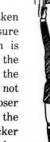

REFEREE SIGNALS

The signals of the Referee are for players, Linesmen, and spectators. Accepted in all parts of the world, they are standardized for control and for the smooth flow of the game.

"Play On, or Advantage"

The Referee indicates that an offense has occurred but that play is allowed to continue. (Don't make the mistake of using this signal when there is no foul, or you'll be using it too often.)

"Direct Free Kick"

This signal is the first movement to be seen from the Referee following the whistle for a foul. There should be no guesswork here as to the direction of the kick.

"Indirect Free Kick"

Use this signal before the kick is taken. Retain it until the ball has been touched by another player or passed out of play. (Notice that the whistle is not on the hand of the up-raised arm.)

"Penalty Kick"

Clear, immediate, and decisive, the signal shows the determination of the Referee to "sell the call." Point directly at the Penalty spot.

"Corner Kick"

This signal sometimes reaffirms the signal of the Linesman. Used for corner kicks in all four corners, not only on the near diagonal.

"Goal Kick"

Point early, so players will not place the ball on the wrong side of the goal area.

REFEREES

1. The Referee and Linesmen should discuss all matters involving mutual cooperation. The following Referee Instructions should be fully covered (takes about 20 minutes).

   a. Linesmen's duties prior to the game (Field Inspection, etc.)
   b. Who shall be senior Linesman in case of need. (Red Flag – NASL and ASL)
   c. The side and end of the field each Linesman will take during each half of the match.
   d. The positions taken for various types of play resumptions.
   e. Signals to be used.
   f. Watch synchronization.

2. Have your Linesmen present, and introduce them, during pre-game instructions to captains.

3. Instruct your Linesmen to enter and to abandon the field with you as a unit, and not as individuals.

4. Before signaling for a goal, always check with your Linesmen.

5. Whenever possible, face your Linesmen as play progresses, keeping the play between the two of you.

6. Never allow your conversations with Linesmen to be overheard.

7. It is recommended that the Referee change his diagonal and that Linesmen change sides but not ends of the field at halftime. If the Referee retains his same diagonal, the Linesmen should remain on their original side of the field.

8. As a need arises and where a special disciplinary problem may exist or be anticipated, the Referee may change diagonals and switch his Linesmen. A need may occur because of bench difficulties.

ADVANTAGES AND DISADVANTAGES OF THE DIAGONAL SYSTEM

Advantages

1. This system is universally accepted by players and coaches, as well as by most countries.

2. The single authority on the field brings consistent interpretation of laws.

Disadvantages

1. Requires three equally qualified Referees who are thoroughly schooled in the laws of the game.

2. To operate most effectively, requires Referee "teams" of three, which are very difficult to assign.

3. Requires Referee to occasionally divide his attention between monitoring play and glancing at his Linesmen to see if they are signaling.

4. Referee is forced to turn his back to a Linesman in order to view play thus missing some "off the ball" signals.

5. Referee often not close enough to play.

6. Linesmen often feel unimportant, and if overruled, will become inattentive.

7. Linesman easily overruled by Referee. Can lead to lack of confidence in both Referee and Linesman by players.

COMMUNICATION

Players communicate constantly, but unfortunately the communication between Referee and linesmen is seldom a part of game control. One reason for this is tradition; the flag is the signal to the Referee, and there is little need to exchange other information. Also, the distance between Referee and linesman is great, making the exchange difficult. Circumstances, however, do present opportunities, and officials should look for those times when it is good to "check in" with the partner.

The ball is out of play for 20 to 30 percent of the time in every game. Throw-ins, corner kicks, and goal kicks and other no-stress times are when a glance in the direction of the linesman or Referee is in order. The communication should not be obvious, nor should it be confused with the communication that is required for the awarding of corner and goal-kicks and throw-ins.

METHODS OF COMMUNICATION

Situation	Signal
Time's up (period is over)	Cover Association patch with hand
Time's out	Hand over wrist
Time's in	Point to wrist
Time remaining (less than 5 minutes)	Fingers using black uniform as background
Great call	Whatever gets the point across
We must talk (it's serious)	Flag parallel to ground, across waist
Flak from bench	Hand over mouth
I saw your flag, but am overruling	Hand in stop position
Give me help (out of bounds)	Flat of hand on stomach (if neither knows, Referee must make immediate decision)

DON'T OFFICIATE INDEPENDENTLY . . . WORK TOGETHER

COMMENTATOR

- Explains all his calls.

- Tells everyone that politics keeps him from getting good assignments.

- Never gets a sore throat.

- Yells "Play On" everytime there is any type of contact.

- Takes a player under his wing and coaches him during the game.

- Spends 20 minutes reciting the laws to the coach before the game.

- Gives advice to God.

- Wife wears ear plugs.

- Interprets *Fair or Foul* for anyone who will listen.

THE ONE REFEREE SYSTEM

A commonly experienced game control situation, unfortunately, involves the "One Referee System," where no neutral Linesmen are present. Under these difficult circumstances, the Referee must be prepared to make all decisions himself. The fact that Club Linesmen are not neutral greatly increases the responsibility of the Referee, and does in fact reduce his effectiveness.

When a Referee finds himself as the only qualified official in a match, he must appoint two Club Linesmen. Their duties are to signal when a ball is out of bounds, either over the touch-line or the goal-line. They shall *not* signal for off-side or for any other violation, nor shall they signal directions for throw-ins, goal-kicks, or corner-kicks. The Referee shall instruct both Linesmen in the above duty before the game, encourage them to keep up with play, not to be distracted in any way from their responsibility and that regardless of their personal opinion, the decision of the Referee is final and must not be questioned.

In whistling under this system, the Referee must make several adjustments in his method of officiating. The following pattern of control is advised:

THE FLEXIBLE DIAGONAL

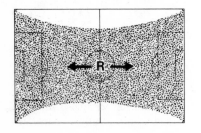

The Referee **(R)** runs either the left-wing or right-wing diagonal, whichever is most appropriate at that moment. It is a 'watered down' diagonal because **(R)** is continually gravitating toward the center of the field, where he will be in a favorable position to recognize infractions. The obvious disadvantage is that he will have to look quickly from side to side to judge offside, but this is unavoidable. He will not be in perfect position to judge every offside but should be able to properly judge the more flagrant violations.

SUGGESTED PREGAME INSTRUCTIONS

"Play the whistle at all times, particularly when a player may be off-side. If your team plays the 'off-side' trap, you do it at your own risk, for a single Referee will sometimes miss an off-side."

The above is an attempt to have the players keep playing, thus cutting down on the amount of suspiciously off-side or claimed off-side goals.

 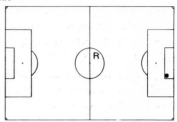

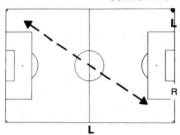

CORNER-KICK

CORNER-KICK

(R) should be *past* the far post. This allows him to see the whole of the corner-kick and the general playing area. He should be on the goal-line so that he is in the best position for judging the ball that temporarily goes out of play on an outswinger, acting as goal judge, and observing any obstruction of the goalkeeper. In any event he must be prepared for an all out sprint when the expected counter-attack materializes.

PENALTY-KICK

The position for the kick is somewhere between the goal-line and the edge of the goal-area. He is 10-15 yards out from the goal post.

He alone is responsible for the monitoring of encroachment, GK movement, and acting as a goal judge.

THROW-IN

- *Near midfield and defensive throws* – Since many attacks and counter-attacks are made following this type of a throw-in, **(R)** should move within 10-15 yards of the thrower and slightly downfield in order to obtain a favorable viewing angle.

- *Attacking, near opponent's penalty-area* – Similar to the above. Do not go to the opposite side of the field, as it places you in a difficult position for match control.

POINTS TO REMEMBER

1. Always play the angle. Try to avoid coming up from directly behind play. Visual perspective is even more important in this system.

2. For all free-kicks, the Referee should position himself downfield, and may use a second whistle to recommence play so that he may position himself correctly.

3. The Referee will often be in doubt on an off-side, and there is no solution to this problem, except that superior field positioning and a careful study of team tactics and abilities is imperative. Do *not* decide to give the advantage to the defense if you are undecided.

4. The off-side more often results from long, rather than short passes. Try to anticipate when a long pass is to be made, and position yourself accordingly.

5. Do not travel to the extreme corners of the field unless it is absolutely necessary. This leaves the opposite corners untended, and violations will be difficult to detect.

6. The Referee may dismiss Club Linesmen at any time, but others must take their place.

7. This system has no advantages over other systems of control, except that with one Referee there is no possibility of disagreement between officials. In the interests of the game, the One Referee System is to be avoided when possible.

"I threw out my club Linesman and I'll throw you out too if you question another one of my calls."

Hard to call when you're alone.

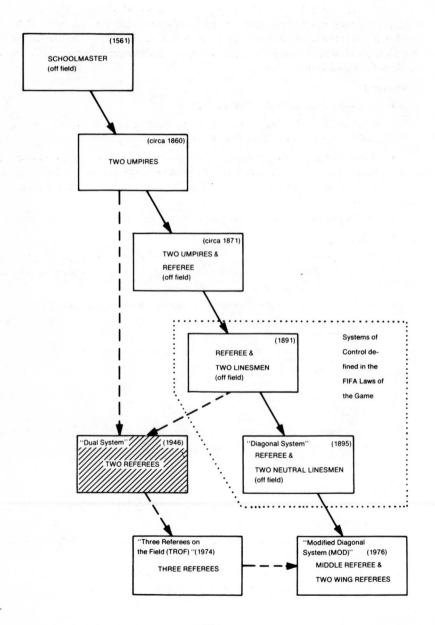

SCHOOLMASTER (off field) (1561)

TWO UMPIRES (circa 1860)

TWO UMPIRES & REFEREE (off field) (circa 1871)

REFEREE & TWO LINESMEN (off field) (1891)

Systems of Control defined in the FIFA Laws of the Game

"Dual System" (1946) TWO REFEREES

"Diagonal System" (1895) REFEREE & TWO NEUTRAL LINESMEN (off field)

"Three Referees on the Field (TROF)" (1974) THREE REFEREES

"Modified Diagonal System (MOD)" (1976) MIDDLE REFEREE & TWO WING REFEREES

THE TWO REFEREE (DUAL) SYSTEM

The Two Referee System of control was first adopted for refereeing in colleges in 1946 by Earle C. Waters, coach of West Chester State Teachers' College in Pennsylvania. Today the two Referee system is an accepted reality in high school. It is extensively used when resources (personnel and money) are limited. Some Referees feel that this is the superior system for officiating. Our purpose here is to examine the system, dispel some myths, point out advantages, disadvantages, and take an in-depth look at field positioning.

Advantages

- A good system for fouls off of the ball.

- Reduced mental strain. Help is given by your partner to take off any of the weight that players or a coach may try to place upon your shoulders.

- Psychological advantage of two officials *on* the field acting together. The Referee team can often overpower a player. If there is any trouble on the field, both officials are there. When a foul is whistled, both officials normally signal in accord.

- Referee teams of two men are easier to assign than three.

Disadvantages

- There is a feeling of being on the outside of the action. It lacks the total feel and and involvement of the diagonal or MOD systems. You must try to get into the game without getting in the way of the players.

- Physical demands. If done properly, the Dual System requires *more* running and sprinting than any other system. It is only an "old man's" or "lazy man's" system when it is operated improperly.

- It is the **worst** system for off-side and out-of-bounds monitoring. If it should become one of the better systems in this respect, then it is being used incorrectly. Game control must take precedent.

- A Referee will sometimes hesitate to call an infraction nearer to his partner than to himself.

- It requires disciplined partnerships (like basketball). The older experienced soccer official is often too inflexable to adapt.

TEAMWORK

Your partner is the most important person at the game.

- Nothing is more satisfying than a well-oiled partnership. You can take on the world (and quite often you have to).

- If the best in your partner is not being brought out, then you yourself are usually to blame.

- Develop rapport with your partner, and a difficult game can be easier. Don't do it and an easy one can become drudgery; a tough one, disaster.

Be in constant communication with your partner.

- Continually have eye contact with him. This suffers the most after a layoff between seasons.

- There is nothing wrong with verbalizing to your partner. "Nice call, Fred"... "I've got the wall, you take the goal-line." Strengthens the officiating bond.

- Flash the time remaining in the period to each other.

- Go towards partner when he is cautioning. Be there when he is ejecting, or if it looks like someone is giving him a hard time.

- Do not allow him to take any abuse from players, coaches, or spectators. The abuse that is heaped upon him falls every bit as heavily upon you, though it's just not that apparent at that moment.

Give partner the trail support that you want him to give you.

AREA OF RESPONSIBILITY

Out of Bounds

- *Touchline* on your side of the field.
- *Goal-line* you move toward as a Lead Referee.

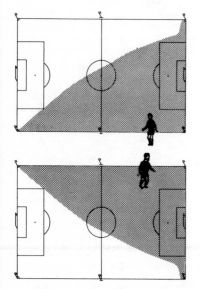

Each Referee works toward his right during one of the periods. He then has the responsibility for monitoring off-side when the attacking team goes toward the goal on his right. The shaded portion indicates his prime area of responsibility. This territorial flow complements the existing FIFA Diagonal System of Control. When the attack is made toward the goal on his right he is known as the Lead (**L**) Referee. When the attack is made toward the goal on his left he is referred to as the Trail (**T**) Referee.

Each Referee works toward his left for the other period. As play moves toward *his* right goal he is in a Trail (**T**) mode and when play goes to his left, he is in a Lead (**L**) capacity.

The partner of each of the above illustrated Referees is on the diagonally opposite side of the field, working in a like manner.

To minimize confusion, all subsequent discussions and illustrations will assume each Referee is working toward his right (top diagram).

To begin the 2nd period, the Referees merely move across to the opposite side of the field. They always retain the same end of the field. This is a high school requirment. The same philosophy is followed in the NASL whereby the Referee runs the right-wing diagonal during the first period and then changes to the more conventional left-wing diagonal for the 2nd period. There are reasons for this switch:

- Off-side calls are equalized (staying where you are is the only way to do this).

- You are placed by a new subset of players. If you run to your right the left wings and right fullbacks have no one near them. When you change to begin the 2nd period, they are now closely under surveillance. "Presence lends conviction."

- Environmental conditions are equalized. (Sun, field, wind, etc.)

- You get away from a particular team bench/coach/group of spectators. This burden is now shared with your partner. Quite often you will discover that his chemistry doesn't agitate them like yours did, or vice versa. If both benches are on the same side of the field, too many pressures are placed upon the Referee who has to contend with them for a complete game.

- Most of us have experienced the problem of pointing in the wrong direction during the first few minutes of the 2nd period. Changing sides of the field eliminates that problem. (e.g., The blue team that went to your right during the 1st period still does in the 2nd.)

The only exception to the above required side changes would be:

- A very poor quadrant of the field that is difficult to run in.

- An extremely weak partner.

BASICS

Jurisdiction

Both officials have equal authority and are responsible for whistling fouls and violations on any part of the field at any time. Fouls are normally not called immediately in front of your partner unless it is clear that he is shielded.

Monitoring Play

Play should be contained between the two Referees, much as it is in basketball. Eye contact should be maintained, particularly in conjunction with advantage clause situations. (L) keeps ahead of play and keeps fairly close to the touch-line. As the ball moves closer to his goal, he moves closer to the touch-line. When play moves into his penalty-area he should be on the goal-line closer to the goal, depending on the position of the last-but-one defender.

(T) is in the field approximately 10 to 20 yards inside the touch-line. He follows beyond midfield as close to the play as possible, taking into consideration field conditions, kicking strength of the players, their speed, his own speed, and that of his partner. He is in a position to reverse his field immediately should a counterattack develop, yet still be ahead of play.

The chief shortcoming of the poor Referee is the hugging of the touch-line. He thinks that the job is:

- Out-of-bounds
- Off-side
- Fouls in his half of the field

. . . . . and he does them in that order. The priorities *should* be

1. Game Control — Call fouls anywhere. Get rid of the my ½, your ½ philosophy. That can destroy the game, your partner, and ultimately you yourself.
2. Off-Side
3. Out-of-Bounds — If you are going to miss something, it is better to miss a meaningless out-of-bounds at midfield as opposed to an 'off-the-ball' foul.

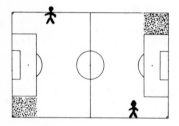

The toughest areas to monitor are the coffin corners. They are nobody's 'prime' area but rather, the responsibility belongs equally to both officials. It requires very tight trail support for calling fouls in these areas.

Calling the Infraction

- Blow the whistle and point in the direction the kick is to be taken.
- Give auditory (optional) and visual signal for the infraction.
  "PUSHING — NUMBER 14" (Give pushing signal)
- Give auditory (optional) and visual signal for the type of kick or throw-in.
  "BLUE KICK — DIRECT"

Simultaneous Whistle — Rule of thumb: Closer Referee immediately points in the proper direction. Any doubts as to who is closer can be resolved by whose half of the field it is in.

If different infractions are indicated, signal the infraction to each other.

- If dissimilar — the more serious prevails.
- If the same type of foul — DROP-BALL quickly by the closer Referee.

It is very important to signal the nature of all fouls. To fail to do so keeps partner from attaining full involvement in the game.

MECHANICS

The shaded areas  indicate the latitude of **(T)** and **(L)** positioning.

Kick-Off

What to look for on a kick-off.

- Do the players encroach?
- Was the ball played in a forward direction?
- Did the ball travel its circumference?

These questions are best answered by **(T)**.

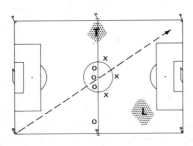

(T) whistles for the kick-off after:

- He receives a signal from **(L)** that his GK is ready and his team has the proper number of players.
- **(T)**s team is ready.
- The timekeeper (if used) is ready.

He is watching from the halfway line approximately 5-15 yards in from the touch-line.

(L) is approximately 20-25 yards downfield and 10 yards in from the touch-line. He watches for left wing encroachment when he is behind **(T)**.

Monitoring Off-Side

The dual system is the *worst* system for off-sides.

(L) may stay parallel with the next-to-last defender.

or

He may stay with the most advanced offensive player. This allows deeper penetration as a trail and puts you closer to play. However, you must be sure that you can get to the next to last defender before any offensive player does.

..... or, because the extensive use of either of the above results in a poor visual perspective, (L) may use a mixture of the two. This consists of staying even with the lead attacker *until he passes* the next-to-last defender; then he stays even with this next-to-last defender until *he re-passes* the lead attacker. Then (L) would switch back and stay with the lead attacker.

(T) comes in from behind and monitors play.

Read the game carefully for a team's off-side philosophy. If they extensively implement the 'trap', then it must be watched closely. The monitoring of play in general as well as off-side may be accomplished by pulling to the center of the field and much backwards running.

Goal-Kick or Corner-Kick?

As previously mentioned, the ends of the diagonal (referred to as the coffin corners) are the most troublesome areas to cover because of the distance away from their respective (L)'s. As the ball crosses the goal-line, the distinction between goal/corner-kick is sometimes a difficult one to make.

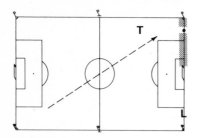 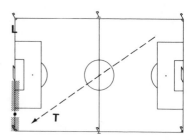

(T) can take some of the pressure off in one of the two ways:

He Makes the Call — If (T) is advanced enough into (L)'s half and clearly sees which man the ball came off of, he may make the call, provided he signals and indicates it quickly and decisively enough. (L) has signaled almost simultaneously the instant the ball went over the goal-line. (L) may now take his cue from (T) because he has him within his line of sight.

or . . .

He Gives a Subtle Indication — If he saw it as a corner-kick he continues his forward momentum and trots toward the corner.

A goal-kick is indicated by falling back toward the halfway line.

To stand perfectly still says, "I have no idea." Once (L) makes the call, (T) immediately becomes supportive in his movements.

Goal-Kick

What to look for in the goal-kick:

- Part of the ball within the goal-area.

- In correct half of the goal-area.

- Ball passing beyond the penalty-area before it is played.

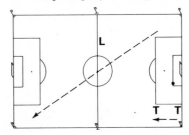

(T) checks for correct ball placement, then rapidly moves to a position at the front of the penalty-area to ensure that the ball leaves the area.

(L) is usually just inside the halfway line for a possible development at midfield and in line with the side of the penalty-area so he can see the ball in relation to the line.

Corner-Kick

(T) assumes the duties of the Referee who is operating under the diagonal or modified diagonal system of control. He is the main official for calling fouls within the goal area. This is because (L) is diluted with:

- Ball in and out of play, particularly the outswinger.

- Off-side potential.

- A goal being scored (100% of ball in?)

- Encroachment, if it is a near side corner-kick.

(T) must come down to the vicinity of the penalty-area. If he doesn't come within 25 of his partners' goal-line, then he should not accept an assignment with the system.

(L) must know where 10 yards in from the sideline is so he can cope with attempted encroachment.

Nearside Kick

(L) checks out ball placement, then . . .

- Is between intersection of goal-area and penalty-area line or is 10 yards in from the corner.

- Is approximately 1 foot behind the touch-line.

- As the ball is played, he pivots 180° on his inside foot following the flight of the ball and stepping into the field.

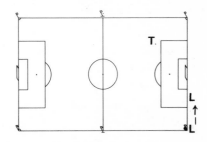

-45-

Farside Kick

(T) normally hates the farside corner-kick because it necessitates more running. He checks out ball placement, then moves back to his normal position, but not too close to the goal-area so as to get in the way of the kick.

(L) is in similar position as the nearside kick; only after the ball is kicked, he moves a little closer to the goal and perhaps a step or two into the field.

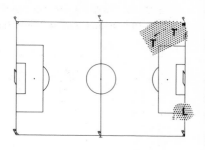

A problem area **(L)** must be aware of is recovery in sufficient time in order to monitor the off-side.

Penalty-Kick

The Referee who whistled the penalty immediately moves toward the penalty-spot, pointing at it. He then gives the signal for the type of foul.

Things to do before the penalty-kick can be taken:

- Everyone out of the penalty-area and penalty-arc.
- Correct ball positioning.
- Correct GK positioning.

(L) . . .

- Takes possession of the ball and makes sure that it is properly placed (either by himself or the kicker).
- Identifies the kicker to the GK.
- Makes sure GK is correctly positioned.
- Takes up position on the goal-line somewhere between the intersection of the goal-area and penalty-area lines.
- Gives the signal for the taking of the kick (after GK has indicated that he is ready).
- Watches for the ball entering the goal and GK foot movement (mostly forward/backward).

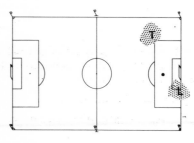

(T) . . .

- Clears out all but the kicker from the penalty-area and penalty-arc.
- Watches for encroachment and
- Lateral movement of the GK's feet.

Throw-Ins

On Opposite Touch-Line

If (T), try to be opposite the point of the throw-in. Come well into the field.

If (L), get downfield and well into the field of play.

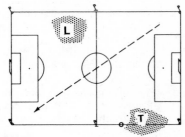

On Your Touch-Line

If (L), lead the throw by 10-20 yards. Stand either straddling or just outside of the touch-line.

If (T), be within 10 yards of the thrower, either straddling the touch-line or just inside the field of play.

Duties

If the throw is from the farside touch-line — be careful in whistling foul throw-ins. Try to limit your calls to those dealing with:

• Not starting from behind the head when the thrower presents his profile to you.

• Obviously releasing the ball from the side of the head.

. . . Otherwise call only the most *blatant* infractions when your partner is inattentive.

(T) has primary responsibility for seeing that the throw-in enters the field at the point it went out of bounds.

Free-Kicks

(L) is either even with the last-but-one defender for the possible off-side and in anticipation of the development of the play, or on the goal-line. As distance to the goal is shortened, he should move nearer to the goal for closer view.

(T) sees that the kick is properly taken. He places the ball if necessary.

The free-kick which results in the forming of a wall presents the Referee with one of his biggest challenges.

Important ingredients for the Referee are:

• Probability of a goal being scored.

• The wall being at least 10 yards back.

• Correct placement of the ball.

• Off-side monitoring.

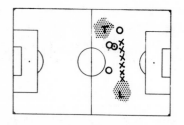

For kicks taken 20-35 yards out from the goal-line:

(T) comes up and monitors ball placement, and assists with pushing the wall back (if necessary).

(L) establishes the wall and monitors off-side.

Kicks taken within 20 yards of the goal-line are the really critical ones. Referees lacking diagonal experience seem to have a lot of trouble with this mechanic. Otherwise, they seem to instrinctively do it properly.

(L) pushes back the wall until (T) comes onto the scene, then he sprints to the end-line to check on the possible scoring of a goal (always top priority).

(T) makes sure that ball placement is OK. Re-pushes the wall back (if necessary) and stays on the wall for off-side monitoring.

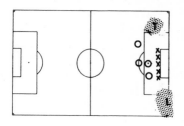

BEFORE, AT HALF, AND AFTER THE GAME

Before the Game

Each Referee identifies the captain and checks out all the players' equipment/apparel of either one or both teams together. The officials inspect field conditions together and verify measurements.

One official might be designated as the Senior Referee. The Senior Referee is responsible for the game report and has final say in matters of dispute. He overrules the other official only relative to interpretation of the laws of the game (not judgment calls). Conventionally he often is the one who delivers any pre-game instructions to the team captains, conducts the coin flips, and is the chief timekeeper.

At Half-Time

The Referee closest to the ball should pick it up. The two Referees run toward each other and then walk off the field together, retiring to an area which is away from players and spectators. The halftime interval should be used to discuss play during the first half and to make any adjustments deemed necessary.

After the Game

The closer Referee picks up the ball. The officials see that it is returned to its rightful owners. Both Referees then leave the field together.

Hint – At all times, avoid the temptation to explain a decision by your fellow Referee.

OTHER ASPECTS OF PLAY

Substitutions

New players enter at midfield. Each Referee has a team which reports to him (if required). During play he maintains a count of players on the team defending his goal from time to time.

Drop-Ball

Usually conducted by (T). (L) generally only puts into play a drop ball if it is quite near his touch-line and relatively deep into his territory. (See Dynamically Switching Diagonals — on the next page.)

Timekeeping

Time is normally kept by the Senior Referee. His partner keeps backup time. Both Referees should flash the time to one another when it gets down to five or less minutes remaining in the period.

This time is indicated by the hand, using the Referee's black uniform as background. Each finger equals one minute. Crossed index fingers means 30 seconds. To indicate that time has expired, the Referee Badge is covered.

If for some reason the prime timekeeper desires his partner to take over the timing responsibility, he indicates it by pointing from his watch to his partner. The partner acknowledges that he is now official timekeeper by first pointing to his own watch and then to himself.

Goalkeeper Fielding the Ball

Whenever the GK fields the ball, (T) lines up with the penalty-area line where he can observe steps as well as a possble handling of the ball in conjunction with the clearing punt/throw.

(L) is downfield in anticipating of a long clearing punt/throw by the GK (same position as for the goal-kick). He is particularly alert for possible off-side situations. (L) lines up with the *side* of the penalty-area whenever the GK if fielding a ball in that vicinity. This is done as a check in GK handling outside of the penalty-area.

Record Keeping

Scoring of Goals — The number of the player scoring each goal is recorded by the appropriate (L). This information is passed on to the other Referee if convenient before the subsequent kick-off.

Cautions and Ejections — Whenever administered by a Referee, he immediately relays data regarding the number of the player to his partner.

Information relating to any Caution *must be communicated* to one's partner before the booking of the player can be considered complete. The partner who is not cautioning must take the majority of this responsibility.

Dynamically Switching Diagonals (For Experienced Referee Teams)

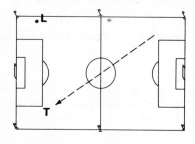

Occasionally a free-kick or a drop-ball occurs relatively deep into (L)'s territory near his touch-line. The three aspects which the Referee team must accomplish are correct: (1) ball placement, (2) location of the wall, and (3) position as goal judge.

For (T) to come all the way over to the other touch-line for administration or (1) and (2) is impractical, plus the added problem of having both officials on the same side of the field.

The well disciplines Referee team may choose to temporarily change diagonals to overcome this situation. To accomplish this, one of the Referees (usually T) signals his partner. (Crossing the index fingers of both hands back and forth accompanied with a vocal "switch" is an acceptable method.) Acceptance can be indicated by a nod of the head.

(L) now becomes (T). If it is a free-kick he is responsible for the wall and positioning of the ball. He then backpedals 10 to 15 yards to the position of a normal trailer. (T), who is now the new (L), moves down on the goal-line. The Referees change back whenever it is convenient (usually when the ball is out of play — throw-in, goal/corner-kick, etc.). Implementing this dynamic switching of diagonals requires both Referees being highly disciplined and continually having eye contact.

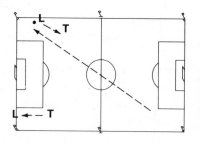

HINTS FOR REFEREES

1. Face the player throwing the ball in from the touch-line, without turning your back on players awaiting the throw-in.

2. Never instruct your partner to "stay out of *my* penalty-area." Rather, remind him that positioning and distance from play are the important factors in whistling under this system.

3. If you are alert, and fifty yards distant, you should be able to call an infraction that occurs in front of your partner, if you believe he was shielded.

4. Use hand signals for the advantage rule. Your partner will know you have seen a foul but have elected to let play continue.

5. Signal for the taking of an IFK especially if the ball went over the end-line. Your partner then knows that it isn't a goal-kick and that the opponents are vulnerable for being off-side.

6. When the Referee is in position for judging off-side, he must know *who* is between him and the touch-line.

7. Practice and be proficient at running backwards quickly.

8. Stay out of the penalty-area as much as possible. When you are there, you are vulnerable to being hit by a surprise shot on goal, and also are in a poor position to call off-side.

9. When a penalty-kick is called by either Referee, the two Referees must act together to administer the penalty. (L) whistles for the kick and acts as goal judge. (T) watches for encroachments and other violations.

MASTER SHEET — TWO REFEREES

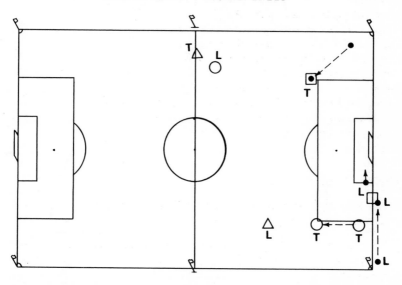

SYMBOLS

L = Lead Referee	△ = Kick-Off	● = Corner-Kick
T = Trail Referee	○ = Goal-Kick	□ = Penalty-Kick

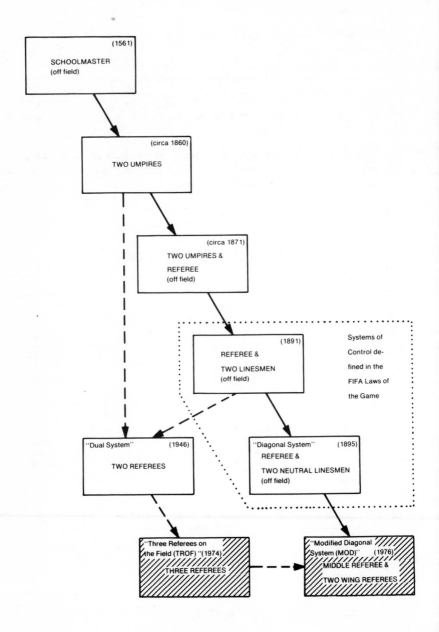

SCHOOLMASTER (off field) (1561)

TWO UMPIRES (circa 1860)

TWO UMPIRES & REFEREE (off field) (circa 1871)

REFEREE & TWO LINESMEN (off field) (1891)

Systems of Control defined in the FIFA Laws of the Game

"Dual System" (1946) TWO REFEREES

"Diagonal System" (1895) REFEREE & TWO NEUTRAL LINESMEN (off field)

"Three Referees on the Field (TROF)" (1974) THREE REFEREES

"Modified Diagonal System (MOD)" (1976) MIDDLE REFEREE & TWO WING REFEREES

THE MODIFIED DIAGONAL (MOD)

"The ultimate system for game control, flexibility, and training."

In June 1973, Joe Bonchonsky of Torrance, California conceptualized a new system of soccer officiating. Here are some of his words indicating a need for such a system.

"While players and coaches have advanced because of their own unbridled ingenuity, the Referee remains in the archaic times of soccer sytems and the big question is 'How long will the sport of soccer be able to live with the old system of refereeing? Modern day technology and its cameras have too often found the Referee allowing the injustices on the field prevailing over the efforts and artistry of better skilled players and coaches. With the MOD, the artists on the field will actually experience less whistling, knowing that the guilty will be punished and that their skills can be exhibitied."

Bonchonsky, a Referee, originally termed the system "Three Referees on the Field." In 1976 the name was subsequently changed to the Modified Diagonal (MOD) through a suggestion by Bill Mason of Palos Verdes, California, but its principles remain somewhat the same. MOD emphasizes the "team" effort in refereeing. The three Referees, all with whistles, must fully cooperate to benefit from the advantages of the system.

The whistle in the hand of the Wing Referee means that the game is stopped when it should be; when an infraction occurs. Also, the Middle Referee will be able to concentrate on the important aspects of play without the worry: "What's happening when I'm glancing for my Linesmen?"

BASIC COVERAGE

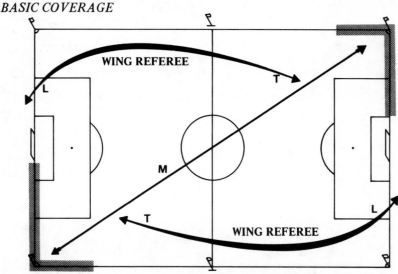

M = Middle Referee. He runs on the diagonal. The Wing Referees. They are located on the nearside and the farside of the field. One is designated *Lead* Referee (L) and the other as *Trail* Referee (T). These roles change instantaneously depending upon the direction of play.

MOD may be used in three main ways.
1. It may be used like a dual system of control plus one. In this mode all officials can and do perform all functions on an equal basis. This suggests not only equivalent ability of all three officials but also a high degree of teamwork.
2. It can be used as an extreme "Referee-Linesman" relationship whereby the wing officials give weak support... calling out-of-bounds, off-sides, and fouls only when they are positive that the middle Referee did not see it.
3. The system might be performed as a mix of the above two approaches. It all depends upon the personnel... their abilities and their rapport with one another.

The training of new officials is accomplished by either:
- Putting the trainee in the center, flanked by two experienced 'dual oriented' Referees who will carry him. He gets the feel of the game and participates to the degree that he feels comfortable.

- Having one or even two trainees on the wing flanking a Referee experienced in the diagonal system of control. He takes over and the wing(s) call out-of-bounds and off-side. Participation is increased as they grow into their refereeing role.

> The authors feel that the MOD system is the answer to modern day soccer officiating and should be very seriously considered by all Referees and soccer organizers.

MASTER SHEET — THREE REFEREES

SYMBOLS

M - Middle Referee

L = Lead Referee

T = Trail Referee

△ = Kick-Off

○ = Goal-Kick

● = Corner-Kick

☐ = Penalty-Kick

IV

During Play

THE USE OF THE WATCH

As with the whistle, the properly equipped Referee carries either two watches, or one with a dual function (time of day and a count up/count down stop watch). After he has synchronized watches with his two linesmen and noted actual time of the kickoff on a regular watch, he may sound his whistle for the commencement of the game. The game begins and he starts his stopwatch at the moment the ball has legally traveled its circumference. The Referee is the sole timekeeper on the field, and he may check time with his Linesmen for accuracy or for any other reason. Although an average of more than 100 stoppages occur on the field during the game, his watch must not be stopped, except for unusual circumstances.

WHEN TO STOP THE WATCH

YES	NO
Treatment of injuries, when a player cannot be safely removed from the field.	Ball out of bounds.
	After a goal. (Yes for High School and College.)
Lost ball, or ball that must be replaced.	
Deliberate wasting of time by either team, whether or not they are at an advantage.	After a foul.
	For the taking of a penalty-kick. (Yes for High School and College.)

Sometimes

When administering a caution or ejection (yes for High School and College) unless it is a very brief disciplinary procedure.

HINTS FOR REFEREES

1. It is quite difficult to observe the game and your watch at the same time. In the absence of a count down timer on your watch, you must observe your watch only during stoppages. If the period is about to end, count down the remaining seconds to yourself as you observe play, and check quickly before sounding the whistle to end the period.

2. **Arrange a signal system with your linesmen so there will be no discrepancies on time of game.**

Linesmen can signal the Referee regarding time remaining by using a hand held on a black uniform background. Use one finger for each minute remaining up to five minutes and either a closed fist or crossed index fingers for half-minute increments. A hand covering the Referee patch indicates that time has expired.

3. Do not indicate when you are making up time. Players who see a Referee checking his watch will deduce that he is aware of an unnatural stoppage.

4. A period can end when a ball is out of play.

5. When time runs out, the period is over, even if the ball is in the air (unless its during the 1978 World Cup).

6. The carrying of two watches (or the equivalent) is extrememly important. The second watch, set to regular time, is used to back up the primary watch. It sometimes happens that a Referee will stop his watch for some reason and then not properly restart it. The back-up watch then allows him to end the game properly and on time, making any allowance for time lost.

7. The Referee should periodically check his watch for accuracy, at least once every three months.

DUAL PURPOSE WATCHES (WRIST ALARM CHRONOGRAPHS)

- 1st Choice - A wristwatch with a countdown alarm.

- 2nd Choice - A normal wrist chronograph.

- Recommendations... Citizen, Seiko or Casio

PURCHASING A BACK-UP STOPWATCH

- Be sure that the 'reset' function doesn't operate when the watch is running.

- Avoid a watch with a 30 second sweep.

- Avoid one that can be stopped accidentally.

- Conventional stopwatch recommendations... Heuer and Minerva.

- The Ingersol is a setable stopwatch that is made in England. The first 45 minutes have a green background and it is very difficult to stop accidentally.

THE USE OF THE WHISTLE

It has been previously observed that the properly equipped Referee must have two whistles. It is recommended that the spare whistle be very accessible, as it is intended for emergencies when the game whistle is defective.

Most experienced Referees carry the whistle in the hand, rather than in the mouth, for the following reasons.

1. A Referee should allow himself time to think and to change his original quick decision. A whistle carried in the mouth is often sounded too hastily.

2. A whistle carried in the mouth is inviting danger.

3. A whistle carried in the mouth makes breathing difficult and unnatural.

4. Heavy breathing with a whistle in the mouth can cause an accidental whistle. If you choose to run with a whistle in your mouth, keep your tongue in the opening of the whistle.

5. A whistle carried on a string around the neck discourages running, for it will bounce, and is distracting. If placed around the neck and held while running, it inhibits free movement on the field. It also detracts from the appearance of the Referee.

It should be obvious that the whistle is the Referee's tool, not his weapon. He should whistle only when necessary, for each time he does, the attention of the participants and spectators switches from game to Referee. One strong short and decisive whistle is usually all that is required. Any Referee who sounds the whistle unnecessarily is seeking attention. It is advisable to whistle longer and louder for a severe foul, and the whistle should say, "I won't allow this to happen again."

HINTS

1. Referees should sound a whistle for the taking of a penalty-kick. This audible signal is for the goalkeeper and for the kicker as well, for they are studying each other and should not have to be distracted from their concentration by having to look at the Referee for a hand signal. If the penalty-kick is taken before the whistle is blown, the kick must be retaken, regardless of the outcome.

2. For emphasis, some Referees prefer to whistle for a goal. This is not recommended, for unfortunately this is sometimes done prematurely, and if the whistle is sounded before the ball is entirely over the goal-line, a drop-ball must be given at the position of the ball when the whistle occurred. Furthermore, an unwhistled goal makes the disputed goal a somewhat easier solution, in that consultation with the Linesman can be carried out with the players' knowing that the Referee has not yet made up his mind on the legality of the goal.

3. The authors recommend the following whistles: the Balillas: Al, Micro, Arbiter, and Balilla/2 (plastic); Acme Thunderer (plastic) and Acme Thunderer Valsport (wide mouth metal).

WHEN WHISTLE SHOULD BE BLOWN

* = Required

Before all kick-offs
- start of game*
- start of half*
- put in play after a goal

For any violation of the Laws of the Game
- improper throw-in*
- to award free-kicks*
- to award penalty-kicks*

Out of Bounds, resulting in . . .
- throw-in ⎫ Unless it is clearly out of
- goal-kick ⎭ bounds
- corner-kick

To put into play . . .
- a penalty-kick
- after a substitution
- after an injury
- a free-kick if the attacking team has asked for the 10 yards. (They shouldn't have to.)
- just prior to dropping the ball

Period Endings*
- half — It's often conventional for the Referee to blow his whistle two times.
- game — Blow whistle three times and point to the center of the field.

If the Referee mistakenly whistles — resume play with a DROP-BALL.

If play is interrupted by a Non-Referee's whistle — PLAY ON.

At first stoppage, have captain of the home team take the necessary action to identify and remove the person blowing the whistle. The Referee has the authority to order the removal of a problem spectator.

*High School/College — The Referee shall blow his whistle whenever the ball is out of play.

SIGNALS & SIGNALING

The laws of the game list only one required hand signal for Referees, this being the upraised arm for the indirect free-kick. The benefits of this signal are obvious, particularly when a kick is to be taken near the goal. The signal is solely for the players, so they will know the options open to them as they attack and defend the goal when the kick is taken.

A whistle is sounded on the field ... is it for pushing? holding? off-side? obstruction? The Referee will sometimes point in the direction where the ball is to be kicked, but this is the only signal that is normally given. When this happens, players, coaches, spectators, and sometimes other officials are all kept uninformed of the situation and of the infraction. When asked, sometimes the Referee will explain to the player the nature of the violation. This, however, is not recommended, even to the team captain, for it leads to further conversation and to more questions.

The purpose of this section is to recommend a series of signals that a Referee may use in the course of a game, signals which will neither slow the game nor call undue attention to the Referee. Rather, they will convey information in a concise and direct manner to both player and spectator. Furthermore, they will improve Referee-player communications, nonverbally.

With the exception of the accepted signal for "play on," signals are best used immediately after the whistle and prior to the Referee's pointing the direction of the kick. While the Referee is using his handsignal, he will be doublechecking in his mind, making sure that he does not erroneously point in the wrong direction. The proper use of these signals will in part lift the veil of secrecy that sometimes exists between violator and Referee (and violated!), and will further extend his authority on the field. All Referees must again be reminded that these signals are offered here only as suggested improvements for the game.

NON-FREE-KICKS

SCORING

Goal
or Point to the
Center Circle.

No Goal

Goal-Kick
Point toward the
halfway-line with
one hand.

Corner-Kick
Point to corner-flag
on side kick is to be
taken.

Penalty-Kick
Point to penalty-mark.

INDIRECT

Dangerous Play

Misconduct

Charging
At inappropriate time

Off-Side

Obstruction
Hit the chest with palms

**Goalkeeper
Steps**

DIRECT

Handling Ball   **Tripping**

Kicking
Show red card

Pushing

Holding

**Charging Violently
Charging from Behind**

Striking

Jumping at

MISCELLANEOUS

Advantage

"Play-On"

Time-Out

HINTS

- Obvious fouls need only the whistle. Everyone knows what has happened. Don't point or gesticulate.

- Subtle fouls, such as an obstruction preceding a charge, need a definite, clear, and immediate signal. Walk or move quickly away from the player (unless you sense possible retaliation), for you will no doubt have the possibility for dissent in such decisions. Players never consider the possibility that you are right.

- Get the habit of walking or moving toward the direction of the team that fouled. This shows everyone that the kick will be taken toward their goal.

- A hand signal indicating direction of kick is all right in most cases. However, do not keep it up after players have fully accepted the direction. Otherwise, the advisable 60° angle of the arm could possibly be interpreted as an IFK signal.

- Do not get in the habit of pointing where the ball should be placed for a kick. "Over there, near the bare spot" is enough. Like the whistle, the hand and arm must be used only when needed.

- Pointing to the goal area and the corner area for kicks is fine, but when everyone knows what's happening, don't do it just "for kicks."

- A penalty-kick, always unwelcome by the defense, demands your pointing to the penalty-spot.

- Keep the "play on" signal to a minimum. Usually no one is looking and no one cares. In most cases you are trying to justify not calling a foul.

If you see a bad situation developing, keep the ball moving before things get worse.

"Dirtiness is a substitute for ability."

Willy Keo

Don't talk about your good games. Let them speak for themselves.

CHEAPSKATER

Make it two coats Fred — this uniform has got to last me for three weeks.

- Carries one card; yellow on one side and red on the other.
- Tapes up socks with roll of adhesive tape 'obtained' from a team trainer four months ago.
- Has his flip-coin attached to a chain.
- Collects discarded screw-in cleats laying in the vicinity of the field.
- Uses 15 year old Acme Thunderer which hangs on a shoelace lanyard.
- Sun has caused shoulder and seat of pants area to turn brown.
- Comes to game carrying Referee gear in paper Safeway bag.
- Borrows a Timex from one of the Linesmen.
- Asks Coach if he has cash, instead of a check.
- Gives wife worn out soccer shoes for use as she does the yard work.
- Uses Xerox copy of Referee Data Card contained in *Fair or Foul*.

REFEREE/LINESMAN DATA CARD

The Data Card is a structured format designed to replace the traditional notebook of blank paper. It is scaled to fit on a 4" x 6" card which is folded in half for convenient pocket insertion. After the match, it can be placed into any standard 4" x 6" card file for future reference.

Colors of the teams are of primary concern. Misconduct and goal information on the left side of the card pertains to the Red team and that on the right to the White team. Numbers of the team captains and their alternates are directly beneath their respective team colors.

An "X" is placed into the appropriate box the the team taking the kick-off. To start the second period, the opposite team kicks-off. The direction the ball is to be kicked-off in is noted in the box marked "Direction." A permanent landmark could be used instead of compass direction if desired. Kick-offs starting a period during regulation play are taken in the same direction.

Time of Day (the backup to your watch with stop action) is recorded on the upper left hand portion of the card. The difference between End Time of the 1st half and Start Time of the 2nd half tells you what the actual halftime interval was.

Match Self Evaluation is accomplished in the upper right hand portion of the card. An overall rating is made (0–10) as well as pertinent comments which may act as the impetus to modify your behavior.

-64-

The Misconduct portion is centralized. It tells you the name and number (#) of the player who was cautioned (C) or ejected (E), the reason, and the time in minutes when the offense occurred (Min.). An added feature is recording the opponent's number (Opp. #) of the player who was the target of the violator's action. Sometimes (as in the case of #6 on the White team), an instigating player can be identified and actively monitored, thus heading off the ejection which unfortunately occurred in the 84th minute.

Your status (R = Referee, L = Linesman, W = Wing Referee (MOD)) is indicated in the box at the bottom labeled 'Status-Self'. Directly to the right of this is located the status and name of your fellow official(s).

The back of the card is a Tie Breaker Kick Record for use when the match is decided by either kicks taken from the penalty-mark or a shootout (as used in the NASL).

Team colors are entered for the winner of the toss (they must kick first) and their opponent. Each kicker has recorded his name, number (#), if he made the shot or not (X = Score, − = Miss), and what the cumulative (running) totals are.

The results are entered on the front of the card (PK Results) directly beneath the Final Score box.

TIE BREAKER KICK RECORD

WINNER OF TOSS CHATHAM				OPPONENT HARRISON			
PLAYER NAME	#	X −	RUNNING TOTAL	PLAYER NAME	#	X −	RUNNING TOTAL
BOB HOLLAND	6	X	1	JIM POST	2	X	1
PHIL BARKSDALE	2	−	1	OTTO HILTON	11	--	1
BOSE KOLDEWEY	3	X	2	BILL WILSON	10	--	1
BILL PARKINSON	8	−	2	JIM HAAS	4	X	2
HARRY GRAHAM	9	X	3	JOHN BAS	8	X	3
HARRY WEAVER	7	X	4	PAUL GILL	7	X	4
AL OLSEN	5	−		MARIO SAVIO	3	X	5

Team colors are entered for the winner of the toss (they must kick first) and their opponent. Each kicker has recorded his name, number (#), if he made the shot or not (X = Score, − = Miss), and what the cumulative (running) totals are.

The results are entered on the front of the card (PK Results) directly beneath the Final Score box.

THOUGHTS ON GAME CONTROL

The problem of game control cannot be over-discussed in Referee clinics, and deserves the closest attention of every soccer official.

The success of every soccer Referee will largely depend on the attitude he carries with him toward the game and its players. The Referee is evaluated from the moment he enters the field of play. He is judged by everyone on his dress, his voice and confidence, and his general demeanor. He should be thorough without reciting the laws, enthusiastic without appearing high strung and nervous, polite without appearing too friendly, and firm while being fair.

The Referee's best friend on the field is not his whistle, for his whistle must be used when all else fails. Anyone can blow a whistle, and many fouls occurring in soccer are obvious. Unlike his whistle, his voice will serve him best, and bring him closer to the players. The good Referee will never let a hard foul go without a word to the player. These warnings help prevent cautions, as cautions help prevent ejections and ejections help prevent player riots. These words of advice to a player should always be direct, and positive: "Let's keep the hands down when going for the ball," or "This isn't the kind of tackle I allow," instead of "Don't use your hands going after the ball," or "If you tackle like that again, you'll be cautioned."

Positioning is vitally important when the Referee talks to a player. He should not always approach the player directly, for this will call attention to the Referee's action. Rather, he should move alongside the player, or he may be moving away from the player while talking. There is no "punishment" involved, and the Referee is saying, "I want to get on with the game, but you first must know how I will react to your acts." Words are administered, if possible, so that both offended and offender can hear. This prevents retaliation, and the offended knows that the Referee is on the field to protect the rights of the players. Even when advantage is allowed, the Referee may say, "Play on, watch the tripping #10." On such an occasion the Referee leaves no doubt that he has seen it, allowed the advantage, and noticed the number of the player who fouled. He has thus gained the respect of both players, and others within earshot, and he probably will not have to warn this player again.

The testing period for the Referee is in the first few minutes of play of each period. If the Referee is firm, the testing period will then be over, and the players will settle down to a fair game. If the Referee fails the testing period, for whatever reason, the game will proceed, but with players waiting for the opening when they can gain the unfair advantage. For the Referee, the game is won in these precious minutes. For the players, they must wait the full duration of the contest.

HINTS:

1. Superior field positioning is essential to good game control. Most players will accept a questionable call when a Referee is in a favorable position to call an infraction. They will always suspect even an inconsequential whistle if the Referee is far from play.

2. There are times when the Referee is best-advised to keep distance from players, and at the same time require them to stay away from him. When a penalty-kick is awarded, dissent usually is prevalent except with the most disciplined of teams. After calling the infraction, and while waiting for players to position themselves, the Referee should move to some isolated portion of the penalty-area, where players seldom congregate. He has created distance between himself and the players. If players try to approach him, he may say, "The foul has been called and it is a penalty. I will not change it. If you approach me, you will be cautioned for dissent." (Ungentlemanly conduct)

3. A smile from the Referee should be seen at least once after he has entered the field. This will prove he is human. Too many Referees assume their responsibility with never a smile nor a bit of humor. This method can break the tension in a game, but should never be attempted when it could be misconstrued as being at the expense of a player.

4. The Referee's main responsibility lies in protecting law abiding players from those who don't.

There will be many challenges to your game control. David Socha, who represented America at the 1982 World Cup, is oblivious to players' reaction.

WARNINGS, CAUTIONS, AND EJECTIONS

The consistent and disciplined attitude of the Referee is best exemplified in his handling of warnings, cautions, and ejections. Since the Referee whistles the game not for the players or spectators but in order to apply the Laws of the Game, he must take extreme measures when a single disruptive act or constant infringement of the laws takes place.

Law XII states rather clearly the conditions under which a player is to be cautioned, and those conditions under which he is to be removed from the game. The Referee should memorize the four basic conditions where a player shall be cautioned and the three where he shall be ejected from a game. He should not hesitate to employ these laws.

The World Cup of 1970 brought a partial answer to communication difficulties on the field, where in international competition an Argentine referee may be trying to caution a Moroccan or a Czech player. Obviously, the language difficulties are great, greater perhaps than the tensions of the game. A system of yellow cards for cautions and red cards for ejections was employed, for the benefit of players, coaches, and spectators alike. If a player was being cautioned, a small 3" x 5" yellow card was held high by the Referee, followed by the booking of the player. No words were to be spoken, in any language. Similarly, a red card was used for a more serious situation, when a player was being sent off the field. Whether it was the threat of the cards, the quality of the refereeing, or the players themselves no one will know for sure, but the red cards were not needed, and a World Cup without serious incident was soon history.

Other soccer organizations have accepted the cards, citing among other reasons the example that is made of the offender as the card is held high. Whatever the reasons, this idea is a very constructive step toward game control, and is highly recommended for all levels of soccer.

The word "warning" appears nowhere in the laws of the game, yet comes up frequently in referee discussions, and sometimes on the field. Warnings as such are rather nebulous, and are usually the easy way out for a Referee who for some reason is hesitating to issue a caution. For our purposes here, a warning is a "soft caution." In his efforts to minimize conversation on the field, the Referee must keep his warnings at a minimum, and with little explanation. It is the Referee's desire to avoid and to anticipate troubles on the field, and he may occasionally warn a player that his actions could lead to something more serious. Play should not be stopped to issue a warning, but these few well chosen words should come during a natural stoppage, and, as with cautions, in a place where players may not gather around the Referee. The warning is enough for most players, but if not, the caution will come as less of a surprise.

HINTS FOR REFEREES:

1. A free-kick, particularly one near the goal, is often the subject of much delay and consternation on the part of both Referee and players. Defenders who stand over or in front of the ball, without yielding ten yards must be cautioned. Other defenders, farther from the ball, often rush forward before the ball is kicked. When they do, the whistle must be sounded immediately, and the offenders cautioned. The Referee must *not* apply the advantage clause and await the outcome of the kick. He shall not prevent the kick from being taken unless asked by the players to step off the ten yards.

2. A player who has been sent off must leave the field. It is not recommended that he be seated with substitutes on the bench.

3. If an expelled player comes back on the field, he is no longer considered a player, and is a foreign object (regardless of his nationality). If he handles the ball, a drop ball is called.

4. If a captain is ejected, a substitute captain must be named among the remaining players.

5. If an extreme situation develops on the field, where cautions and ejections seem only to lead to more problems, the Referee may call both teams or both captains to the center of the field. He may then warn them that further violence will result in termination of the game.

6. The Referee should go to the player to administer a caution or an ejection. To require him to come to you is to abuse him.

7. When a player is cautioned or ejected, the name of the offender, and not just the number, must be recorded, as well as the offense and time elapsed.

8. Carry your two cards in separate pockets. This eliminates the problem of confusion and embarassing mistakes.

9. While it is sometimes advisable to be slow (ceremonial) in issuing a card, needless delay is unwise. Remember, that time is not out for such sanctions.

☆ ★ ☆ ★ ☆ ★ ☆ ★ ☆ ★ ☆ ★ ☆ ★ ☆ ★ ☆ ★ ☆ ★ ☆ ★ ☆ ★ ☆

Some think it's a positive move...

In Argentina, an addition was introduced to the Laws of the Game. When a player holds the arm or any other part of the body of an opponent, the Referee automatically cautions the offender, and also makes the appropriate gesture to caution the whole team. From this moment, any other player from the cautioned team who commits a similar infringement will immediately be sent off the field by the Referee.

☆ ★ ☆ ★ ☆ ★ ☆ ★ ☆ ★ ☆ ★ ☆ ★ ☆ ★ ☆ ★ ☆ ★ ☆ ★ ☆

GOALKEEPERS AND THE LAWS

In the eyes of many Referees, goalkeepers are privileged. Certainly it is easier to call an infraction in favor of the goalkeeper rather than against him, and intelligent goalkeepers know this. Referees should be keenly aware of the variety of infractions in connection with the play near goal.

Basic Observations:

- Goalkeepers, by nature, are more aggressive than many other players. They see themselves as leaders of the defense. As such, they cal. teammates off balls in the air and on the ground.

- Goalkeepers occasionally place themselves in dangerous positions. This is done at their own risk, and not to be called "dangerous play."

- Goalkeepers are skilled with the feet. If they trip someone, it is a desperate move, and can be intentional.

- Some goalkeepers guard the goal, others the whole Penalty Area. The wider the range of the goalkeeper, and the more he commits himself, the more likely he is to commit fouls.

Some Common Violations

By Goalkeepers

- Jumping at an opponent, (usually over the back), (Penalty Kick)

- Raising a leg to fend off an opponent, (dangerous play), (Indirect Free Kick)

- Deliberately handling the ball outside of the Penalty Area to stop a one-on-one attack (Direct Free Kick and a caution)

- Any foul when a crowded Goal Area may mean escape from detection

- Following through on a fisted ball, and striking an opponent. (Striking an Opponent, Penalty Kick, Caution, possible ejection)

By Attackers

- Playing the ball dangerously, even when the goalkeeper is not in possession. (Dangerous Play. Indirect Free Kick)

- Jumping at the goalkeeper. Attacker usually coming in at speed, and goalkeeper is vulnerable because he is jumping up, and subject to injury. (Direct Free Kick)

- Pushing or holding the goalkeeper. (Direct Free Kick)

- "Innocently" standing in the immediate vicinity of the goalkeeper, usually after a save. (Law 12, IBD 8 is directed toward these players. Players must be cautioned if they persist) (Obstruction. Indirect Free Kick)

- Obstructing goalkeeper on corner kicks, long throw-ins, and on goalmouth skirmishes. (Everyone must play the ball) (Obstruction, Indirect Free Kick)
- Turning one's back, and charging at goalkeeper, just after a high ball has been saved. (Charging violently, Direct Free Kick)
- Failing to stop or turn away from a goalkeeper when a save has been made, and when the ball is in possession. (Obstruction, Indirect Free Kick)

Goalkeeper Possession

Goalkeeper possession occurs when one or both hands are holding the ball and keeping it from moving. Once the goalkeeper possesses the ball and releases it into play (by putting it on the ground) it may not be touched with the hands until it has been touched or played by another player.

Allowed:

Bouncing with the hand (steps counted)
Throwing the ball in the air and catching it (steps counted)
Dribbling with the feet (steps not counted)

Not Allowed: (Sanction - Indirect Free Kick)

Tapping the ball along with the hands
Throwing the ball in the air, letting it hit the ground, then picking it up.

Goalkeeper Control

Goalkeepers must be allowed the opportunity to bring the ball under control before being penalized. If a ball is caught in the air, but lost upon landing, it may be regrasped without penalty. A hard shot, not immediately controlled, may be regrasped, without penalty.

Fouls involving the goalkeeper may bring retaliation. A peacemaker moves in to avoid a confrontation.

Do you know what a goalkeeper may and may not do?

9.15 METERS, PLEASE!

Make no mistake about it, the administering of free-kicks (including penalties) is probably the single act which separates the superior from the average Referee. Since free-kicks are "set" situations, which, if properly executed, result in goals, the defense may use a variety of "gamesmanship" moves to prevent the goal.

Defensive players are required to be 10 yards (9.15 meters) away from the ball for the taking of all free-kicks and corner-kicks. The alert Referee must know that some players have been coached to distract the offense, delay the game, and generally to cause confusion so the defense may be made ready. This is particularly true with all "ceremonial" kicks near goal, where the wall is being set up and where offensive players are equally as confused. In fact, there usually seems to be guesswork on the part of the attacking team . . . who will take the kick, and how will it be taken?

WHEN THE FOUL IS AWARDED

1. Immediately point the direction of the kick. If it is indirect, raise the arm and say, "Indirect kick."

2. Indicate the place where the kick is to be taken.

3. Move away from the play, so you will not interfere with a quick free-kick. While you are doing so, if necessary, remind the defense to quickly retreat, or they will be cautioned.

IF YOU ARE ASKED TO MARK TEN YARDS
(Only the kicking team has the right to ask)

1. Indicate, "All right, but wait for my signal (FIFA recommends a whistle) before kicking." (They have now reduced the chances for surprise.)

2. Mark it off by quickly running 5-6 steps (or, you should be able to estimate the distance of ten yards within less than 2 feet). Never stride it off. Never push players back with hands or arms.

3. Say, "They're back. They won't encroach." (Players who hear this won't *dare* encroach!)

HINTS:

- If the kicking team has to ask for the ten yards, you probably haven't done your job. Laws XIII IBD2 and Law XVII require that players retreat, and they cannot be allowed to waste time.

- If you stand over the ball and try to move the wall, you are preventing a kick and inviting the defense to defy your own estimate of ten yards.

- Be careful about using your whistle to move the wall. You may be whistling when your back is turned on the ball, and some enterprising attacker has sent the ball on the way to the goal. Use your voice.

THE WALL

Closely allied with the "ten yards" ritual is the wall itself, always set up to prevent an easy shot at goal. Most important is the concept of the advantages which accrue to the attacking team. The attacking team may:

- Take the kick at any time, unless they have asked for ten yards.
- Station players within the defensive wall, if space allows.
- Form their own wall, in front of the "ten yard" wall.
- Ask for "ten yards" from the Referee.
- Delay the taking of the kick for a reasonable period of time in order to confuse the defense.

The well-prepared Referee must expect the unexpected when a free-kick is awarded near goal. The most common abuses are:

Defensive

(a) Players standing over or near the ball to delay.

Remedy: As already stated, move them back quickly, with a firm voice. Don't threaten them, but caution them if you must.

(b) All the players in the wall refuse to retreat the proper distance.

Remedy: Stop the taking of the kick, if you are convinced that the offense will not be disrupted . Caution all defensive players who have not moved. You may also want to stop time. If you do so, make sure they know that these tactics will serve no good, for time is out.

(c) Players rush at the kicker (the ball) as he moves to kick, and before the ball is in play.

Remedy: Whistle immediately, before the ball is in play, and then caution. If whistle is late (after the kick), caution, and have the kick taken from the spot where the infraction occurred. If ball goes directly in goal following offender's action, allow goal (provided that you haven't whistled), then caution.

Offensive

(a) Occasionally more than one player "runs over" the ball in an attempt to confuse the defense. You may feel this is ungentlemanly conduct. Generally, Referees let this go, but remember the offense does not have unlimited advantages for the taking of the free-kick.

(b) Players try to force their way into a wall. A linking of arms by the defense seems fair, and is generally done to prevent the ball going through the wall. Players on the offense in a defensive wall will invariably cause elbowing, pushing, and striking. Discourage it.

FURTHER HINTS:

- Off-side sometimes occurs directly from a free-kick, when both teams are within a wall. The attacking players must move forward just prior to the kick to avoid the possibility of being called for off-side.

- If an indirect free-kick is taken within 10 yards of the opponent's goal, the Referee should say, "Defense, ten yards away or on the goal-line." It is not necessary to add that players, if on the goal-line, should be between the goal posts. If an infringement occurs, deal with it on an individual basis. *Both feet* must be on the goal-line.

- Young players under 14 have little concept of the wall and of tactics. Show them what is right, and they will comply.

- Most problems in the wall can be anticipated. Be ahead of the players in your thinking, and take care of problesm before they happen.

L.A. Aztecs

The wall continually poses problems for Referees. Here, the Referee has made the players comply with the 9.15 meters, and he is holding up play and turning his back in order to run into position for the taking of the free-kick. Can you see the offensive player in the wall? What do you think the players in white will do when the Referee has turned his back?

INJURIES

Soccer is not without its injuries, and they may result by means which are fair or foul, sometimes through inexperience and clumsiness, and sometimes through deviousness and premeditation.

The problem facing the Referee is how to stop the game at the proper time when an injury occurs in the field of play. A slight injury deserves only token notice by the Referee until a natural stoppage occurs, at which time he may stop the game. A more serious injury normally deserves immediate attention and the game should be stopped without delay. However, if the injury occurs at a place where there is no longer game activity and to a player who is not involved in the play when the injury is noticed, the game should be stopped only when the ball is out of play *or* when the player or his team is suddenly at a disadvantage through the injury. This is especially important when the goalkeeper is incapacitated and the play is suddenly shifted in his direction.

HINTS TO REFEREES

1. When the Referee stops play due to an injury, he must give a drop-ball at the point of play when the game was stopped. (High school — if one team has clear possession of the ball, give them an indirect-free-kick.)

   Drop-balls within the penalty-area are to be avoided, if possible. Stop play for an injury after the goalkeeper has made his clearing move.

2. Try to avoid touching a player. If he is injured and in need of medical attention, signal for help from a club trainer or coach.

3. Do not allow teams to group and refresh themselves during an injury timeout. Make every effort to have the injured player(s) removed from the field so that play may resume.

4. Do not allow the team trainer or coach on the field unless you suspect that the injured player cannot attend to himself.

5. Do not allow players from either team to crowd around an injured player.

6. Do not answer players' queries about the game during this stoppage of play.

7. An opponent who lifts a player from the ground to humiliate him and to minimize his injuries must be cautioned for ungentlemanly conduct.

8. Soccer injuries, as with ski injuries, are more frequent later in the day, when muscles become tired and reactions slow. Players also will sometimes feign injuries at this time to regain strength and wind.

9. In youth soccer the Referee should consider the age of the player in stopping play for injury. Generally, the younger the player, the quicker the game should be stopped.

Horst Müller

Circumstances surrounding injuries are as varied as the injuries themselves. Bad luck, player inadequacy, fatigue, or player intention can all be a part of what leads up to the drama of the game stoppage for injury. In a World Cup game (top), the Referee chooses to signal for the trainer. In a youth game (below), the Referee, though lacking somewhat in perfect dress, wisely decides to stop the game immediately and attend to a player who was hit in the nose by the ball. If a Referee has seen what caused the injury, he is better able to determine at what point to stop play.

WHAT TO DO AT HALFTIME

Law VII states that halftime shall not exceed five minutes, except by consent of the Referee. If, due to special circumstances, the Referee deems it necessary to extend the halftime period beyond five minutes, he will probably meet with little resistance, for this period usually lasts ten to fifteen minutes.

Some experienced Referees have the habit of announcing, upon the period's end, that "Time is up . . . five minutes between halves." They will then immediately start timing this interval, and will reconvene the players four minutes later, allowing a minute for re-assembly and organization of the two teams. All of the above is advisable, for it establishes the Referee's authority even during halftime, and allows no extra time for rest.

The Referee should be seen only with his two neutral linesmen at halftime. They shall not accept refreshment from either team, nor shall they be seen discussing the game with managers, players, coaches, or spectators. This valuable time is to be spent exchanging mutual constructive criticisms on the progress of the game.

Probably the singlemost important topic at halftime should be a discussion of players' behavior and play. If there are problems or anticipated problems, (the second half invariably presents more of a challenge than the first), they should be brought out. Warnings, cautions, and ejections should be discussed in detail. Often Referees are seen at halftime with seemingly little to discuss. Two topics should be in mind: (1) "What did we do in the first half?" and (2) "How are we going to do in the second half?"

HINTS ON WHAT TO DO AT HALFTIME

1. Always retain the game ball at halftime, for you are responsible for the ball until game's end.

2. During the five minute interval, warm up again by running from one goal to the other as you re-inspect the nets, which may have become loose with halftime activities.

3. Never be afraid to ask a fellow Referee at half time if he is noticing things on the field that you are not seeing. If he is, it is his duty to report them to you.

4. If a Linesman is doing his job, he should be complimented at halftime by the Referee. If he is not, the Referee should try to be constructive in his approach to him. The Referee needs his support, for an uncooperative Linesman can destroy the efforts of the best Referee.

5. Be extra alert during the opening minutes of each half. This is the time when players will test your alertness and your strict enforcement of the rules of the game.

6. Never smoke within view of players or spectators.

THE "RICE PUDDING" GAME

Ken Aston has wisely grouped the dull, easy, unchallenging contests into the category of "rice pudding" games. These games, while always containing the possibility of unexpected isolated incidents, make the Referee wish he were elsewhere. Challenging the Assessor as much as the Referee, they do occur, and sometimes frequently. One international Referee was known to deliberately call a foul the wrong way, just to add some spice to a listless game. (We do not advocate this.)

We feel that at least one in four or five games doesn't present much of a challenge to you. During these games, you can still be challenged, and you can improve. Consider these areas:

1. **Cooperation.** Use the game to develop special ways of cooperation and communication with the Linesmen. (See chapter on Communication.)

2. **Fitness.** In a game that is not hotly contested, the ball will not go from end to end as quickly. Experiment with new ways of running. Try longer strides, running backwards, or perhaps being ahead of play more than usual.

3. **Mechanics.** While concentrating on play, practice a constant eye communication (peripheral vision) with Linesmen. Is it possible to watch your Linesmen without taking your eyes off the play? It can be done, and now is the time to practice this skill.

4. **Attentiveness.** Listen to everything going on near the touchline and in the field of play. Sharpen your awareness of the banter going on among the players. A Referee who says he never hears what's going on both on and off the field is missing a lot.

5. **Communication with players.** Chances are that the players are as bored with the whole thing as you are. Try some new ways of talking with players. One Referee we know loosened things up considerably during a game by saying to a halfback during an attack: "I'll race you to the goal-line." Have you ever thought of the facial expression you tote around with you? It might be time to try something new.

Finally, sharpen that attitude, and keep alert. A lot of games explode when all seems well, and almost everyone's asleep.

 Expect the unexpected in your games.

"Don't just stand there, say something."
Experienced FIFA Referee John Davies of San Francisco knows when to turn it off.

V

Don't Just Do Something...
Stand There!

THE ADVANTAGE CLAUSE

"It must be clear, immediate, and effective."

The advantage clause is a very effective tool for the Referee, for it allows him to ignore the whistle for the good of the game.

Law V states that "a Referee may refrain from penalizing in cases where he is satisfied that by doing so he would give an advantage to the offending team."

The advantage clause is self-explanatory. Contrary to the "no harm, no foul" situation in basketball, there can indeed be harm, but as long as the offended player or team will retain the advantage, or have more of an advantage by retaining the ball without game stoppage, no foul is called.

The correct application of this clause within Law V is most difficult for the inexperienced Referee, and real understanding of its meaning will come only through extensive game experience. The new Referee should know here that he can only *assume* what *might* happen if he allows play to go on, and that he is always technically right by ignoring the clause and whistling for all violations, regardless of the position of the offended. Most qualified referees admit that in cases where extreme discipline problems prevail and when a player may retaliate for an unpunished offense, it is always better to call the foul and ignore the clause.

Generally speaking, the more advanced the level of the game, the more the advantage clause will be applied, for the players will expect it. In lower levels of soccer such as youth competition, the official should endeavor to teach the players that all fouls are unfair, and must be penalized.

"Play On."

Horst Muller

HINTS TO REFEREES

1. In applying the advantage, it is always advisable to acknowledge having seen a foul. Recommended signals are either raising an arm, or waving arms and hands at waist level with a verbal indication of "Advantage, Play On." This will indicate to both players and spectators that you have noticed the foul.

2. Once you have elected to apply the advantage, you may not change your decision, even though a player may stop play, lose his own advantage, and ask for a whistle.

3. When in doubt, do not use the advantage. The player must have clear possession and the clear advantage that he had before the infraction.

4. Early in the game, apply the advantage only when a direct scoring chance is evident, but not at midfield. After the authority of the Referee has been established, a more liberal application of advantage may be used.

5. In a hard fought game where extreme contact is frequent, it is often advisable to neglect the advantage as a preventive measure to keep the game in control.

6. If the advantage is applied, and a sanction is in order, the Referee should wait until the ball is out of play to caution or eject.

7. The advantage is also applied when a player is fouled but a teammate obtains or retains control of the ball.

8. On a foul that takes place in the penalty-area, the Referee should apply the advantage clause only if he is almost certain that a goal will be scored. The biggest advantage is at the penalty-mark.

9. The Referee must be more concerned about the effect of an illegal act than about the act itself.

10. Do not be confused by the wording of the advantage clause. Although it mentions only the "offending" team, think of it this way: If you take the advantage (through the foul or infraction) away from the offending team (by the whistle) you give it to the "offended" team. If you don't whistle, they have gained nothing by their foul.

CONCACAF RECOMMENDED EXCEPTIONS TO THE ADVANTAGE

1. No advantage if a clear off-side.

2. No advantage during dangerous play.

3. No advantage if a player is kicked deliberately.

Minimal body contact in a game often sends players down, for they are going at high speed. Don't get fooled by this in a game.

THE OTHER ADVANTAGE

The advantage clause says that the Referee should . . .

> *"Refrain from penalizing in cases where he is satisfied that, by doing so, he would be giving an advantage to the offending team."*

The "other" advantage has to do with a practical game flow, but most of all with good common sense.

Law V IBD 8 says,

> *"The laws of the game are intended to provide that games should be played with as little interference as possible, and in this view it is the duty of the Referees to penalize only deliberate breaches of the law. Constant whistling for trifling and doubtful breaches produces bad feeling and loss of temper on the part of the players and spoils the pleasure of the spectators."*

The common interpretation tends to be to not whistle so many 'ticky-tack' fouls. This in part is a correct interpretation, however it is often used as carte blanche for doing nothing. This occasionally results in chaos.

V-8 is the hardest of all to implement properly. It is ten times more difficult than the advantage clause, and even that is a concept not fully comprehended by most Referees.

It is the feel and flow of the game, and as it goes, so goes your game control. It, like the advantage, takes on more importance as you officiate the older and more experienced player. V-8 can't be taught. It comes only with a continued awareness of it . . . and much experience. There are certain ancillary aspects of V-8 that lend themselves as practical hints in this section. A better title might be . . .

- Flow with the game or drown or
- Delay leads to decay or
- Things which annoy Referee Assessors.

SIGNALING A FOUL WITH REPEATED BLASTS OF THE WHISTLE

Everyone's attention is drawn toward you. It distracts the players' concentration. It often brings the game to a halt. One of the worst things it does is to diminish the effect of the whistle when it is really needed.

Law VIII *Every player shall be in his own half of the field and not less than 10 yards from the ball until the ball is kicked off.*

Ask yourself as a Referee, "Is an advantage being gained?" If not, then call the kick back only if the encroachment is blatant. This is only done because it might cause your credibility as a Referee to be questioned.

Law XVII   The whole of the ball shall be placed within the quarter circle.

Is a player gaining an advantage because the ball is not 100% within the area? If you think so, then don't allow the kick until the situation is rectified. The main thing is that you don't require the letter of the law just because you are aware of its existence.

Law XVI   The ball is to be kicked from a point within that half of the goal-area that is nearest to where it crossed the line.

If 1 or 2 yards more or less from the middle of the goal, don't make a big deal about it. Let the defensive player go to the side that is closest for him. It means more playing time for the players and does away with another unnecessary delay. Of course, if you are asked by the defense or you perceive dissention about to creep in, then by all means quickly render your irrevocable decision.

Law XII   If the goalkeeper takes more than 4 steps when holding, etc. . . .

The purpose is to prevent the goalkeeper from wasting time. As long as this is complied with don't count stutter steps or be overly pickey about the number of steps taken . . . unless your Referee credibility can be seriously questioned. When did you last see a professional Referee call steps on a goalkeeper?

Your fellow official makes a non-serious mistake.

If possible, do not correct it until halftime or at game's end. For example,

- Your linesman points in an incorrect direction.
- Your partner in a multiple Referee system forces a player to put the ball in the exact corner of the goal-area for a goal-kick.

If the players, coaches, or spectators don't make a big deal out of it . . . why should you? On the spot overrulings should only be done for a reason . . . and not merely to assert your authority or law knowledge.

Law XI   Off-side position, but goalkeeper can easily reach the ball first.

This has to be used carefully. Although CONCACAF recommends no type of an advantage on an off-side, many Referees feel that it aids game flow. If the Referee discovers that he made a mistake by not calling the off-side, he may still redeem himself with the late whistle . . . because the moment of judgment extends until the next moment of judgment.

"I said ten centimeters to the left."

Probably the most notable aspect of the 'other' advantage is the . . .

EXACT BLADE OF GRASS SYNDROME!!

Law XII   A free-kick is awarded to the opposing team from the place where the offense occurred.

How many times have you seen an over-zealous Referee run over to a spot and *demand* the ball be placed at that exact location? How many times have you seen him require that the ball be meaninglessly moved a yard or so to comply with the Referees' requirement? If an off-side occurred around the 30 yard line, who cares if the ball is placed 5-6 yards forward or back? Who cares if the ball is displaced laterally by 10-15 yards as long as no advantage is being gained? Only the officious Referee.

There are instances, however, not to be casual about —

- Defenders usually would prefer that the ball be placed just outside of the penalty-area as opposed to within. Don't compromise. If the foul was committed within the area, have the free-kick taken from inside the area.
- Don't ever let an off-side near the halfway-line result in the ball being kicked from within the offender's own half of the field.
- If one player is off-side and another player is merely in an off-side position, make sure that the ball is placed in the immediate vicinity of the player who was whistled for being off-side. If not, you will be chipping away at your own credibility.
- The closer to the goal that a foul is committed, the tighter the Referee should become regarding ball placement.

The foul that is committed near midfield or by the attacking team in the defender's territory should be given the same latitude as the routine off-side.

Law XV   The ball shall be thrown in from the point where it crossed the line.

Does the thrower's team gain an unfair advantage? If he 'crabs' 5-10 yards in either direction . . . .

- at midfield? . . . . . . NO
- close to the opponent's goal? . . . . . . YES, if in the direction of the opponent's goal (an unfair advantage). Otherwise, NO.
- close to his own goal? . . . . . . YES if it puts him within throwing range of his own goalkeeper (an unfair advantage). Otherwise, NO.

There are two questions you must ask yourself.

1. Is a team being taken advantage of? This you should not allow.
2. Am I being taken advantage of? We make outselves look bad enough without having to be helped along by the players. Don't be officious, but don't let them do a number on you either.

"ALLOW THEM TO CHEAT . . . . . . BUT NOT TO STEAL!!!!!"

—Joe Reed
National Federation Baseball Rules Committee

-87-

When in doubt, ask yourself, "Is It Fair?"

VI

Really Knowing
Fair from Foul

LESS FLAK FOR THE MAN IN BLACK!

If Mecca is proper field execution, perhaps now is the time to reflect upon our strong and weak points.

The diagram below depicts that there are five major ingredients necessary for the fully prepared Referee. The largest barrier for the Referee who wishes to successfully implement these tools is, of course, attitude. It totally encloses proper field execution. Attitude colors, distorts, and enhances all that we do on the field.

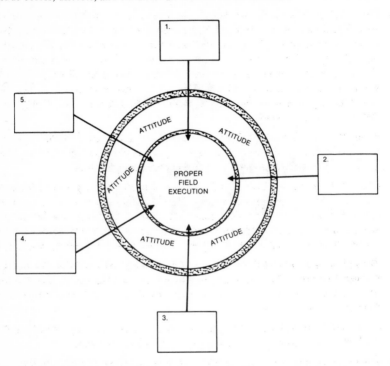

Review the following attitudinal points regularly. They are every bit as important as the rules contained within FIFA Law.

THE TEN COMMANDMENTS OF ATTITUDE

1. ***Thou shalt have a good image*** — What do we convey to the players, coaches, and spectators? . . . . Do we look the part? . . . . Are cards hanging out of our pockets? . . . . Socks at half-mast? . . . . Ill-fitting uniform? . . . . Are you viewed as a little Caesar or a Casper Milktoast?

2. ***Thou shalt have rapport with fellow officials*** — How do you appear to your partner(s)? Are you capable of relaxing them? Do you bring out the best in them? If you don't, it's usually *your* fault.

3. *Thou shalt concentrate* — Are you able to sustain concentration throughout the game? Do you totally dedicate yourself to the task at hand for a full 90 minutes or do you occasionally find yourself standing around just watching play? How successful are you in fighting off mental fatigue? Both authors find that to do more than two (sometimes one) game in a day results in not staying sharp. When doing multiple games, are you with it or just a body putting in time? Don't accept too heavy a load. It does the game a disservice. If you must do it in a tournament . . . try to pace yourself.

4. *Thou shalt be emotionally stable* — We have all seen the unstable symptoms on the field. The Referee who appeared in house slippers to officiate a college game. He told a coach at halftime that he would beat him up if he received a bad rating (an interesting switch) . . . . The Referee who received 7 unsatisfactory ratings out of 10 . . . . The local Referee who was red-lined ("Do not assign") by all six of the schools within a particular high school league because he was so abrasive . . . . The Referee who gets players and coaches mad even before the game has started. The unstable Referee is not disciplined.

5. *Thou shalt be self-disciplined* — Can you control yourself on the field? Do you overreact to the abuse that is often heaped upon you? Do you intelligently apply the laws in a calm, professional manner? . . . . or do your glands take over?

6. *Thou shalt have confidence in self* — Do you think well of yourself? Do you like you? . . . . Don't overdo it though, the flipside of the coin is being pompous on an ego trip. Do you emulate a field general by wearing more than one Referee patch? If so, you have a poor self-image. People measure your ability by deeds on the field, not by how many badges you display. The confident Referee is not defensive.

7. *Thou shalt be non-defensive* — Are you able to be self-effacing? Can you admit your mistakes? (Where, when, how, and to whom is another matter) . . . . or is it always 'them' (players, coaches, spectators, or partner(s))? By his actions, the non-defensive Referee exudes confidence.

8. *Thou shalt be motivated* — Are you motivated to give your very best effort? If not, don't work the game . . . . even if you are donating your time.

9. *Thou shalt be flexible* — Do you have the ability to modify your behavior? . . . . or are you rigid, being unable to adapt to each new and unexpected situation as it occurs?

10. *Thou shalt not use the name of the Referee in vain* — How badly do you chew up the Referee when you are functioning as a coach or a spectator? Do you discretely keep it to yourself or only for the ears of a close companion? Some Referees are the most venomous critics imaginable. Why is this done? . . . Insecurity!!! It's usually the weakest Referees that chip away. Normally the louder and more vicious they are, the poorer is their own officiating. To openly criticize is to drive nails into your own coffin . . . . and into those of all the other men in black.

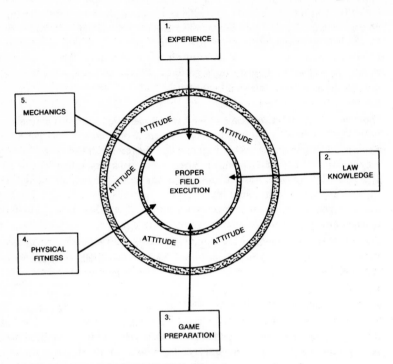

THE FIVE MAJOR INGREDIENTS *(See diagram above)*

1. ***Experience*** is the ***most important*** ingredient. Unfortunately it only comes so quickly. It takes much time to assimilate all that you have been exposed to. Often your very assignments are restrictive. You can't mature as an official if you never have tough or challenging games. Seek out the potentially difficult games. It may be painful, but with the proper attitude, it will cause you to grow. Vicarious experience can be gained from watching other Referees in action. Empathize with them during the game. What can you learn from them? What could they have learned from you?

2. ***Law Knowledge*** links up very closely with experience in order to be effective. You can't be a quality Referee without knowing the laws cold. You can however, know the laws inside and out and be quite ineffective on the field. A frequently heard put-down of a Referee by a fellow official is: "He is no good because he is a book Referee." Although this statement is often true, it seems to always come from a speaker who is attempting to absolve *his* less than adequate knowledge of the laws. The same parallel can be drawn between him and the Referee who screams at the ineptness of another official. The 'book Referee' statement is particularly offensive because it demeans one's knowledge of the laws of the game . . . . and that knowledge is essential.

3. *Game Preparation* — Do you psych up for all your games? Billy Cooke, ASL Referee, spends most of his day prior to his officiating assignment just thinking and concentrating upon his upcoming game. Do you just walk onto the field and slide into the match? It's no problem if the game doesn't test you, but if it does, you could be in hot water.

4. *Physical Fitness* is the *least important* of the five components for proper field execution. How many times have you seen a Referee who could not make it physically? One out of 50? Many Referees seem unfit, but it is because of their attitude. It is of course important to be in tip-top shape . . . . but you can only perform up to your physiological potential. Being in just 'average' shape is probably adequate for your officiating better than 95% of the time. Being lazy or 'dogging it' is prevalent, but only by Referees who are breaking many of the attitude commandments.

5. *Mechanics* — A well-known Referee assessor recently said, "Of all the sports I've observed, soccer officials are worse in mechanics than any other group of officials." Unfortunately, he is right!! The importance of mechanics has been recognized by various local high school officials' associations. Football and basketball tests have 25-30% of their test items devoted to mechanics. The baseball association allocates approximately 35% of its qualification exam to this important area. Mechanics should be learned so that it becomes reflexive in nature. Deviation from the 'accepted' is fine as long as you have a very good reason for doing so . . . . other than being lazy or having a lack of mental concentration.

Mechanics is the link between 'pure academia' and game control.

There is absolutely no excuse for having deficiencies in either law knowledge or mechanics because they can be studied out of a book . . . anytime . . . anyplace you desire. They are at *your* beck and call. Wouldn't it be nice if we could gain experience in the same manner?

Perhaps it seems that mechanics is being overstated a bit . . . but chances are that if you asked the question, "How can I gain a noticeable improvement in my soccer officiating skills in the shortest period of time?" . . . the answer for the majority would be . . . STUDY MECHANICS!!!

 "Perfection is impossible. Excellence is not."

— Vince Lombardi
Late, Green Bay Packers

 "It's not who won or lost, but how you let the game be played."

— F. G. Rawling

The concentration of the Referee must exceed that of the players.

CONCENTRATION

"There's nothing that concentrates a man's mind more than the knowledge that he's going to be hanged the next morning."

—Samuel Johnson

Concentration is usually something that is learned, like the law. Unlike the player, whose concentration usually breaks when his team loses the ball, the Referee can briefly relax only when the ball is not in play. And, like players, concentration diminishes when fatigue sets in. If you cannot keep up with play physically, you can't keep up mentally.

The "warming up" period for players should be used constructively by the Referee. You can learn much from the players at this time: Do they seem well-disciplined? Are they self-motivated, or responding to a leader or the coach? (highly important) How skilled are they? Merely asking these questions to yourself will cause you to think about the task at hand, and the accumulated bits of information will serve you in the game. It is all part of the "mental rehearsal" that Tom Tutko, noted sports psychologist, talks about in his book, *Sports Psyching* (J. B. Tarcher, 1976). While Tutko explains what is necessary for the athlete, his words fit the Referee as well.

Concentration really begins when you imagine what will happen on the field . . . what kinds of fouls are most likely to happen . . . . what is the best position for calling them . . . . . what are the most difficult situations for this age group and level . . . . what must I do to properly assess an "advantage" situation?

Of course, you are not to anticipate what is going to happen, but you must anticipate what *can* happen. Unfortunately, most Referees go into a game the way some people get behind the wheel of a car . . . . "I won't think about events and demands upon me until they happen." The Referee who thinks about refereeing only on the day of the game will seldom improve, and the Referee who thinks about his game only when it is being played is also less likely to advance.

Your concentration on all matters of play will lead to confidence. You are to lead the game at all times. The concentration takes many forms. Very quickly you are able to assess the weak and strong players, conditions of field, support you may expect from fellow officials, influence of crowd upon players, and how you are going to fare in the first stressful moment.

Look carefully for that first foul. How and when you see it and how you handle it will make a difference for the remainder of the game. You should be the first one on the field to anticipate that foul. If you referee like Gordon Hill, you will know a lot about fouls before they happen. Once Hill even stopped an important match because he *knew* what a player was *thinking* of doing.

It is possible to hear all, yet respond only to those stimuli which aid you. If a coach says, "Time's up, Ref!", don't take a glance at your watch at that moment. Wait, then when the coach is no longer looking at you (he'll not look at you unless you respond immediately), check your watch. It is possible that time IS up, but immediate response to such a command is a sign of weakness. Concentrate also on what is said and done on the sideline. It may help you.

THE TEN MOST DIFFICULT DECISIONS

There are certain calls (or lack of calls) that have continually plagued Referees. In this section we present our view of the 'top ten'. The judging of the fair tackle, the intentional hand ball, and endangering the goalkeeper are not to be ignored because these, too, are difficult. We feel that the following present the Referee with an even more difficult challenge.

1. LETTING THE GAME FLOW

This is the 'uncall'. (See 'The Other Advantage' in Chapter V.) "Referee, is thy name nit-picker?" Do you always insist on ball placement for a free-kick on that exact spot? How tolerant are you of a reflexive outcry of a four letter word overheard by only a few and directed at no one in particular? Does every centimeter of the ball have to be within the quarter-circle on a corner-kick? Do you allow a reasonable amount of 'crabbing' along the touch-line for a throw-in? Do you whistle every niggling little foul? Do you react to every dissenting word? Remember, it is often wise to look and hear the other way. Can you successfully make the distinction between letting the game flow and the discipline that is needed for game control? The majority of us have trouble, for this is *the* most difficult decision of all. "ALLOW THEM TO CHEAT, BUT NOT TO STEAL."

2. APPLYING THE ADVANTAGE

The advantage must be immediate, clear, and effective. Once you give it you may not change your mind. If you have doubt as to giving it . . . . don't!! Very rarely should it be given deep in one's own territory. The advantage often does not exist at the beginning of a period. The experienced Referee has the advantage on a string. He lets it out gradually as the players demonstrate they can handle it and immediately reels it in when nastiness or immaturity is exhibited. When it is applied there should be a verbal "advantage" to the players accompanied by a signal to both players and spectators that he has noticed the infraction and has chosen to let it pass.

3. THE SECOND CAUTION

How often have you ejected a player when he commits a second cautionable offense? Now ask yourself how often you have done it *prior* to consulting your Referee Data Card during the booking process. Your mind as well as your notebook should contain the names of cautioned players. Many players exploit the fact that they have a caution because they sense the psychological pressures that are brought to bear upon the Referee. To them, the caution doesn't say, "Cool it." It says, "Push the bounds a little bit further." They feel a certain immunity because the typical Referee is reluctant to eject unless the action is of a violent nature and can at least be marginally identified as such by players, coaches, and spectators alike.

4. THE DOUBLE STANDARD

Almost all of us are guilty of this. When we are, we are allowing defenders to control the game. What is a foul at midfield is often acceptable when committed within the penalty area. It is a combination of bein gprudent and lacking the necessary intestinal fortitude. How often have you seen an attacker get 'heel nipped' in the penalty area which is just enough to destroy his timing causing him to shoot wide or not to shoot at all? Have you ever given a penalty-kick for it? Do the players take advantage of you and their opponents when they are within the penalty area? We have to strive more for consistency. There is no secret formula. Each Referee must introspect and make the decision for himself. It is axiomatic that more fouls called in the penalty area mean fewer fouls.

5. OFF-SIDE, IF PARTICIPATES

Since our last edition we have officiated with many experienced and respected Referees. More of them than we would like to admit appear to have a very limited practical grasp of the off-side law. They whistle it too often. The direct shot on goal that scores. It is so hard that no one can lay a finger on it. How many times has that goal been disallowed because a player was merely in an off-side position? Even the classical case of the non-participating wing, far away from play, why is he sanctioned? Rule of thumb: *Could* the player in question get to the ball first? If not, don't penalize.

6. TACKLING FROM BEHIND

The tackle from behind usually occurs when a player is beaten. It is also a predictable foul, since the tackler is seen to be moving in desperation, in a "catch-up" situation. Finally, once the tackle takes place, even though the dribbler may retain the ball, retaliation often happens. The tackle brings problems to hesitant referees because (1) often the ball is played along with the trip, and (2) the advantage is sometimes applied. The tackler from behind is in a low-percentage situation. Most attempts from behind should be penalized, for the legs and/or feet are contacted. The clever player will keep the non-tackling foot raised high, to bring down the opponent, even though the ball itself may be clearly played. Often more than a free-kick is warranted. A player tripped from behing at high speed can be injured, and a hard trip to a player at any speed results in possible injury. A stern warning where there is no hurt or more severe sanctions where there is injury will help bring the game under control.

7. THE CHARGE

Is it fair or foul? Were both players playing the ball? Where was the ball? Many officials incorrectly penalize the fair charge. If a big guy and a little guy go after the ball, the smaller one may very well be knocked on his wallet. If a player looks at the opponent just prior to charging him, then it is very likely going to be a foul charge. When judging the charge, 'read' intent in the eyes and face and look for non-shoulder contact.

8. DANGEROUS PLAY

Dangerous play is any action that creates a potential or an actual danger to an opponent, a teammate, or to oneself. It most often involves the 'high kick.' Just the act of raising the foot to chest level or higher does not make it dangerous. It must pose a real threat. The 'bicycle kick' is usually dangerous when it is done in close quarters. The real 'guts call,' however, is when a player *puts himself* in jeopardy by putting his head down at waist or lower levels close to a player who is attempting to kick the ball. How will you call it?

9. OBSTRUCTION

The players who think they are semi-sophisticated about the laws (usually between 16 and 19 years of age) will give you more flak about real or imagined obstructions than even the accursed hand ball. The player may legally obstruct when the ball is within playing distance. The laws say that obstruction must be intentional. The experienced Referee often determines intent by looking at the eyes and facial expression of the player in question. A common occurrence of the 'uncalled obstruction', particularly with adult players, is the defender who attempts to 'protect his goalkeeper'. In basketball the 'pick' and 'screen' are intentional and are allowed. If you see it in a soccer match that you are officiating, call it and give an IFK.

10. DANGEROUS PLAY OR OBSTRUCTION?

How often in one of your games has a player fallen to the gound, partially withholding the ball from play? It is very likely unintentional and he is thrashing about trying to kick it away. At the same time an opponent is also trying to kick the ball. Is it obstruction on the player on the ground? Is he guilty of dangerous play because he is putting himself in jeopardy? Is it dangerous play on the part of the opponent? Should a drop-ball be given? Sometimes the situation takes care of itself. Often it doesn't, and you become painfully aware that something must be done. Who gets the IFK? Whatever you do, do it quickly. Fans and players will be off your back and better yet, no one will be hurt.

Bill Smith

When is this considered dangerous?

XII (k) . . . . HAVE YOU FORGOTTEN IT?

The "intelligent and gifted" player will develop talents and skills to the fullest, exploiting the opponents' weaknesses as well. The "crafty" or "smart" competitor may also be tempted to exploit the laws for his own benefit, sometimes taking advantage of the Referee.

There are players who, from the opening whistle, are on the fringes of being warned or cautioned. Some, when cautioned, know that Referees lack the courage to eject. They are therefore "protected," and allowed more freedom than the player who never receives the caution.

You are expected to judge the intent of all players. This expectation must be carried one step further: You must judge when a player is deliberately and persistently infringing on the laws. When this happens, you must invoke the most commonly forgotten aspect of LAW XII: SECTION K. "A player shall be cautioned if he persistently infringes on the Laws of the Game."

It is your duty to stop the player who fouls as a defensive tactic, and who really has lost nothing through the foul. Stopping an opponent at all costs is a tactic which ruins the game for spectators and causes injury and ill-feeling. The free-kick dutifully awarded is never enough!

REMEMBER: The violations do not have to be the same. (i.e., a tripping foul or two plus an intentional hand ball and an unfair charge by one player may be all you need. Don't you agree that a player who commits these three violations in a fairly short period of time is persistently infringing on the laws of the game?)

Have you ever officiated a perfect game?

Comment: If you feel you have, tell others about it, for some Referees have been struggling for the perfect game for more than 20 years. There is always something to be learned from little mistakes, a wrong move or a wrong gesture which was ill-timed. Some experienced top officials make a large number of mistakes, but they are usually inconsequential to the control and outcome of the game.

 Players must not be allowed to take the game over 100%, but they will try to.

"YOU'VE GOT TO FEEL THE FOUL."

"YOU'VE GOT TO FEEL THE FOUL"

The argument goes on. Some Referees who are new to the game immediately grasp the essence of play, while others experienced in the game make poor officials. Conversely, some Referees place undue emphasis on laws too early, and never make it, and others who have played can identify with the "fair charge," the "sliding tackle," or the unfair tactic of the goalkeeper. Thus the argument: "What is the best background for training?"

Generalities are not particularly helpful here, but one fact remains: A Referee who has played, however modestly, can improve skills of officiating and understanding of play. If you've felt a foul, or know what an extended foot can do to a shin or ankle, you'll look for them in games. If you know how easy it is to be playing the ball and to honestly stumble into someone, you may have reached a new level. If you've taken a throw-in and raised your foot just after doing so, you'll know what the split-second means. If you've struggled, as a goalkeeper, to keep feet and arms still for the taking of a penalty, you may not call this inconsequential, minor infraction.

A Referee's field training should not be confined to the business end of the whistle. If you compete in friendly games on the field with other Referees, you'll develop a more sensitive attitude toward all that goes on. Play, but remember to keep it safe! You're needed for your games!

"If you will kindly spit him out and give him his shirt back, I'll restart the game with a drop-ball."

FOULS THAT MEAN TROUBLE FOR YOU

Most of the play in your games is safe, fairly easy to follow, and without incident. However, you will sometimes see players committing fouls that are intentional, dangerous, and which will lead to hard feelings. Many of the most common ones are pictured here. Think about them, be ready for them, and be prepared to deal with them before they happen in your games.

The tackle from the side, with the leg crossing over the opponent's.

The foot kicking "over the ball," onto an opponent's shin. Variation: In an exaggerated manner, the player follows through after kicking the ball.

The tackle from behind, where the foot hits the opponent in the Achilles area.

The two-footed tackle, where the player jumps over the ball to get the opponent.

The goalkeeper jumping in at an opponent, presumably to protect himself as he makes the save.

The sliding tackle which misses the ball and catches the opponent in the lower leg or knee.

The late tackle from the side, where the opponent is hit in the thigh. This usually results from a bouncing ball that is not being perfectly controlled by the opponent.

A knee in the thigh from behind, in a feigned attempt to play the ball.

"Making a back" (stopping) in front of an opponent. Sometimes a player will lean down behind an opponent who is moving backward to play a ball.

The sliding tackle from behind, usually causing damage to the opponent's ankle, and sometimes to oneself.

A teammate tries to keep it from beginning again.

VII

After It's Over...
Before It Begins Again

REFEREE MEETINGS

"Criticism will come from coaches if it doesn't first come from our own ranks."

The word "meeting" does not exactly conjure up squeals of delight, whether a person be a businessman, teacher, union member, churchgoer, or Referee. Unfortunately to a soccer official it is often that time when Referees get together to air grievances, boast about top assignments that were handled with ease, complain about the deterioration of play and conduct of players and to quibble about their *own* interpretations of the Laws of the Game. (Without a rule book, of course.) Another sad fact is that too many Referees are too set in their ways, and their own learning process terminated years ago.

To any serious observer of the game, there is something new to be learned from each contest. Moreover, the good Referee will realize that even a seasoned veteran of international matches will make mistakes, and that the only substantive difference among Referees is often the degree and frequency of these mistakes. If a group of Referees openly admit that their Referee Association meetings can provide a vehicle for freely admitting mistakes and correcting ingorance, they will find their field efforts improved, and jealousies will dwindle.

The Referee's privileged position in the game must not be taken lightly. His never-ending education is gained through the study of the Laws of the Game, his observation of other Referees, game experience, and in communication with fellow Referees. Our objectives here is to offer some suggestions as to how this communication process can be effected through group meetings.

SUGGESTED ACTIVITIES FOR REFEREE MEETINGS
(exclusive of training sessions for new Referees)

1. A *written test,* such as the one contained in this book, is an excellent method for initiating rules discussion. Since time is valuable, tests should be taken individually and brought to the meeting, having been corrected by the Referee. Test score totals need not be discussed. Each item should be discussed individually, and new items may be added for future tests.

2. A *review of certain laws of the game* is advisable, particularly at the beginning of the season. Law XII, Fouls and Misconduct, and Law XI, Off-Side, are the most obvious for generating lively discussion.

3. *Audio-visual material* such as movies will aid in clarifying the certain points of disagreement. The movies need not necessarily be on the laws, and may not be directed toward referees, but could be game movies which can be studied from the standpoint of game control and law application.

4. *Reviews of Books.* A few books now exist on refereeing, and can be reported upon by a member. FIFA News now carries interesting and timely information on rule interpretations, and this should be regularly brought to the attention of the association.

5. *Outside Speakers.* These people may have distinguished themselves in areas outside of refereeing. An accomplished Referee or umpire in another sport may also bring new insights into game-control Referee education.

6. *Game Situations.* Each meeting should have at least a short period devoted to recent situations on the field.

7. *Referee Evaluation – On Field.* If time and conditions permit, the group should observe a senior Referee in a game, and his performance should be evaluated.

8. *Individual Contributions by Member Referees.* In order for maximum efficiency to be achieved within the association, each member must participate actively at least once during the year. Each member should be given a topic for presentation, either in writing or as an instructional device at a meeting. A list of topics for presentation could include:

   a. Referee-Linesman cooperation
   b. Pre-game instructions to players
   c. Pre-game instructions from a Referee to his Linesmen
   d. Dealing with injuries
   e. How to handle club Linesmen
   f. Administering a caution
   g. When to make up time
   h. Writing disciplinary reports
   i. When is a charge a fair charge?
   j. Fundamental differences among the three systems of control
   k. How to evaluate a fellow official

HINTS

1. Many times an individual with limited or non-existent refereeing experience can best run your meetings. Like any administrator, he should be able to organize, delegate authority, and bring out the best in the membership.

2. Newsletters provide the needed communication during the offseason.

3. Try to include at least one social event each year in your calendar of activities. The sacrificing soccer wife should certainly be included.

4. Some Referee groups award an annual trophy or award to an outstandingly sportsmanlike player, team, or coach.

5. Coaches, players, and other administrators should be invited to attend meetings. For obvious reasons, game mistakes and game situations are not to be discussed in their presence.

 "The egoist is one who cannot bring himself to communicate or cooperate with others; all his anxieties are those of sustaining his own ego, not those of striving for perfection."

Bishop Fulton Sheen

COACHES' REFEREE EVALUATION

Certain leagues and Referee associations require periodic Referee evaluation. However, this is done in a haphazard manner, and often the methods are open to question. Since few organizations in soccer can afford Referee evaluators, Referees will have to rely on fellow Referees on the field and on coaches for constructive criticism. The criticism leveled at a fellow Referee is often misinterpreted, and can lead to a lack of cooperation on his part. The natural reaction of most Referees is to defend themselves when suggestions are made. Each Referee must decide if and how to ask for criticism and how to respond to it.

Coaches within Southern California are provided the opportunity to evaluate high school and college Referees every game during the season. The coach rates each Referee on a 5-point scale (see form on the opposite page). He may also make comments if he chooses (they are required whenever an unsatisfactory rating is given).

This information is then weighted and tabulated. Each Referee receives an evaluation package upon completion of the season. It contains all the specific ratings, by Referee as well as by school. All comments, good, bad, and otherwise are also printed. A Referee not only receives feedback regarding his assignments but also for every other Referee as well. This peer pressure, in many cases, has provided the impetus for improving one's performance on the field. Other times, unfortunately, it is rationalized away.

Sometimes a coach's comment on a card tickled our funny bone. Listed below are some of these comments which were extracted from several thousand rating cards. They combine both humor and pathos. All comments are verbatim . . . including spelling.

- _____ was 20 minutes late – Underwear hung beneath his shorts. His shirt was unbuttoned to the _waste_. He could not see fouls. Let the game get out of hand. Why not assign people who know soccer?

- There was a Ref. named Mr. Bliss, A lot of calls he did miss.

- Had a name-calling contest with the players. He is well known for his name-calling. My name is not S.O.B. crazy.

- Seems inconsistent – 'ticky-tacky' to 'blind' . . .

- . . . He _thinks_ he is _good_, which makes matters worse . . . and a giant ego . . .

- . . . Have you ever seen an official roll the ball from 3 yards away for a drop ball?

- . . . . . . wore what appeared to be house slippers . . .

- . . . used a crackerjack whistle

- He said, "No offside because your team put him off-side on purpose, so it doesn't count."

- 1,783 calls went against us and one was for us.

- He refused to _due_ the JV game

- I probably should protest however the man's a priest so what can I say?

COACHES EVALUATION OF REFEREES

Game Date: _____ / _____ / _____
Month   Day   Year

Game: _____ ( ) ____ At _____ ( )
(Visitor)   Score   (Home)   Score

OVERALL RATING (Obtained from Side 2)

Name of Official		Outstanding 56-64 pts.	Good 41-55 pts.	Average 24-40 pts.	Weak 9-23 pts.	Unsatisfactory 0-8 pts.
A	Referee					
B	(Referee) (Line)					
C	(Referee) (Line)					

If total (from side 2) equals...

56-64 = Outstanding
41-55 = Good
24-40 = Average
9-23 = Weak
0- 8 = Unsatisfactory

NOTE: EXPLANATIONS ARE REQUIRED ON ALL UNSATISFACTORY RATINGS

Constructive comments: _____
_____
_____
_____

PLEASE COMPLETE AND RETURN TO:
SCSOA-COMMISSIONER OF CERTIFICATION
1217 3rd St.
MANHATTAN BEACH. CA 90266

SIDE 1

Signed: _____
Title: _____
School: _____

SIDE 2

- Circle the numerical equivalent for each of the eight traits.
- Do this for all officials.
- Add up the numbers and put the totals at the bottom.

	A Outstanding	Good	Average	Weak	Unsatisfactory	B Outstanding	Good	Average	Weak	Unsatisfactory	C Outstanding	Good	Average	Weak	Unsatisfactory
1. Game Control (Ref) or Balls out Assistance- off-side (Line)	16	12	8	4	0	16	12	8	4	0	16	12	8	4	0
2. Rule Application (Ref) or Fouls & Assistance-Misconduct (Line)	12	9	6	3	0	12	9	6	3	0	12	9	6	3	0
3. Teamwork	8	6	4	2	0	8	6	4	2	0	8	6	4	2	0
4. Hustle	8	6	4	2	0	8	6	4	2	0	8	6	4	2	0
5. Signals	8	6	4	2	0	8	6	4	2	0	8	6	4	2	0
6. Decisiveness	4	3	2	1	0	4	3	2	1	0	4	3	2	1	0
7. Professionalism	4	3	2	1	0	4	3	2	1	0	4	3	2	1	0
8. Impartiality	4	3	2	1	0	4	3	2	1	0	4	3	2	1	0

Total _____   Total _____   Total _____

TRANSFER THE 'TOTAL' INFORMATION TO SIDE 1.

-109-

- Should refrain from engaging in a discourse with each offending player to share with him many years of soccer experience.

- He calls what he sees, but I don't thing that he sees well.

- Despite the rain and mud, Mr._____ rose to new levels of incompetence.

- When I told my player to lay down, he gave me a yellow card.

- Made uncalled for remarks about the sexual gender of the JV coach.

- He walked away laughing after the other Ref. made a penalty call.

- Must have had a competition with the other Ref. to see who could blow his whistle the most.

- He is also *arogant* . . . nothing personal.

- He claimed he had a flat 2 weeks in a row. With the money he makes from coming late he should invest in some tires.

A yellow card for the coach. The prelude to a negative evaluation.

SPECTATOR

- If he had one more eye, he would be a cyclops.
- Never sees the fouls that the coaches and the spectators do.

- Often can't find the field.

- Pulls the ball outside from six yards within the Penalty-Area.

- Can't find his car in the parking lot.

- Always points in the wrong direction.

- Tells Coach that he is not properly dressed for the match.

- Books his fellow Linesman by mistake.

- Knows there is a God out there somewhere but has yet to see the light.

- Can't find his wife.

- When observed reading *Fair or Foul*, the book is upside-down.

"Sorry, but I can't start the match until you put more air in this game ball."

REFEREEING THE REFEREES

"If the intent is to criticize, don't do it. If it is to help, do it."

Jimmy Walder, the most famous Referee in America's soccer history, was once asked how many times he was "assessed" during his more than 50 years with the whistle. "Each game," he mused, "and that depended on the number of people that were watching the game." Actually, Walder was never assessed. He officiated in an era where each Referee was on his own, and the only help came from within. Fortunately, assessment for soccer Referees is now a reality, and efforts by many groups are being made toward standardization.

Though a single sheet of paper is the Assessor's report, the most valuable tool the Assessor brings to the task is his attitude. Objective criticism of another's performance is a highly sensitive issue, but can be the major force in a Referee's development. The Assessor is just one part of the officiating team, and his chief job is to help. There are various ways of quantifying performance, and it is felt that providing officials with a "score" needs careful examination. Instead, the intent here is to present some basic observations on elements common to the task of controlling a soccer game.

A Brief Guide for Assessors

Key Elements for Judging a Performance

1. Appearance. The purchase and maintenance of a good uniform is required. What first impressions does this Referee create?

2. Signals. A demonstrative Referee is compensating for weaknesses. Do the signals indicate confidence and does the whistle speak with authority, and is it varied?

3. Stoppages. When the ball is out of play, trouble begins. Is the game quickly, fairly, and accurately restarted?

4. The Advantage. Many fouls are easily recognizable. They are not to be whistled unless an advantage is gained through the foul. Does the Referee have a real feel for the advantage, using it neither too little nor too much?

5. Cooperation with Linesmen. The "team" concept begins with pre-game instructions, where Linesmen are given responsibility and respect. It carries over to all other aspects of handling the game. Does eye contact and signalling show that communication is evident in all situations?

6. Application of the Laws.
   The Penal Offenses. Does the Referee really understand the intent of the players' actions?

   Technical Offenses. Obstruction and dangerous play exist largely in the mind of the Referee. Does he understand when these are extreme enough to be called?

   Misconduct and Game Control. Referees often appear to be interferring with play, and create hard feelings. Is he looking for trouble in areas where it is better to turn the back? Are situations dealt with fairly and quickly?

Positioning. A basic problem of Referees is the inability to move off the diagonal to the play, and to be looking in the right place at the right time. Does the Referee appear to anticipate an incident before it happens?

Personal control comes before game control.

Experience alone cannot carry you in today's complex game. You need assessments, rule review, conditioning, and a continuing positive attitude toward everyone in the game.

 A good Referee knows which players are likely to foul.

Players like to intimidate one another. An implied threat is one thing, but a successful threat is another.

TRIO
A Method of Evaluating Referees
"You can't quantify Referee Performance or Personality."

The American Youth Soccer Organization (AYSO), though recruiting and training volunteers, has taken a vital interest in all areas of referee improvement. Efforts have centered on realistic observations of referees during game situations. TRIO, an acronym for "Training Referees Through Improved Observation", was begun because (a) Referees must improve and reach maximum potential, (b) The organization should identify its better officials, and (c) Referees should be encouraged to help one another. TRIO provides basic guidelines for both the official and the observer on the sideline.

Important to success of TRIO is the exchange between referee and observer. "Self analysis" on the reverse side of the observer report will encourage the referee to look critically at his own performance. Following this, the observer develops his own points for encouragement and improvement, and common points are discussed.

USE OF THE TRIO FORM:

1. Before any discussion, the offical completes the reverse side of the form. This should take no more than 3-4 minutes.

2. Discussion should follow. the observer should not read the official's comments until his own comments have been written, following discussion.

3. **ATTITUDE** shows in dress, voice and expression, communication with the observer and the other officials, and in relationships with the game participants.

   ABILITY TO REACT indicates the referee's understanding of what is happening both on and off the field. the official should be able to handle any situation accurately (the Laws), and with authority (control), and must inspire total confidence in other officials, players, and coaches.

   ACCESS TO PLAY involves conditioning and reading of the game. The official should be near all important action and should demonstrate flexibility in thought and movement. Sound mechanics are expected.

Points to Remember

The official should know he is being evaluated.

Be in on pre-game instructions to Linesmen, but only to observe.

During game, stay in background, and do not draw attention to your presence. Locate yourself where problems are likely to occur, such as the spectator/coach side.

Where improvement is needed, cover only two or three points in discussion.

Invite all officials to participate in discussion.

Do not discuss overall rating.

Be discreet, positive, friendly, supportive, thorough, and professional.

Observer _____   Game Date _____ Division _____

Address _____ _____   Teams _____

_____   Region(s) _____

_____ *(print)* Name of Official _____

Region _____   Address _____

Telephone ( )_____   _____

_____

Attitude	1	2	3
Ability to React	1	2	3
Access to Play	1	2	3

1 Effective — 2 Adequate — 3 Inadequate

INCIDENTS WHICH CHALLENGED THE OFFICIAL (Include Disciplinary Actions)

1.

2.

3.

4.

POINTS COVERED IN DISCUSSION FOLLOWING GAME:

1.

2.

3.

4.

OVERALL COMMENTS:

Recommendation: ☐ Pass   ☐ Further Observation

Date Submitted _____ Signature_____

REFEREE AND LINESMAN SELF-ANALYSIS

Area _____

Name of Official _____ Region _____

Address _____

_____ Zip Code _____

Telephone ( ) _____ Current Patch _____
            Area

My Reaction to the Game:

Areas Where I Proved Strong:

Areas Where I Need Improvement:

Further Comments:

Signature _____

ASSESSMENT, OBSERVATION, EVALUATION, EXAMINATION . . . You name it.

The recent World Cup Final brought a record number of assessors to the screen, almost 1.75 billion. In the stadium were 90,000 more, a few of whom were objective. Referees, while they should be selective in their consideration of advice, often could learn from the players themselves. What do you think of this unedited letter, recently written to a Referee from a young player away at college?

Dear Dad,

We played our first game Sunday, and I want to ask you a few questions. First of all, I'm frustrated. I missed an easy breakaway shot. Our goalkeeper got a yellow for swearing at a teammate. The ref was enough of a brat to throw her out, but he didn't

One of our fullbacks was down on the ground after being hit hard. The ref wouldn't stop the game. She stayed on the ground. The ball went out of play, and he still didn't stop. He helped her off the field with the play still going on on her side of the field even. As he was carrying her off, they shot, and the ref was in the goalkeeper's way and she couldn't see a thing. They scored. I thought that was totally unfair. Isn't that against the rules? Doesn't he have to stop when the ball goes out of play if she is on the ground? That's what I thought.

At the beginning of the game, he thought he was being Mr. Joe Referee, checking everyone's cleats and jewelry. Well, one girl had a cast on her arm that she covered up with an Ace bandage. She and Ann went for the ball at the same time. Ann got whacked, and got the wind knocked out of her. When we got back, I took her to the hospital, and she had separated cartilage at the sternum, and two broken ribs. I'll tell you though, the Drs. here don't know what they're even talking about, and they were very rude to me.

Any way, the other team played well together, and won, 5-1. It was impossible for us to play in the 103° heat anyway. Do you think any of it was the referee's fault? I would like to have you come over to ref our games, but that wouldn't be very fair, either, I guess.

Love,

[Name Withheld]

What can you tell about this Referee without seeing the game? Do you get clues about referees or teams or players through such reports?

WRITING GAME REPORTS

> *"The game report is a very important part of Referee makeup. The average soccer Referee does not render a good report. It is perhaps the most neglected aspect of Referee training."*

> — *Pat Smith, Chief Assessor*
> *North American Soccer League*

Referees dislike paperwork, and would rather talk about incidents than take matters to the proper authorities through a report. The writing of these reports is probably the most unwelcome task of the Referee. Most league rules require a reporting of all incidents resulting in cautions and ejections, and for good reason. These reports form the "Word Picture" of what actually happened. The report, usually acted upon at a hearing or some other meeting, must contain all of the elements of the situation.

ELEMENTS OF AN EFFECTIVE GAME REPORT

Punctuality. The reports should be legibly written and mailed immediately following the game, when the facts are clear in mind.

Accuracy. Names, numbers, time, score, and the citing of the law which was violated are all vital to the report. A drawing of the field may help, if you feel this is important.

Brevity. No one wants to know the full history of the game or player in question. Don't build a case. Just say what happened.

Honesty. The Referee must deal only with the incident, and must not "invent" circumstances which support his position.

Uniformity. Although no two persons see the same incident alike, credibility is there if the incidents were similarly viewed and interpreted by Referee and Linesmen.

HINTS FOR REFEREES

1. Misconduct of officials and spectators are to be reported, as well as that of players.

2. Do not rely on your memory on the field. Record the time of the incident, as well as any words that were spoken to you and gestures made at the time of the incident.

3. The Referee must act upon the testimony of his neutral Linesman, even though the Referee may not have seen the incident.

4. Incidents must not be discussed, after the match, even with other Referees. Reports from other Referees or Linesmen must be filed separately, usually within 24 hours.

5. All cautions and ejections must be reported.

6. The Referee's report must include all incidents on and off the field, and must contain only the facts.

7. When the Referee's report has been made and submitted, the job has been completed.

8. When a player is cautioned or ejected, cite the reason, and be accurate. For instance, a player may not be cautioned for dangerous play.

VIII

The Rules Almanac

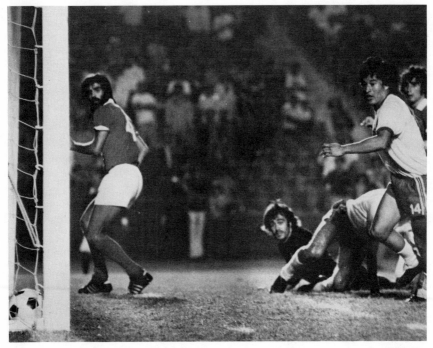

A ball sitting on the goal-line, a nemesis for the Referee who is out of position. Where must the Referee or Linesman be to judge whether or not this goal is valid?

Hidden and implied rules, International Board Decisions, Referee Commission interpretations, and other bits and pieces of information about the Laws of the Game are hard to find. While some of the materials in this synopsis section may be found in other parts of the book, it is offered here in basic summary fashion as an adjunct to the Laws.

Important information from the seventeen Laws of the Game is summarized in order, and may be referred to accordingly. An effort has been made to be concise yet complete in our examination of these Laws. For the new or for the experienced Referee, it is best read and studied after reviewing the Laws. It will then serve as a refresher, and an understanding of the synopsis is an important prelude to the taking of the two soccer tests.

<table>
<tr><td>Law I</td><td>THE FIELD OF PLAY
The Field of Play</td><td>Law X</td><td>METHOD OF SCORING
Scoring</td></tr>
<tr><td></td><td></td><td>Law XI</td><td>OFF-SIDE
Off-Side</td></tr>
<tr><td>Law II</td><td>THE BALL
The Ball</td><td>Law XII</td><td>FOULS AND MISCONDUCT
Fouls and Misconduct</td></tr>
<tr><td>Law III</td><td>THE NUMBER OF PLAYERS
Players
Substitutions
Illness/Injury
The Goalkeeper</td><td></td><td>Warnings
Cautions
Ejections
Entering/Leaving the Field</td></tr>
<tr><td></td><td></td><td>Law XIII</td><td>FREE-KICK
Free-Kicks – General
Indirect Free-Kick</td></tr>
<tr><td>Law IV</td><td>PLAYERS' EQUIPMENT
Equipment/Apparel</td><td></td><td>Misconduct</td></tr>
<tr><td>Law V</td><td>REFEREES
Referee
Advantage Clause
Termination of Game</td><td></td><td>Dangerous Play
Direct Free-Kick
Charging</td></tr>
<tr><td>Law VI</td><td>LINESMEN</td><td>Law XIV</td><td>PENALTY-KICK
Penalty-Kick</td></tr>
<tr><td>Law VII</td><td>DURATION OF THE GAME
Timing</td><td>Law XV</td><td>THROW-IN
Throw-In</td></tr>
<tr><td>Law VIII</td><td>THE START OF PLAY
Kick-Off
Drop-Ball
Outside Agent</td><td>Law XVI</td><td>GOAL-KICK
Goal-Kick</td></tr>
<tr><td></td><td></td><td>Law XVII</td><td>CORNER-KICK
Corner-Kick and
Corner-Post</td></tr>
<tr><td>Law IX</td><td>BALL IN AND OUT OF PLAY
In/Out of Play</td><td></td><td></td></tr>
</table>

FIELD OF PLAY

(ALL UNDESIGNATED DISTANCES IN YARDS)

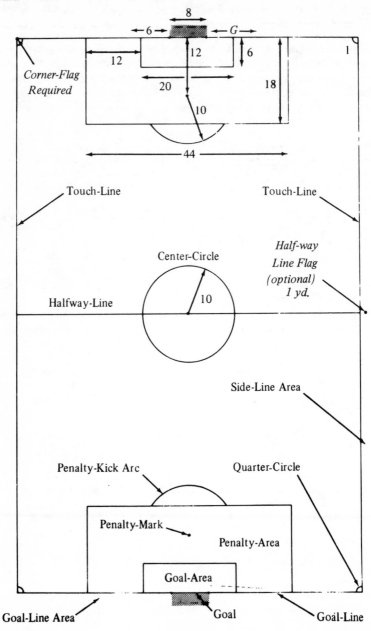

Field of Play

AREAS

GOAL	8 Yards—Wide 8 Feet—Height
GOAL-AREA	20 Yards—Wide 6 Yards—Deep
PENALTY-AREA	44 Yards—Wide 18 Yards—Deep
CORNER-AREA	1 Yard Radius from corner
PENALTY-MARK	12 Yards from Goal-Line
CENTER-CIRCLE	10 Yard Radius

- Length and height are inside measurements.
- Width and depth of posts and cross-bars are a maximum of 5 inches.
- A rope is not a satisfactory substitute for a cross-bar when played under competitive rules.
- A net, if used, should extend not less than 5 feet beyond the goal-line.
- Posts and bars are made of wood, metal, or other approved material.
- There are no rules re: the color of the goalposts or crossbar.

- - - - - - - - - - - - - - - - - - -

- The space within the inside areas of the field of play includes the width of the lines marking those areas.

- - - - - - - - - - - - - - - - - - -

- From front of goal-area. or
- From front of penalty-area. } 6 Yards
- Mark = 9 inch diameter spot (approx.) is conventional
- College and High-School uses a penalty-kick line (2 ft. long).

- - - - - - - - - - - - - - - - - - -

Lines - Maximum of 5 inches in width (2½ to 3 inches advised), Part of the areas they limit. Goal-lines must be the same width as the goal-posts and cross-bar. Touch-lines and goal-lines belong to the field of play.

	FIFA	INTERNATIONAL MATCHES	HIGH SCHOOL	COLLEGE
TOUCH-LINE	100 yards minimum 130 yards maximum	110 Yards 120 Yards	100 Yards 120 Yards	110 Yards 120 Yards
GOAL-LINE	50 yards minimum 100 yards maximum	70 Yards 80 Yards	65 Yards 75 Yards	65 Yards 75 Yards

(The field of play shall be rectangular)

OLYMPIC FINALS AND WORLD CUP 115 x 74 Yards (105 x 68 Meters)

Youth Leagues may use a smaller field and a smaller goal.

FLAGS

CORNER	5 feet high (minimum) – Blunted end.
HALFWAY-LINE (Optional)	1 yard (minimum) from the touch-line at midfield.

Protests for irregularities in measurement must be made in writing prior to the start of the game. See FIFA Laws for yard/meter conversion.

Sometimes the ball appears to be incidental to play.

THE BALL

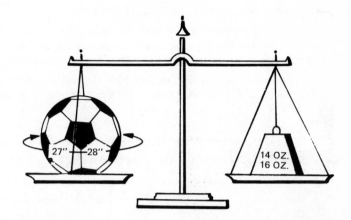

Pressure —

9-10.5 psi at sea level.

Hand pressure should dent the ball's surface 1/4 to 1/2 inch.

College — Ball must bounce between 60-65" when dropped onto a cement floor from 100 inches.

Diameter is 8-3/4"

	Youth		
26.5-28"	13 yrs. & older	14-16 oz.	A size 5 ball
25-26.5"	9-12 yrs. old	12-14 oz.	A size 4 ball
23.5-25"	8 yrs. & younger	10-12 oz.	A size 3 ball

Outer Casing — Leather or other approved material.

Color — None specified.

A minimum of three balls are required. *College* - Ball must be of the same make.

If the game is played on a neutral field, each team must supply at least two balls in good condition. Captains select one of two balls.

The ball shall not be changed during the game unless authorized by the Referee.

Variation of weight during the game is usually not enough to consider the ball unfit because it was official at the start of the game, unless the Referee considers it otherwise.

If the ball bursts or becomes deflated during the course of a match, the game shall be stopped and restarted with a drop-ball.

If this happens during a stoppage of the game, the game shall be restarted accordingly.

 "Inflation pressure is right if it feels good to the Referee.
Ken Aston

PLAYERS

(A player is one who is currently participating in the game.)

Two teams are comprised of not more than 11 nor less than 7 players (recommended by FIFA) on each team. One must be the goalkeeper. (High School - the game can't be started with fewer than 11 on a side.)

On the bench may be the coach, trainer, 1 additional official of the team and up to 5 substitutes. (College - 7 substitutes — High School - unlimited substitutes)

Captain

- Should be indicated in the line-up along with a substitute captain.
- Responsible for the discipline of his teammates.
- The Referee may need his assistance.
- Has no special rights... technically, this includes being allowed to talk to the Referee.

An ineligible player on the opposing team should be protested in writing before the game starts.

Horst Müller

The pause for substitution does not have to be a somber affair.

SUBSTITUTIONS

(To substitute is to bring in a player from the bench.)

A substitute is considered an outside agent until he has officially entered the game. Substitution is:

- Done during a play stoppage.
- The Referee must be informed before the change is made.
- The player being substituted for must leave the field before his replacement enters.
- Substitutes are to enter at the halfway-line.

A substitute is considered to be part of the team when

- He enters the field and...
- After the player he is replacing has left the field.

It is not necessary to wait until the Referee restarts play for the substitute to be considered a player.

A player who has been substituted for can take no further part in the game. (FIFA)

A player who has been ordered off the field after the starting kick-off may not be substituted.

A player who has been ordered off the field *before play begins* may be substituted.

Number of Substitutes

FIFA = 2 of possible 5

Youth = 4

High School = No limit. Substitution is the same as college plus after a disqualification. Exception:
- There must be possession in order to substitute during a throw-in or a corner-kick.
- An injured player *must* be replaced.

Goalkeeper Substitution
See Goalkeeper (this chapter).

College = Up to 7. May subsitute on a Goal-Kick, Corner-Kick, Goal, between periods, and for an injury or a cautioned player. (Opponents can substitute a like number if there is a substitution for an injury or a caution.

ILLNESS/INJURY

1. Stop the game if a player has been seriously injured. Restart with a drop-ball.
   (***High School*** — IFK if there is clear possession.)

2. If a player other than the GK is *slightly* injured, play shall not be stopped until the ball has ceased to be in play.

3. A player who is able to reach the side-line area under his own power shall not be treated on the field.

4. No person may enter the field to help an injured player unless permission has been granted by the Referee.

5. Time allowances are made for injuries.

6. If the GK is obviously injured or passed out - Immediately whistle. Play is resumed with a drop-ball.

Play must be immediately stopped if a goalkeeper is injured.

Horst Müller

"Let's drag him over there."

"We have lots of real 'personalities' among the Referees, and they tend to go their own way. By putting themselves in the ground they make it much more difficult to reach uniformity. This is why the aim of every Referee's meeting, of every conference and discussion must be to try to reach uniformity in the interpretation of the soccer laws."

— Frederich Seipelt
European Referee Instructor

There is enough competition on the field. Referees do not need to compete with each other or with players for attention.

GOALKEEPER

Steps/Dual Possession - IFK

If more than 4 steps are taken, (Steps taken to regain balance do not count.) only deliberate violations should be penalized (XII-IBD 8). If the ball is quickly distributed, don't penalize a trifling offense. (A quick 5th or 6th step).

or

The goalkeeper is guilty of Dual Possession. Once the Goalkeeper releases the ball into play (puts it on the ground), he can't again touch the ball with his hands until it has been touched or played by another player.

Possession

To have the ball within his hands or cradled within his arms.

Possession is also a finger, hand, arm or leg on a stationary ball brought under the control of the Goalkeeper.

When there is possession, an opponent can not attempt to play the ball.

ACTION WITH BALL	POSSESSION	COUNT STEPS	
HOLDING IT	YES		
BOUNCING IT	NO (H.S./COL. = YES)	YES	
THROWING IT UP AND CATCHING IT	YES		

To bounce the ball or throw it up and catch it is *not* considered as being a release of the ball.

Delaying Tactics

- He only has the time necessary to put the ball back into play.
- Holds the ball too long.
- Baits an opponent by withholding the ball from play.
- Repeatedly kicks the ball back and forth with another player is not to be penalized. It is time consuming, not time wasting.

Charging (See also Charging - this chaper.)

He may be charged: ▨

LOCATION	HE OBSTRUCTS	HAS POSSESSION OF BALL	DOES NOT HAVE POSSESSION OF BALL
WITHIN THE GOAL-AREA	//////	//////	CAN *NOT* BE CHARGED – IFK
IN ALL OTHER PORTIONS OF THE PENALTY-AREA	//////	//////	//////

Unintentional body contact is not to be penalized.

- Youth, High School, College - Goalkeeper may not be charged inside the penalty-area.

-130-

GOALKEEPER (Cont.)

	COLLEGE AND H.S.	YOUTH
INTENTIONAL CHARGING	EJECT AND DIRECT	CAUTION AND DIRECT
_UN_INTENTIONAL CHARGING	DIRECT	IFK

Changing/Substitution

Must be done when ball is not in play.

May be substituted for whenever there is a stoppage in play including:

- When a PK has been awarded to the opposing team. (Not for High School.)
- If a PK is retaken. (Not for High School.)

Referee must be notified. A change of jersey does not constitute official notification (but the player wearing the jersey is the Goalkeeper and has all the Goalkeeper privileges).

If a Goalkeeper is substituted without notifying the Referee:

- If he *changes places* with another player - caution both players when ball is out of play.

  If replaced by a *substitute* - the Goalkeeper is cautioned and if the Referee stopped play exclusively to administer this caution then IFK is given where the ball was when the game was stopped.

Ungentlemanly Conduct - Caution and IFK

Hits ball with an object held in the hand.

Holds onto upright or cross-bar to gain an unfair advantage.

Leans on shoulders of teammate to gain an unfair advantage.

Lying down in front of his goal as a contemptuous gesture in a very one-sided game.

Miscellaneous

Goalkeeper shall wear colors which distinguish him from the other players (including the other Goalkeeper and the Referee. If the jerseys of the two Goalkeepers are the same and they are unable to change, the Referee must accept the situation.

A Goalkeeper may score in opponent's goal by throwing or making a clearing kick, provided he is within his own PA.

If Goalkeeper is injured or passes out - immediately stop play. Resume with a dropball.

A Goalkeeper who deliberately throws the ball at an opponent who is outside the P.A. is sanctioned with a P.K.

EQUIPMENT/APPAREL

The Referee should inspect player equipment prior to the start of the game.

A player may wear glasses (at his own risk). It is up to the Referee as to whether restraining straps are necessary. No metal bracelets, wrist watches or any object that may be dangerous to himself or to the other players.

A player should not play without a jersey. If the Referee allows it, it must be reported.

Shirt numbers are not to be changed except when substituting or changing places with the goalkeeper. If changed — CAUTION, require them to change back and IFK if the game was in progress.

Players can't take part in a game without shoes (one or both) unless none of the players have them. A goal counts, however, even if scored by a player who has lost his shoe(s). No goal is allowed if a flying shoe distracted the GK.

Any Referee who is asked to examine a player's shoes should always do so.

Shoes

	MATERIAL	MINIMUM DIAMETER	MAXIMUM PROTRUSION	
STUDS (Screw-In)	LEATHER RUBBER ALUMINUM PLASTIC	1/2 inch		• Must be solid
STUDS (Moulded)	RUBBER PLASTIC POLYURETHANE	1/2 inch (if less than 10 studs) otherwise, 3/8 inch	3/4 inch (size of a penny)	
BARS	LEATHER RUBBER			• Must extend the total width of the sole.

American football shoes having a distinctive screw-in toe cleat are not allowed.

Shoes with metal posts extending from the soles upon which a threaded stud is screwed onto, are illegal.

NO ☝ ☝ YES

The Referee is authorized to order jerseys changed if similarity of colors impairs the control of the game. Home team should change.

A cast is not permitted if the Referee decides it is dangerous to the other players. (High School and Youth — Casts, even if padded, are not allowed.)

ROTTENTATOR

- Always needs a shave.

- Is chronically late for every game.

- Wears stolen FIFA patch.

- Never washes his uniform.

- B.O. causes coach to stay away from him.

- Shrugs shoulders when Referee makes an unpopular call.

- Leaves after game saying he will shower at home.

- Blames God for everything.

  Wife avoids him.

- Tells people that he wrote *Fair or Foul.*

REFEREE

1. The Referee's authority commences as soon as he is in the vicinity of the field of play.

2. Players (including the captain) technically do not have the right to address the Referee. If any do... the Referee is within his right to CAUTION and IFK.

3. A Referee can only reverse his decision as long as the game has not been restarted.

4. The Referee has no authority to declare a winner in a game he terminates. He must however, make a detailed report to the proper authority. (*High School and College* - He may declare a forfeit.)

5. If he is late and the game is in progress, he may not take over.

   Club Game - If the Referee doesn't show, a substitute Referee may officiate provided both captains agree in writing.

6. The Referee may name a substitute Linesman to replace one who did not show up, who may act until the designated Linesman arrives.

7. He has discretionary powers in regard to dangerous playing. He can punish it with a CAUTION in addition to IFK.

8. To terminate a game for bad visibility he can use as a suggested minimum standard of not being able to see both goals from the center circle.

9. It is the duty of the Referee to act upon the information of a *neutral* Linesman with regard to incidents that do not come under the personal notice of the Referee.

   If an immediate decision is rendered, he may penalize, as appropriate. If, however, play had continued, all he can do is CAUTION or EJECT.

10. A Referee, not having seen a score, may only allow the goal if reported by a *neutral* Linesman.

11. He must not allow both Linesmen to place themselves on the same touch-line. (Reference System once used in Russia.)

12. Coaching from the boundary lines is not allowed (FIFA) - First WARN, then CAUTION, then EJECT.

13. The Referee should not allow players to waste time. The law requires that opposing players retreat the required 10 yards when a free kick is being taken. The Referee must assert his personality and apply the laws of the game.

ADVANTAGE CLAUSE (LAW V) *See Chapter V - Advantage.*

The Referee shall refrain from penalizing when it would be an advantage to the offending team. - ADVANTAGE CLAUSE.

In order to justify the decision for applying the advantage clause, the advantage should be evident, clear and immediate.

Application if within:
• Defensive 1/3 of field - *Almost Never*
• Midfield - *Infrequently*
• Attacking 1/3 of field (non PA) - *Most Often*
• Within the PA - only if Referee is almost positive that a goal will be scored.

The advantage may not be applied prior to or during the process of putting the ball back into play, (e.g., throw-in, kick-off).

Remember, *It is a clause, not a law.*

TERMINATION/SUSPENSION OF GAME

When may the Referee terminate/suspend a game?

• CONTROL

1. When he considers that he will not be able to exert complete vigilance over the game.

2. When the field is invaded by spectators or players, and the official feels that he cannot restore order.

3. When a player refuses to leave the game, and play cannot be continued.

• ENVIRONMENT

1. If the Referee cannot see both goals while standing in the center circle. (A recommendation.)

2. If the field is not longer properly marked, through rain or other elements and cannot be remarked.

3. When the ground becomes so wet that the ball will not bounce.

4. If a wind condition will not allow a stationary ball to remain so.

5. When smog prevails to the extent that the players' health is endangered.

• OTHER

1 If one team has less than seven players. (If specified in the rules of composition.)

2 If there are no more game balls that are acceptable to the Referee.

3. When the Referee is incapacitated, and cannot continue, unless a neutral Linesman replaces him.

If a game is terminated prematurely, the League must decide whter the game will be replayed in full or the score at the time of the stoppage will be allowed to stand.

TIMING

At the start of each half or overtime period, playing time begins from the moment the ball is legally put into play (travels its circumference in a forward direction), not on the sounding of the whistle. There is a running clock, and time is stopped only at the Referee's discretion.

Time Allowance

- Treatment of injuries when a player cannot be safely removed from the field.
- Lost (or not easily recovered) ball or one in need of replacement.
- Time wasting by either team.
- Extension of time for penalty-kick.

High school and college soccer . . . the clock is stopped after a goal and for the taking of a penalty-kick and for cautions/ejections.

If, at the end of a period, an error in timing (shortage) is noted, and called to the Referee's attention by a neutral Linesman and acknowledged, the players must be called back onto the field and play must continue for the duration of the shortage.

Time losses occurring in the one period may not be added to another.

The duration of the game can't be protested.

Game Time

FIFA and College	High School	Youth
Two equal periods of 45 minutes each	Two periods of 40 minutes each or Four quarters of 20 minutes each	Division 1 — Two periods of 40 minutes each Division 2 — Two periods of 35 minutes each Division 3 — Two periods of 30 minutes each Division 4,5 — Two periods of 25 minutes each Division 6 — Two periods of 20 minutes each

Halftime

FIFA	College	High School	Youth
5 minutes (May be extended to not more than 15 minutes)	Maximum of 10 minutes	10 minutes (2 minutes between quarters)	Minimum — 5 minutes Maximum — 10 minutes

Captains of both teams *may not* agree to forego the half-time interval if any player objects.

If Necessary to Establish a Winner (Overtime)

FIFA	College	High School	Youth
Two periods of 15 minutes each. (Generally accepted) 5 minutes between regulation period and overtime is recommended.	Two periods of 10 minutes each.	Two periods of 5 minutes each.	(Sudden Death) *Division* *2 Periods of:* 1 10 min. 2-3 9 min. 4-5 8 min. 6 7 min.

KICK-OFF

WHEN TAKEN		• To start the game. • To re-start after half-time. • After a team scores a goal. • To start overtime periods.
WHERE TAKEN	Center of the field	• Each player must be in his own half of the field - RETAKE. • A player having one foot in each half of the field is still in his own half of the field.
IN-PLAY	CIRCUMFERENCE and into opponent's half of play.	• If travels along the center-line and goes out of bounds, RETAKE because ball must be kicked forward. • If any player touches the ball before it is in play — RETAKE.
PLAYS BALL TWICE IN SUCCESSION	IFK	• If played 2nd time before moving its circumference - RETAKE.
SCORE DIRECTLY?	NO	• Opponent's goal - GOAL-KICK. • Own goal - RETAKE - Not in play.
DISTANCE AWAY	Opponent's = 10 Yards	

If there is successive encroachment or the ball isn't kicked into the opponent's half of play . . .

- 1st time — WARN and RETAKE

- 2nd time — CAUTION and RETAKE

- 3rd time — EJECT and RETAKE

The home team captain normally flips the coin. The captain of the visiting team calls the toss. The winner of the coin toss has the choice of kick-off or end of field. If end is chosen, the other team must kick-off. After the captain winning the flip has made hs decision, he may not change his mind.

At half-time, ends are changed and the opposite team kicks-off. Note that this kick-off is in the same direction as it was to begin the game.

If there is overtime, a coin toss will again be taken.

DROP-BALL

WHEN TAKEN?	* (see below)	
HOW TAKEN?	Dropped, not thrown	• Drop from waist height of the players.
WHERE TAKEN?	Where ball was when play was stopped	(College, High School, Youth - At nearest point outside the penalty area.
IN PLAY	When touches the ground.	• If goes over goal/touch-line before touched by any player — RETAKE. • If played before touches ground . . . 1st time WARN and RETAKE 2nd time CAUTION and RETAKE 3rd time EJECT and RETAKE
OFF-SIDE DIRECTLY?	No	• This pertains only to the *first* player to play the ball.
DISTANCE AWAY	No prescribed distance that players must be away from the ball.	• Players may not interfere with the dropping of the ball.

If, during a DROP-BALL, but before the ball is actually dropped, a foul is committed — Referee can CAUTION or EJECT but can't award a free-kick because the ball isn't in play.

When taken . . .

- Temporary suspension not covered elsewhere in soccer laws.

- Illegal field entry by a substitute.

- Ball out of bounds — Referee unable to identify the team who last played it.

- Ball out of bounds after simultaneously coming off of 2 opponents. (A rarity.)

- Player(s) accidentally falls on ball and play is stopped before it becomes dangerous.

- After stoppage for illness/injury.

- Ball hits a corner-post or an upright and breaks it.

- Ball strikes an outside agent or the outside agent causes interference.

- Simultaneous fouls of the same gravity. (This is a rarity.)

- When the ball bursts or becomes deflated during the course of a match. (If the ball bursts or becomes deflated as the game is being restarted and *before the ball has been played or touched by a player* — RETAKE . . . even if it hits a foreign object. Exception: The ball bursts on the cross-bar when taking a Penalty-Kick = DROP-BALL.)

DROP BALL (Cont.)

- If the Referee mistakenly whistles.
- If the Referee prematurely awards a goal.
- The instant the Referee notices the inside of the goal is altered, if done prior to the ball going into the goal (other than GK moving the cross-bar).

The Drop Ball

1. The Drop Ball occurs at the position where the ball was when the play was stopped. (College, High School and Youth - Ball is dropped at the nearest point outside of the Penalty-Area.)

2. It is often advisable to quickly say "Drop-ball," and to drop it immediately. Although the laws do not require that a player from each team is present, it is customary. (High School - requires one from each team.)

3. When the ball is to be dropped within the Penalty-Area, be sure that a defender is present.

4. If a drop-ball is taken near the goal-line, hits a rock, and then goes directly into the goal without being played by any player - RETAKE. (After having rock removed.)

5. To give a drop-ball when two players simultaineously kick a ball out of bounds (as indicated by Law VIII) tends to indicate Referee indecision. Most experienced Referees will award the throw-in or the goal-kick to the defensive team should this situation occur. If a drop-ball is given, it should be done at the point it left the field of play.

6. When using the diagonal system with neutral linesmen, always face one of your linesmen when dropping the ball.

7. A goalkeeper within the PA may pick up a drop-ball directly after it hits the ground, for the ball is in play.

8. The player who first plays the ball may continue to play it without it having to be played by a 2nd player.

POTENTATOR

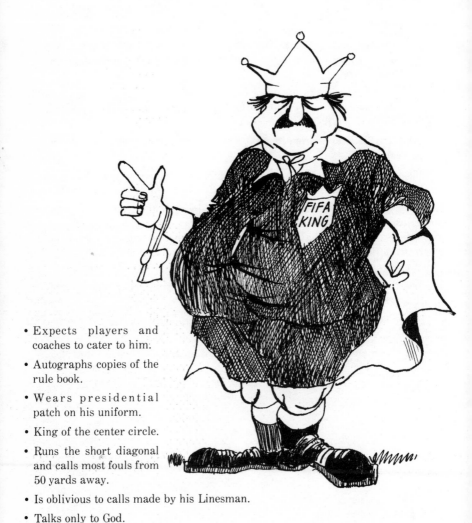

- Expects players and coaches to cater to him.
- Autographs copies of the rule book.
- Wears presidential patch on his uniform.
- King of the center circle.
- Runs the short diagonal and calls most fouls from 50 yards away.
- Is oblivious to calls made by his Linesman.
- Talks only to God.
- Has two wives.
- Claims to have been the prime consultant for the writing of *Fair or Foul.*

OUTSIDE AGENT (FOREIGN OBJECTS)

If a spectator, substitute, animal, reserve-ball, or any other object enters the field of play — Referee, if necessary, will stop play and will award a DROP-BALL.

A limb of a tree would be considered a foreign object if it overhung into the field and was touched by an in play ball.

The bodies of the Referees and Linesmen are **not** considered foreign objects. They are neutral objects and are part of the field if they are within the field of play.

A goal can't be awarded in any case if the ball has been prevented by some outside agent from passing over the goal-line, or if the agent touched the ball.

Following a restart, if the ball is in play and touches an outside agent prior to any other player having touched it . . .

- If a penalty-kick — RETAKE
- All other situations — DROP-BALL
  (Kick-off, goal-kick, corner-kick, etc.)

Substitutes and ejected players are outside agents.

Oto Maxmilian

"Don't worry, Gentlemen, I'll take care of this outside agent."

IN/OUT OF PLAY

It is the position of the ball that is important, not the position of the player.

Ball in Play	After...
KICK-OFF	Circumference and into opponent's half of the field.
GOAL-KICK	Clears the penalty-area.
FREE-KICK	Circumference.
FREE-KICK (taken inside own penalty-area)	Circumference and clears the penalty-area.
PENALTY-KICK	Circumference and forward.
THROW-IN	Has been released and enters the field of play (touches or passes the outside edge of the touch-line).
CORNER-KICK	Circumference.
DROP-BALL	Touches ground.
Ball Out of Play	
Wholly crosses the touch or goal-line (ground or air).	If the ball completely crosses the boundary lines in the air, but, because of the wind, returns to the field of play, it shall be considered out of bounds.
When game has been stopped by the Referee	Temporary suspension not covered elsewhere in soccer laws - DROP-BALL.

Ball is in play at all other times including:

- If it rebounds from a goal-post, cross bar, or corner flag into the field of play.
- If it rebounds off of a Referee or Linesman who is in the field of play.
- An infringment of the laws until the whistle is sounded.

 "THE MOST DANGEROUS TIME OF ALL IS WHEN THE BALL IS OUT OF PLAY."

Ken Aston

SCORING

A goal is scored when the *whole* of the ball has completely passed over the back edge of the goal-line between the goal-posts and under the cross-bar.

A goal scored immediately after an infraction is noticed by the Referee does not count (unless he has applied the Advantage Clause).

If the Goalkeeper is obviously injured or passes out, the game should be stopped at once. After the GK has recovered or has been replaced, resume play with a DROP-BALL.

A Referee having not seen a score may allow the goal only if reported by a neutral linesman.

The score of a forfeit is 1-0. (College and High School)

Advantage

If a 'hand ball' by a defensive player goes into his own goal, the score shall count. (An application of the Advantage Clause)

Premature Awarding of a Score

If a score is awarded prematurely by the Referee, which the goalkeeper managed to stop on or near the goal-line, a DROP-BALL must be given where the ball was when the Referee whistled. For High School, College and Youth, the DROP-BALL must be given at the nearest point outside the penalty-area.

Outside Agent

A goal cannot be awarded in any case if the ball has been prevented by some outside agent from passing over the goal-line or if it crosses the goal-line after having contacted an outside agent.

Early Whistle

A goal cannot be awarded if the Referee blows his whistle prior to the ball crossing the goal line.

Field Entry/Exit Without Permission

- Unauthorized entry
  - If score in own goal = GOAL and CAUTION
  - If score in opponent's goal = NO GOAL, CAUTION, INDIRECT
- 12th participant (actually a substitute) entry followed by the scoring of a goal...

  — *If play has not been resumed* — NO GOAL. Have captain send one participant off the field. Resume play with IFK from where the ball was played into the goal.

  — *If play has been resumed* — GOAL. Have captain send one participant off the field. Resume play with a Drop Ball from where the ball was when play was stopped.

Whenever the identity of the 12th participant is known - CAUTION him.

OFF-SIDE

A player is in an off-side position if he is nearer the opponent's goal-line than THE BALL (Diagram 1=D1) at the *moment* the ball is played D3)

The off-side is called if the player is in an off-side position and he:

- Takes advantage of his position.
- Participates in play.
- Influences or interferes with play or with an opponent.
- Trys to gain an (effective) advantage.

Not in Off-side Position (exceptions)

Two opponents are nearer their goal-line than he is. (D2) (D3)	Being in line with an opponent means that no part of an opponent is between the plaer and the goal-line. (D5)
He is in his own half of the field of play. (D11)	The halfway line is considered to be part of both halves of the field. • Both feet on or behind the line is *not* off-side position. • One foot in each half of the field is to be in an off-side position.

Not Off-side, even if in Off-side Position

Receives the ball directly from a...
 	
   GOAL-KICK
   CORNER-KICK   (D8)
   THROW-IN   (D7)
   DROP-BALL   (D10)
	• This protection ends when another player plays the ball. (D9)
	
	• A player may be penalized for being off-side when the ball is played directly to or toward him from a free-kick or a penalty-kick.

The ball was last played by an opponent. (D12)	• This does not apply if attacker is judged to have been interfering with play or an opponent. • A player who is in an off-side position must be judged off-side if he receives the ball directly from a rebound from the up-right or cross-bar.

OFF-SIDE (Cont.)

RULE OF THUMB

If the player in the off-side position has *no* chance of reaching the ball before anyone else, then he is not to be penalized for off-side.

Moment of Judgement

The moment of judgement is the moment the ball is played. Participation is judged until the next time the ball is played.
You may penalize at a later time.

Off-Side Position, Player is Off-Side — Low Frequency of Occurance

Interferes with the play or with an opponent	A player who advances toward an opponent or the ball may be deemed as influencing the course of the game.
Distracts an opposing player	• Standing in front of the GK may affect his line of vision and concentration. • A close-by attacker may be taking advantage of his position if the GK has to allow for his presence. — It could be considered GK distraction if the opponent is inside the goal area. — It shouldn't be considered GK distraction if the opponent is outside the penalty area.

HINTS

A player is not off-side if he is in line with the *ball.* (D-6)

A player who is in an off-side position at the moment the ball was played can't run back in an attempt to "erase" the off-side position. (D-4)

Be aware of a team's employment of the 'off-side trap.' (Defenses move up in unison before the ball is played in order to put an attacker in an off-side position.) This is a legal tactic. It is also called the 'Hungarian Off-side."

A player may step off of the field in order to *avoid* an off-side. But a player may not step off the field in order to *cause* an off-side (D14).

If a player's momentum carries him into the goal itself, he may remain without being penalized as long as he does not distract the GK. (D13).

The player is not off-side if the ball was last played by himself (e.g., player with the ball falls and ball goes behind him. He may get back up, go back and retrieve the ball).

When a defensive wall is formed on the goal-line and an offensive player is part of that wall, the offensive player is in an off-side position the moment the ball is played, unless he moves on-side before the ball is played.

1. RELATIONSHIP TO THE BALL

A passes the ball. B runs from position 1 to position 2 and kicks the ball into the Goal. *Not off-side* because even though there were not two opponents between B and the goal-line, he was *behind* (not ahead) of the ball.

2. OFF-SIDE PASS

A passes to B who is off-side because he is ahead of the ball at the moment it is played by a teammate and there aren't two opponents between him and the goal-line when the ball was passed.

3. MOMENT OF PASS

A runs the ball up and passes the ball. B then runs from position 1 to position 2. B is not off-side because *at the moment of the pass* even though he was ahead of the ball, he had two opponents between him and the goal-line. *Not off-side.*

4. CAN'T GET BACK ON-SIDE

A passes toward B who is in an off-side position. B comes back to get the ball but is whistled off-side because he was in an off-side position at the moment the ball was played by a teammate, and he participated in play.

5. BEING 'IN-LINE' WITH A DEFENDER

A passes the ball to B who is 'in line' with his opponent. B is *off-side* because only one player, the goalkeeper, is between him and the goal-line.

6. BEING 'IN-LINE' WITH THE BALL

A passes the ball B then runs from position 1 to position 2. Although B did not have 2 opponents between him and the goal-line, he is *not off-side* because he was not ahead (he was in-line) of the ball.

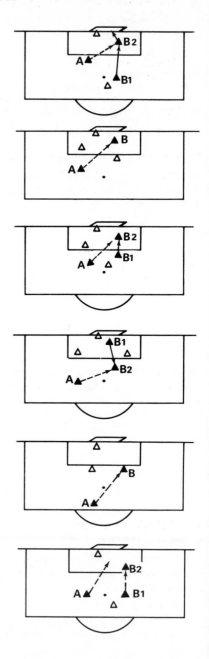

7. DIRECTLY FROM A THROW-IN

A throws the ball to B who kicks it into the goal. *Not off-side* because the ball was received directly from A throw-in.

8. DIRECTLY FROM A CORNER-KICK

A kicks the corner-kick to B who heads it into the goal. *Not off-side* because the ball was received directly from a corner-kick.

9. *AFTER* A CORNER-KICK

A kicks the corner-kick to B who passes to A at position 2. B received the ball directly and is not off-side.

A was in front of the ball and didn't have two opponents between himself and the goal-line so is off-side the instant B plays the ball. A is *off-side* at position 2 because he is ahead of the ball and there are not two defensive players between him and the goal-line.

10. RESUMING PLAY WITH A DROP-BALL

The Referee (R) drops the ball and A kicks the ball directly to B who shoots and scores. A is not off-side as he played the ball directly from the drop, but B is off-side because immunity from off-side was removed as soon as the ball was touched by player A.

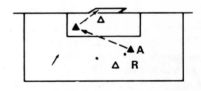

11. OWN HALF OF FIELD

A passes the ball. B then goes from position 1 to position 2. B is not off-side because he was within his half of the field at the moment of the pass.

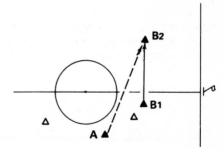

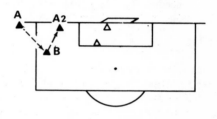

12. GOALKEEPER DEFLECTION AND NON-PARTICIPATION

A kicks toward the goal. The ball is deflected by the goalkeeper to **B** who kicks the ball into the goal.

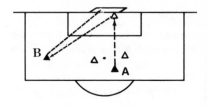

Although **B** is in an off-side position he is not to be penalized because the ball was last played by opponent and **B** was judged too far out of play to be participating at the moment of the shot.

If, however, the Referee feels that **B** would have been able to get to the ball before the GK deflection, then the off-side would have been called.

If the ball had been deflected by a cross-bar instead of an opponent, it would be considered to be the same as a direct pass and an off-side would be whistled.

INFREQUENTLY OCCURRING SITUATIONS

13. OFFENSIVE PLAYER GOES INSIDE GOAL

A runs the ball to position 1 and passes to **B**. **A**, realizing he is in an off-side position, runs into the goal and remains there passively. *Not off-side* because **A** was not interfering in play nor was he interfering with the opponents. If, at any time, the Referee feels that **A2** is actively distracting the goalkeeper, (mere presence is not sufficient), then he shall call off-side. Play would be resumed with an IFK within the half of the goal area on the side where the offense occurred, even though the infraction occurred outside the field of play.

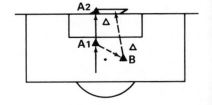

"No advantage shall be given on an off-side."

Concacaf

14. DEFENSE MAY NOT PUT MAN OFF-SIDE BY LEAVING THE FIELD

Defensive player **D** moves from position 1 to position 2 in an attempt to put **B** off-side. This is not allowed. Not off-side.

MISCONDUCT – CAUTION

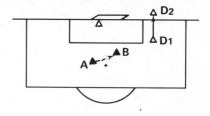

"THE INTENT OF THE OFF-SIDE IS TO PREVENT THE SCORING OF A GOAL BY A PLAYER WHO HAS NOT HONESTLY WORKED FOR IT."

Ken Aston

Sometimes at midfield an incorrectly placed ball will show you don't know the laws of the game. If the kick is going to the right, and the infraction was for off-side, it is important for your credibility that the ball be correctly placed.

CONDENSED OFF-SIDE
(See diagram ⟶)

I. To be off-side is to take advantage of being in an off-side position.

Taking advantage means the same as writers and lecturers who say...

- "Participates in play"....

- "Influences play"....

- "Seeks to gain an (effective) advantage"...

- "Interferes with play"

A rule of thumb that we often use is the question, "When the ball is played, do you think that the player in the off-side position *might* be able to get to it first?

A "yes" answer means the whistle is blown and an off-side is called.

II. *What is the Off-Side position?*

It is being *ahead* of the ball... not even or behind the ball, but ahead. The player is closer to the opponents' goal-line than the ball is....

WHEN?

... the moment the ball is played by a teammate. This is the moment of judgment, and it lasts until the next moment of judgment, which is the *next* time the ball is played.

III. *Not Off-Side*

A. There are two ways of escaping from this off-side position. Both give the player immunity from being in an off-side position.

B. One can be in an off-side position but still be immune from being whistled off-side.

- When the ball is received directly from the Corner-Kick, Goal-Kick, Throw-In, or Drop Ball, it is significant to note that no one can be in an off-side position until the ball is played.

- If the ball was last played by an opponent there can be no off-side unless the attacker is judged to have been interfering with play or with an opponent.

I
> Player *takes advantage*
> of being in an off-side *position*

II.
> Off-side Position
>
> What: Player is closer to the opponents
>   goal-line than the **ball** is.
>
> When: The **moment** the ball is played
>   by a teammate.

III. NOT OFF-SIDE

a. ESCAPE

- 2 defenders nearer own
  goal-line than the player.
- Player in own half of field.

b. STILL IN OFF-SIDE POSITION

- Receive the ball *directly* from a:
  - Corner-kick
  - Throw-in
  - Goal-kick
  - Drop ball
- Ball last played by an opponent.

"This is not a cleat inspection."

-152-

"If you don't protect the players, they will protect themselves, and this means trouble with a capital 'T'."

Ken Aston

FOULS AND MISCONDUCT

1. An offense or attempted offense **is committed at the place where the player concerned initiated the action.**

2. An **unintentional** hand ball, trip, push, kick, or charge from behind — no infringement. Intention comprises as much of the foul as the contact itself. Sometimes seemingly violent play is not penalized as a penal offense because there is no intention. This is often due to the players not knowing how to play the game, which often results in dangerous play.

3. An offense normally punishable by a free-kick or a penalty-kick, if committed while play is suspended, can result only in a warning, caution or ejection.

4. Substitutes cannot commit a foul. They may be cautioned or ejected, but play is always resumed with a drop-ball.

5. An offense occurring outside a Referee's field of vision is indicated by a neutral linesman. The Referee can award a free-kick or a penalty-kick, if done via an immediate decision.

6. Two **opposing** players are **outside the boundary** of the field of play and one intentionally commits misconduct or violent conduct upon the other; stop the game, caution or eject and resume with drop-ball.

7. Retaliation when fouled is not permitted. A player shall not retaliate in any way.

8. If two infractions of a different nature are committed at the same time, the Referee will punish the more serious offense.

9. Two players on the same team simultaneously commit offenses having equal status against members of the opposite team. Award the opposition that which gives them the greatest advantage.

10. Two players on the same team commit offenses upon one another while the ball is in play. Caution or eject, then restart play with an IFK in favor of the opponents.

11. Hard or particularly dangerous fouls are left up to the Referee's discretion as to whether he administers a caution or not.

12. The captain is responsible for the conduct of his team. (See Players — this chapter.)

13. Always caution or eject for any foul that is committed:
    - Off the ball.
    - With malice aforethought.
    - By going over the ball.

14. In the Penalty-Area — to ignore the foul is better than to compromise with a lesser foul (an IFK, when a PK should have been awarded).

15. Never 'pull' the ball out of the Penalty-Area if you are convinced that the foul occurred inside the Penalty-Area.

INTENTIONAL VS DELIBERATE

The intentional foul — The player determines to act in a certain way.

The deliberate foul — It is intentionally committed with careful and thorough consideration. It is characterized by **awareness of the consequences.** More conscious will is involved with the deliberate foul.

There is a rather fine line to be drawn between the intentional foul (as mentioned in Law XII) and one that is done deliberately. The deliberate foul should be penalized at least with a caution and quite often an ejection.

WARNINGS OR "SOFT CAUTIONS"

Warn the first time a . . .

- *Kick-off* — is intentionally not played into opponent's half of the field or is subject to encroachment. RETAKE

- *Corner-Kick* — has defensive encroachment. RETAKE or ADVANTAGE CLAUSE

- *Goal-Kick* or *Free-Kick (within own Penalty-Area)* — intentionally not kicked beyond Penalty-Area or an opposing player encroaches, or any player touches the ball within the Penalty-Area.

- *Drop-Ball* — is touched or played before hitting the ground. RETAKE

 If you have to use the yellow card, your game control has slipped.

A caution means that "You've been given two chances, and you've used up one of them already."

CAUTIONS (YELLOW CARD)

Cause . . .	Action If Ball in Play	
Ungentlemanly conduct	IFK	● See 'Ungentlemanly Conduct' – this chapter.
Constantly infringes the laws of the game	(As per offense)	
Dissent	IFK	● Shows by word or movements of the body.
Player Field entry or exit without permission	IFK	● Apply advantage clause if applicable.
Field entry by a substitute	DROP-BALL	
Deliberately fouling	(As per offense)	● Deliberately catching the ball to prevent an attack from developing. At midfield the Referee can be more lenient.
Dangerous play (Referee option)	IFK	● See 'Dangerous Play.'
Deliberately fouling	(As per offense)	● Deliberately catching the ball to prevent an attack from developing.
Dangerous play (if Referee desires)	IFK	● See 'Dangerous Play'.
Player (other than the goalkeeper changes shirt numbers.	IFK	● Require them to change back.
Coaching from the side-line.	DROP-BALL	
Delaying the taking of a free-kick. (Defensive player wasting time getting back 10 yards from the ball.		● The law requires that the players get back. The Referee must assert his personality and apply the laws of the game.

Caution during a penalty-kick if there is an encroachment, the wrong person kicks, or any distraction either to or by the GK

If a player receives a third caution during the season, most leagues require him to sit out the next game.

Caution the Second Time in Succession a . . .

- *Kick-Off* – is intentionally not played into opponent's half of the field or is subject to encroachment. RETAKE

- *Corner-Kick* – has defensive encroachment. RETAKE or ADVANTAGE CLAUSE

- *Goal-Kick* or *Free-Kick (within own penalty-area)* – is intentionally not kicked beyond penalty-area or an opposing player encroaches, or any player touches the ball within the penalty-area.

- *Drop-Ball* – is touched or played before hitting the ground. RETAKE

The cautioning of a player takes at least 15 seconds away from play, and it frequently takes 60 seconds.

EJECTION (RED CARD)

Condition

VIOLENT CONDUCT OR SERIOUS FOUL PLAY Maliciously strikes or attempts to strike (includes spitting at). Maliciously kicks or attempts to kick.	If player strikes an opponent far away from play, and the advantage is applicable, do not eject immediately, wait until a counter attack or the first stoppage of play. Two teammates fighting with one another. Throwing of an object at any player.
Persists in misconduct after having received a caution.	NOTE: A player is never given a second caution. This second offense requires an ejection.
Foul or abusive language and/or gestures.	The same applies to foul language coming from outside the field of play.

The game is restarted with a DIRECT FREE-KICK if the strike or kick offenses are committed against an opponent. It is restarted with an IFK in all other situations when the infraction is committed on the field of play. (Striking or kicking a Referee, Linesman, spectator or teammate — even if in the Penalty-Area.)

If a Player is Ejected . . .

- Before game starts — he can be replaced by a named substitute.
- Any time after play has started — he cannot be replaced.

If ejected, a player may not occupy the side-line or goal-line area. He must leave the general area of play.

An ejected player is considered an outside agent.

Miscellaneous Ejections

- If a player starts to go after another player in a violent manner.
- Intentional charging of the goalkeeper (youth/high school/college).

Oto Maxmilian

Many have said that soccer's future is in the hands of competent officials. Hopefully, incidents like this, where a player is ejected, will be less and less frequent as the game matures.

ENTERING/LEAVING THE FIELD

Referee orders a player off the field (Ejection)

Before play starts	May be replaced by a named substitute
After play begins	May not be replaced
At half time	

Substitute entry without permission

Referee Notices	No goal is allowed Caution Resume play with drop-ball

If a goal was scored and if it is then determined that there were 12 participants on the field, have the captain send 1 player off the field and...

... If play has *not* been restarted — NO GOAL. Resume play with a drop ball from where the ball was kicked or headed into the goal.

... If play has been restarted — GOAL. Resume play with a drop ball from where the ball was when it was noticed that there were 12 participants.

Trainer/Coach unauthorized entry

Warn, not caution the first time it occurs.

Report the incident to match organizers.

Player leaves the field

- Without Permission — CAUTION and IFK. This includes when it is due to disagreements with teammates. The Referee may allow the player to reenter.

- Injury — May return during a stoppage but only after the Referee signals to do so.

- Equipment Adjustments — Must present himself to the Referee for inspection prior to re-entry.

FREE-KICKS — GENERAL (NON PENALTY-KICK)

Conditions	Kick, in relation to own penalty-area	
	OUTSIDE	**INSIDE**
Where is kick taken?	At the point of infraction (except by defensive team inside its own goal area).	
In play	Circumference	Circumference and outside the penalty-area.
Plays ball a second time	IFK	RETAKE (if hasn't passed penalty-area) Otherwise — IFK
Opponent's distance from ball until it is in play.	10 Yards	10 Yards and outside the penalty-area
Opponent encroachment and Referee stops play before kick is taken.	DELAY KICK	
Opponent encroachment and Referee unable to stop play before kick is taken.	CAUTION AND RETAKE	
Goes directly into one's own goal.	CORNER	RETAKE
Score goal directly against an opponent	DIRECT — Yes IFK — No — GOAL-KICK	
Can teammate be off-side?	YES	
Ball is kicked back to goalkeeper who takes it into his hands within his own penalty-area.	O.K.	RETAKE

- The ball must be stationary. Taken by any player and in any direction.
- Player taking the kick may step outside the boundary lines.
- If taken on or near the boundary lines and goes out of bounds before traveling its own circumference — RETAKE.

- Player taking the kick may voltunarily renounce the distance advantage allowed him.
- If an offensive player requests 10 yards and then kicks the ball while the Referee is establishing the wall . . . CAUTION and RETAKE.
- If a free-kick is taken within 10 yards of the defending team's goal, the defending players may be on the goal-line between the goal-posts. They must however, have both feet on the goal-line.

- Encroachment only applies to defensive players.

- Kick taken from within own penalty-area goes outside of the penalty-area and for some reason comes back and goes directly into own goal (e.g., wind) — CORNER.

To play a ball is to cause it to move. On free kicks, if the first player to kick the ball does not move the ball its circumference, the kick must be retaken.

INDIRECT FREE-KICK (IFK)

A goal cannot be scored unless the ball has been played or touched by a player from either team other than the kicker before passing into the goal.

Referee signals by raising his arm. He keeps it raised until the kick either is played by a second player or the ball goes out of bounds. (If the Referee fails to raise his arm and a goal is scored directly, he should have the kick RETAKEN.)

The following results in an INDIRECT FREE-KICK . . .

After putting the ball into play, immediately plays it again.	If done during the taking of a kick-off, throw-in, free-kick, corner-kick, penalty-kick, or goal-kick going outside the PA.
Off-side	From location of player who was called off-side.
Ungentlemanly conduct	CAUTION - See the next page.
Dangerous play (see this chapter)	The Referee sometimes cautions.
Goalkeepper takes more than 4 steps with ball or has dual possession.	The 4 Step Rule applies until the ball has been played by someone else. While holding, bouncing, or throwing the ball and catching it again.
Fair charges at the wrong moment.	• When not obstructed or ball wasn't within playing distance. • Charging the GK is allowed *except* when... He is not in possession of the ball within his goal-area. Youth, High School & College - Goalkeeper can never be charged within his own penalty-area.
Dissent with decision by... • Throwing the ball away (GK) • Leaving the field • Other	CAUTION
Illegal Obstruction	If done intentionally and *not within playing distance. (Hint* - Look at the players eyes and facial expression if possible*)* • Using his body as an obstacle. • With or without the ball, he backs into an opponent. • If occurs when the ball is not within playing distance of the 2 players involved. • After corner-kick, if opponent then stands in front of the making no attempt to play the ball. • Running across an opponents path to retard his progress. • Attempting to prevent the goalkeeper from putting the ball into play (e.g. player standing directly in front of the GK).
Changing numbers (non-goalkeeper)	CAUTION - For ungentlemanly conduct. Require the players to change back.
Restarting game after violent conduct directed against non-opponents. • Referee • Linesman • Spectators • One's own teammates	• Maliciously Hitting or Spitting • Maliciously Kicking EJECT • Foul language and/or gestures • Insult

If an IFK is taken on the opponent's goal-line, the ball must be kicked backwards or to the side. The ball could never be in play if it was kicked forward.

UNGENTLEMANLY CONDUCT (ALSO CAUTION)

Basic

Restart with an IFK unless the occurrence involved a penal offense or happened when the ball is out of play.

Ungentlemanly conduct applies when directed toward opposing players, teammates, Referees, linesmen or spectators. It occurs when the game is brought into disrepute by unexpected or unprecedented behavior. It offends against the spirit of the game. (e.g., A defender within his penalty-area fists a ball out of the goal. He should be cautioned. Even if the penalty-kick is converted, the defender has lost his reputation as a sportsman and the whole game is the poorer.)

Deliberate Hand Ball

- To prevent a goal from being scored.
- To prevent an attack from developing.
- To make a mockery of the game.

Delaying Tactics

When in possession of the ball, Goalkeeper baits opponent by withholding the ball from play.

Holding ball — Goalkeeper holds too long or any player holds the ball with his legs, or lies on the ball for an unreasonable length of time.

Defenders not retreating 10 yards for a free-kick or a corner-kick.

- Do not leave or too slow in retiring.
- Stand on or in front of the ball.

Harassment

Distracting opponents by dancing about gesticulating, shouting or other actions. (Opponents moving back and forth - even if 10 yards away.)

Jumping in front of a player taking a corner, free-kick, or throw-in.

Worrying or obstructing Goalkeeper. To interfere or attempt to interfere with his clearing move. (May warn on first offense if not blatant.)

Most attempts to prevent the Goalkeeper from putting the ball into play (e.g. offensive players sticks out his leg to inhibit the kick).

Adopting a threatening attitude toward another.

Leverage Used Unfairly

Leaning on shoulders of teammate.

Holds onto uprights or to the crossbar to gain an unfair advantage. (Steadies himself to kick the ball or in order to jump higher.)

UNGENTLEMANLY CONDUCT (Cont.)

Field Entry/Exit

Going off the field without the Referee's permission.

After having received the Referee's permission to leave the field but before having actually left, playing the ball. It is all right as long as the player was not trying to achieve a position of illegal advantage.

Substitute enters the field of play without the Referee's permission (drop ball rather than an IFK).

Injury

Opponent pulling an injured player from the field in order to humiliate him or pulling him to his feet in order to minimize his injury.

Faking an injury.

At the Taking of a Penalty Kick

Goalkeeper swings his hands about in a disruptive manner.

Player other than the one who is designated kicks the ball.

The kicker fakes a kick to get the GK to move his feet.

Objects

GK (within his penalty-area) hits the ball with an object in his hand.

Throwing an object at the ball.

Hiding a dangerous object upon his person (this may also result in an ejection).

Miscellaneous

To keep playing the ball after hearing the whistle.

Making any reference to the religion, morals, or heritage of any individual.

GK lying down near his goal as a contempt-showing action when the game is very one-sided.

Fullback going behind his goal-line to create an off-side.

Defender rushes forward from a wall before the ball is kicked.

After asking for 10 yards, kicking the ball before the Referee has given the signal. (Apply the advantage if applicable.)

Two players carrying on a conversation which indirectly dissents with the decision of a Referee 'Over his head.'

Lighting a cigarette.

Even if these two players were teammates, a foul should be called for dangerous play.

DANGEROUS PLAY

(Cautions are frequently administered. It is up to the Referee if he chooses to use his discretionary powers.)

1. Restart with INDIRECT unless occurrence is when ball is out of play.

2. The Referee has discretionary powers regarding a negligent action associated with dangerous play.

   a. Player comes to the ball in a manner which is dangerous to another player.

   b. Whenever a player puts himself in danger (e.g., head down at waist level or lower (normally OK for Goalkeeper).

   c. Scissors-kick (bicycle, double kick), if it causes another player to move away. If he kicks the opponent - still an IFK because it wasn't intentional.

   d. High kicking or knee at head level if it endangers another player.

   e. Kicking ball or at ball when in possession of the Goalkeeper.

   f. Heading ball when held aloft by Goalkeeper is almost always dangerous play.

   g. Goalkeeper or field player lifting knee or leg to fend off an opponent.

   h. Stretching out a leg toward the opponent when it could be dangerous to him.

   i. Accidentally jumping at an opponent is often dangerous.

3. Dangerous play does not have to be committed against an opponent. It can be dangerous even if done against a teammate. (College—must be committed against an opponent.)

   "IF IT LOOKS DANGEROUS, IT IS!"

— *Ken Aston*

DIRECT FREE-KICK

Kicking
(Show red card)

Tripping
(No red card)

Jumping at

Pushing

Holding

Charging Violently
Charging from Behind

Striking

Handling Ball

DIRECT FREE-KICK

A goal can be scored 'directly' into the opponent's goal.

A direct free kick results from any of the following *intentionally* committed offenses against an opponent:

Infraction	If Attempted	Comments
1. KICKING	X	EJECT, if it is viewed as serious foul play. Kicks must be directed only at the ball. 'Foot Over' (the ball) kick is considered kicking.
2. TRIPPING	X	No clear intention to play the ball. Sliding tackle – ball not played. Also stooping in front of or behind an opponent. Tackle from behind • If trip and ball is not played – DIRECT/PK – OR – • The ball is played, but in the process contact is first made with with an opponent, – OR – • Play ball with 1 foot and trip with the other, – OR – • If play ball first, followed by an unintentional trip – PLAY ON
3. JUMPING AT		• To play the ball is to be looking at it. • To "accidentally" jump at an opponent is to be guilty of dangerous play.
4. CHARGING VIOLENTLY or dangerously		• Termed an unfair charge. • Hip action; bumping.
5. CHARGING FROM BACK		• Unless fair charging an opponent who is obstructing. • If a player deliberately turns his back to an opponent when he is about to be tackled, he may be charged, but not in a dangerous manner.
6. STRIKING OR SPITTING AT	X	EJECT, if it is viewed as serious foul play. • Also throwing an object including a ball at a player. • Throw-in violently at a player - Take kick from touch-line. • Spitting is always worth an Ejection.
7. HOLDING 8. PUSHING		• Grabbing any part of clothing. • Leaning on opponent's shoulders. • Arm stretched across the chest which retards the opponent's progress. • Two teammates boxing in or fair charging an opponent simultaneously. • Placing a hand on opponent while in pursuit of ball.
9. HANDLES THE BALL • Deliberately handling the ball in order to prevent an attack from developing on a goal. CAUTION – At midfield, the Referee can be more lenient. • Handling the ball before it is put into play is not considered a 'Hand-Ball.'		• Doesn't apply to goalkeeper in his penalty-area. • To fall and accidentally touch the ball is not a hand-ball. • The hand is taken to be the whole of the arm, from the shoulders down through the fingers. • It is intentional when a player extends his arms to present a larger target to the ball or intentionally moves his hands/arms toward the ball (hand striking the ball instead of ball striking the hand). • Instinctive movements of the hands or arms to protect against being hit in the face or groin (breast – women) shall not be considered as intent in handling the ball. The hands used 'palms-outward' is normally intent. If defensive player should score in his own goal with his hands, the score shall count – ADVANTAGE. • A held object is considered as being an extension of the hand.

"Violence in a game is seldom an isolated occurrence. Patterns develop in a game, and the Referee is often the last person to know about it."

Paul Gardner, soccer writer

This charge is violent, and in the middle of the back. The player (right) makes no attempt to play the ball.

CHARGING

In order for a charge to be made fairly, the player:

- May not have hands or arms extended away from the body.
- Must execute only with the shoulder against another shoulder; chest, arms, hands, and hips may not be used. A charge must not be made with or against the chest.
- Must have one or both feet in contact with the ground.

Fair Charge

- A field player who is not playing the ball and is not obstructing is Fair Charged...

  —From behind - DIRECT
  —From the front - IFK

- If a player deliberately turns his back when about to be tackled, he may be charged in a nondangerous manner.
- To look at opponent as you charge him is not playing the ball.
- A fair charge doesn't have to be weak. It can be hard, but it may not be violent.

Goalkeeper

- He may be fairly charged:

LOCATION	HE OBSTRUCTS	HAS POSSESSION OF BALL	DOES NOT HAVE POSSESSION OF BALL
WITHIN THE GOAL AREA	/////	/////	*CAN NOT* BE CHARGED (IFK)
IN ALL OTHER PORTIONS OF THE PENALTY AREA	/////	/////	/////

- If charged while corner-kick is in the air — IFK because he is within his own goal area and didn't have the ball.
- Unintentional body contact is not to be penalized.

Youth, High School, College—Goalkeeper may not be charged within his own penalty area.

Intentional Charging

- College and High School — EJECT
- Youth — CAUTION

Unfair Charge

If charged violently, dangerously, or from behind (unless obstructing) - DIRECT.

PENALTY-KICK

Penalty-Kick
Point to penalty-spot

A penalty-kick results whenever one of the nine (9) penal infractions is committed by the defending team inside their own penalty-area when the ball is in play. Taken from the penalty mark (spot) - (12 yards from the goal-line). The ball may not be placed elsewhere regardless of the condition of the spot.

Referee does not whistle for the kick to be taken until all players are properly positioned. (This includes the Goalkeeper having his feet on the goal-line.)

It is recommended that the Referee hand the ball to the kicker, allowing him to position it on the spot. This also serves to identify the kicker to the goalkeeper.

The Referee must verify that no player is outside the field of play.

Correct Positioning

	In the field of play.	• Kicker may step outside of the penalty-area or the 10 yard arc in order to gain momentum as long as it is not done prior to the whistle for the taking of the kick.
All players except kicker and goalkeeper must be . . .	At least 10 yards away from the penalty-spot.	
	Outside the penalty-area.	• See encroachment

Goalkeeper must stand on the goal-line between the goal-posts without moving his feet until the ball is kicked (circumference). If the Goalkeeper gets into an improper position on the goal-line after the signal for the kick but before the ball is kicked, the Referee awaits the results of the kick. If no goal is scored — RETAKE.

A goalkeeper may be substituted for on a Penalty-Kick. (High School/College = Not from the bench.)

Any player may take the Penalty-Kick. (This includes the opposing Goalkeeper.)

If a penalty-kick is retaken, either the Goalkeeper or the kicker may be changed.

(Note: This does not apply to kicks from the penalty mark to decide a tied game.)

ENALTY KICK (Cont.)

The Kick	Action
If not in a forward direction	RETAKE
In play	CIRCUMFERENCE
The ball is played by the kicker a second time in succession	IFK
OFF-SIDE	IFK
Ball touches an outside agent.	
● As goes toward goal.	RETAKE
● As rebounds into play.	DROP-BALL
Ball bursts directly on a goal-post or the cross-bar.	DROP-BALL

● After the ball is kicked in a forward direction, a teammate may run in from outside the penalty-area and kick the ball.

● If kicker plays the ball to a player who is in an off-side position.
● Ball rebounds from goal-posts or cross-bar to a player who is judged to be in an off-side position.
● If the ball is deflected to him by the GK, there is no off-side.

HINT FOR REFEREES

Quite often a penalty kick situation results in protest and confusion on the field, and the Referee will have difficulty restoring order and may have to caution or eject players on the defensive team. It is advisable to pick up the ball immediately after whistling for the penalty, retaining possession until the players from both teams have cleared the area. The ball should then be given to the kicker for him to place on the penalty-mark in readiness for the kick. This serves to identity the kicker to the goalkeeper. The Referee then positions himself, and after both kicker and goalkeeper are ready, he gives the signal for the kick to be taken. With young players it is recommended that the Referee remind the Goalkeeper to wait until the ball is kicked before moving his feet.

Not Enough Penalty Kicks are Awarded in Games. Why is This?
1. Referees are too far away from the action.
2. Referees think too much, and wonder, "Will my decision be accepted?"
3. Referees have a basic lack of courage.

Fritz Seipelt

PENALTY KICK (Cont.)

ENCROACHMENT

A Caution is given for all encroachments (except for High School and College).

After having whistled for the kick to be taken, the Referee does not intervene for an encroachment. He awaits the result of the kick.

Result	Encroachment By...		
	An Attacker	A Defender or GK Movement	Attacker and Defender
GOAL	RETAKE	GOAL	
NO GOAL: • Save by GK or ball rebounds into play. • GK touches the ball which goes over the goal-line.	IFK	RETAKE	RETAKE
• Ball goes directly over the goal-line, but not into the goal.	GOAL-KICK		

Attacker encroachment in conjunction with the GK moving his feet — RETAKE whatever the result.

The ratio of free kicks against attackers in the Penalty Area compared with those given against defenders is about 50:1. If more Penalty Kicks were called, players could exhibit their skills near goal. As it is, there is too much contact which is ignored.

PENALTY KICK (Cont.)

UNGENTLEMANLY CONDUCT

All ungentlemanly conduct results in a Caution.

Kicker fakes a kick to get the goalkeeper to move his feet.

Distraction by shouting or making motions.

— Normal body movements or swaying are all right. The swinging of arms that are obviously distracting are not.

Player other than the one designated takes the kick (rare)

— Referee must be informed as to who is taking the Penalty Kick.

— Goalkeeper may request that the kicker be identified to him.

Ungentlemanly conduct directed against...

Result

	.... The Goalkeeper	.... The Kicker
GOAL	RETAKE	GOAL
NO GOAL: • Save by GK or ball rebounds into play.	IFK	RETAKE
• Ball crosses goal-line untouched by goalkeeper.	GK	
• Ball crosses goal-line after being touched by goalkeeper.	IFK	

A penalty kick is awarded. The Referee often has a lot of help in making the decision.

IMITATOR

- Tries to please everyone.

- Calls off-side whenever defensive player throws up his hand.

- Emphasizes a foreign accent.

- Calls obstruction in the Penalty-Area instead of tripping.

- Calls coach "Doctor" unless he knows his first name.

- Only calls what the Linesman flags.

- Agrees with God.

- Agrees with wife.

- Paid to have his name mentioned in the acknowledgment section of *Fair or Foul.*

TIME EXTENSION FOR PENALTY-KICK

(Referee should notify both captains prior to the taking of the kick that time has been extended.)

> When a match is extended to allow a penalty-kick to be taken or retaken (be it at halftime or games end), the extension shall last until the moment when the penalty-kick has been completed. The players should be cleared out of the immediate vicinity to eliminate possible encroachment and other violations.

Ball

• Kicked out of bounds.
• Kicked toward goal and is clearly saved by the Goalkeeper
• Hits upright or cross-bar and . . .
  Goes out of bounds.
  Rebounds into play.
• Not kicked strongly enough to reach goal.
• Kicked toward teammate instead of towards goal.
• Hits upright or cross-bar and bursts.
	END OF PERIOD

• Ball goes directly into the goal. • Kicked toward goal, touched by GK, goes into the goal. • Hits upright or cross-bar and goes into the goal.	GOAL & END OF PERIOD
• Ball touches an outside agent.	RETAKE

FIFA Championships must not be decided by kicks from the penalty-mark. In the event that a non-championship game must be settled by kicks from penalty-mark, the following conditions must prevail.

1. The Referee shall choose the goal at which all of the kicks from the penalty-mark shall be taken.

2. The Referee shall toss a coin, and the team whose captain wins the toss must take the first kick.

3. Each team shall take five kicks from the penalty-mark. The kicks shall be taken alternately.

4. The team which scores the greater number of goals shall be declared the winner.

5. Only the players who are on the field at the end of the match, (or extra time), shall be eligible to take part in the kicking from the penalty-mark. Exception - an injured Goalkeeper may be replaced.

6. If after each team has taken five kicks, each has scored the same number of goals, the taking of kicks from the penalty mark shall continue, in the same order (on a sudden death basis) until such time as each has taken the same number of kicks and one team has scored a goal more than the other. The kicks shall not continue after one team has scored a total of goals which establish them as winners.

7. Each kick shall be taken by a different player, and not until all eligible players of any team have taken a kick may a player of the same team have a second kick.

8. Any player who was on the field at the end of the match (see paragraph 5 above) may change places with his Goalkeeper at any time during the taking of kicks from the penalty-mark.

9. Other than the player taking a kick, and the two goalkeepers, all players shall remain within the center circle while the taking of the kicks from the penalty-mark is in progress. The Goalkeeper who is a teammate of the kicker must be at least 18 yards from the goal line and 10 yards from the ball.

10. Unless stated to the contrary herein, the conditions of Laws X and XIV will apply in the taking of these kicks. The relevant paragraphs of the board decisions in relation to Law XIV shall be interpreted by analogy.

THROW-IN

BASIC	A member of the opposing team last touched the ball prior to it going completely out of bounds (air or ground) outside the touch-line.
WHERE IS THE BALL THROWN INTO THE FIELD OF PLAY?	At the point where it crossed the touch-line going out of bounds. If taken at some other point... RETAKE.
IN PLAY	After it has been released - as soon as it passes or touches any point of the touch-line in flight.
THROWER PLAYS A SECOND TIME	IFK
SCORE A GOAL DIRECTLY?	NO { Thrown directly into opponents goal - GOAL-KICK. Thrown directly into own goal - CORNER-KICK.
OFF-SIDE DIRECTLY?	NO
DISTANCE AWAY	• Thrower must be allowed to deliver the ball properly. • If opponents dance about or jump in a way calculated to distract or impede the thrower — CAUTION — ungentlemanly conduct.

The thrower, at the moment of delivery, must . . .

- Face the field of play with some part of the body.
- Have part of *each* foot on or outside the touch-line and on the ground. (If one or both heels are on the touch-line it quite often will result in a foul throw-in due to the player rising on his toes and losing contact with the touchline.

     Feet may be apart.

     May not deliver the ball while running (both feet in motion).

     Taken within 1 meter of the touch-line.

     High School — No contact with touch-line.

- Use both hands and shall deliver the ball from behind and over his head.

     Ball must be delivered with equal force and simultaneously with both hands.

     It may not be delivered with one hand and directed with the other. (Very pronounced right to left or left to right spin is often penalized.)

- Throw-in is not allowed to be merely dropped, it must be thrown.

     If a continuous movement, it does not matter at what point it is released.

     A very 'gentle' throw is *not* considered to be a drop, it is still a throw.

THROW-IN (Cont.)

Miscellaneous

Takes throw-in improperly	Other team takes THROW IN.
Intentionally throws ball away from the field of play	CAUTION – RETAKE
Throw intentionally at Referee	EJECT – IFK
Throw ball at an opponent	
• If as a tactic	O.K. if done in a non-dangerous manner
• If violence against an opponent	DIRECT from the touch-line. EJECT.
Throw-in hits Referee, Linesman or corner-flag.	
• Remains in play.	'PLAY ON' ·
• Goes out of bounds.	TURNOVER
Throw-in	
• Goes directly into opponent's goal	GOAL-KICK
• Goes directly into own goal.	CORNER

The ball must be thrown into the field of play. If the ball hits the ground before it enters the field of play — RETAKE.

On the throw-in — If the ball is not played by any player and...

* It never was considered to have entered the field of play — RETAKE

* It went in and out of the field of play. Other team takes throw-in. (Any part of the ball touching or penetrating the outside edge of the touch-line following its release is considered to have entered the field of play.)

The throw-in can be a surprise to the Referee, both in distance, timing, and technique.

GOAL-KICK

BASIC	Offense last played the whole of the ball over the goal-line (air or ground) excluding the scoring of a goal.	
WHERE TAKEN	Within that half of the goal-area nearest where it crossed the goal-line.	• In taking the kick, only some part of the ball or its projection need be within the proper half of the goal-area.
IN PLAY	Beyond the penalty-area into the field of play.	• If doesn't go beyond penalty-area — RETAKE. • If crosses the goal-line . . . Inside the penalty-area — RETAKE. Outside the penalty-area — CORNER.
KICKER PLAYS BALL TWICE IN SUCCESSION	IFK	• If the ball is not yet in play (hasn't left P.A.) — RETAKE. • If takes kick properly and ball is returned by a strong wind and he plays it again — IFK.
SCORE GOAL DIRECTLY?	In opponents goal — GOAL-KICK. In own goal — RETAKE.	• Kick goes beyond penalty-area and for any reason comes back directly into one's own goal. (Rare) — CORNER.
DIRECTLY OFF-SIDE?	NO	
OPPONENTS DISTANCE AWAY	Outside of penalty-area until ball clears the penalty-area.	• If opponent is trying to leave the P.A., let the kick go, the opponent must be trying to gain an unfair advantage in order to be penalized.
TEAMMATES	Any distance.	• May remain inside P.A.

The ball must be stationary, but it is quite in order for the Goalkeeper to hold down the ball with one hand and simultaneously kick it in order to quickly put the ball into play.

If the ball is intentionally not kicked beyond the penalty-area, or an offensive player encroaches or any player touches ball before passing penalty-area . . .

- 1st time — WARN ⎫
- 2nd time — CAUTION ⎬ RETAKE
- 3rd time — EJECT ⎭

CORNER-KICK AND CORNER-FLAG POST

> **During a corner-kick, watch the players, not the flight of the ball.**

Corner-Kick

BASIC		The defense last played the whole of the ball over the goal-line (air or ground) excluding going into the goal.
WHERE IS KICK TAKEN?		The *whole* of the ball must be within the quarter circle at the nearest corner-flag post.
		Youth — Under 9 years old. Kicks are taken from the intersection of the goal-line and the penalty-area.
IN PLAY	CIRCUMFERENCE	
KICKER PLAYS THE BALL A SECOND TIME IN SUCCESSION	IFK	The kicker is not allowed to play it a second time including if the corner-kick hits a goal-post, Referee, or Linesman.
SCORE A GOAL DIRECTLY?	YES	Even into your own goal (not likely)
OFF-SIDE DIRECTLY?	NO	
DISTANCE AWAY	Opponents	10 YARDS	It is O.K. for an attacker to place himself in the way of the Goalkeeper. Once the ball is kicked, the attacker must move toward the ball. To remain stationary is to obstruct. — IFK.
	Teammates	ANY DISTANCE	Otherwise a player may occupy any location within the field. • If opponent encroaches . . . 1st time — WARN 2nd time — CAUTION RETAKE 3rd time — EJECT

Goalkeeper charged while the kick is in the air . . .

- Fair charge — IFK (Because goalkeeper was within own goal-area and didn't have the ball.)

- Charged violently — DIRECT

If the ball crosses over the middle of the cross-bar after having been last played by a defensive player, the Referee immediately signals from which corner it is to be taken.

Corner-Post

Corner flag-post must not be moved — WARN . . . then CAUTION. (To move means to alter from its stationary straight-up position.)

Ball hits corner flag-post and . . .

- Rebounds into field of play — IN PLAY.

- Breaks it — DROP BALL — Play is suspended until post is either mended, removed or replaced.

- Knocks down or tilts the corner-post away from the field of play in a non-dangerous manner — PLAY ON and refix at first opportunity

If ball goes out of bounds by knocking down or going over the corner-flag . . .

- Last played by attacker — GOAL-KICK

- Last played by defense — THROW-IN by offense.

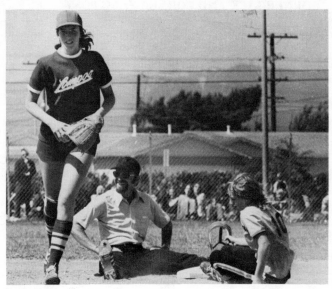

No matter how much you know about rules, things can still go wrong.

Referee Larry Harris who also umpires baseball, hit the dirt in this high school state championship game when his cletes came into contact with a rough spot on the field. He was running backwards at the time.

☆ ★ ☆ ★ ☆ ★ ☆ ★ ☆ ★ ☆ ★ ☆ ★ ☆ ★ ☆ ★ ☆ ★ ☆ ★ ☆ ★ ☆ ★ ☆ ★

If you have never fallen down on a soccer field, then you probably do not run backwards as much as you should.

☆ ★ ☆ ★ ☆ ★ ☆ ★ ☆ ★ ☆ ★ ☆ ★ ☆ ★ ☆ ★ ☆ ★ ☆ ★ ☆ ★ ☆ ★ ☆ ★

☆ ★ ☆ ★ ☆ ★ ☆ ★ ☆ ★ ☆ ★ ☆ ★ ☆ ★ ☆ ★ ☆ ★ ☆ ★ ☆ ★ ☆ ★ ☆ ★ ☆ ★ ☆ ★ ☆ ★ ☆ ★

Have you studied officials in other sports?

Comment: You will notice several references in this book to sports and officials other than in soccer. If you referee other sports, you will find that it will help you immeasurably in your conduct of soccer games. If you referee only in soccer, study top officials in other sports. Your game control, mechanics, and conduct will improve.

☆ ★ ☆ ★ ☆ ★ ☆ ★ ☆ ★ ☆ ★ ☆ ★ ☆ ★ ☆ ★ ☆ ★ ☆ ★ ☆ ★ ☆ ★ ☆ ★ ☆ ★ ☆ ★ ☆ ★

IX

Testing Your Knowledge

WHAT'S THE DIFFERENCE BETWEEN A NOOK AND A CRANNY?
A Test For Us All

For those of you who are interested, a nook is a corner, a quiet secluded place, and a cranny is a small opening, usually in a rock. What's that have to do with refereeing, and in particular, our test? Probably not a lot, except that there are little nooks and crannies in the laws, and you will find most of them discussed in the book. We thought it would be unfair to test you on them, so we decided to stick to the basics of law knowledge and the mechanics of the diagonal system as set forth in the FIFA Laws of the Game. No trick questions here, only a desire to test you on a few things you should know. Expect your score to be in the 90% range the frist time, and perfect the next. Good luck to you!

Use the following play resumption code for answers requiring a fill-in.

IFK — Indirect Free-Kick
DFK — Direct Free-Kick
PK — Penalty-Kick
GK — Goal-Kick
CK — Corner-Kick
TI — Throw-In
DB — Drop Ball
KO — Kick-Off (A goal has just been scored)
PO — Play On (play is not restarted)
R — Retake the action in question

BASIC LAWS — F.I.F.A.

LAW I. — FIELD OF PLAY   LAW II. — THE BALL
LAW III. — NUMBER OF PLAYERS   LAW IV. — PLAYERS EQUIPMENT

1. If a player is ejected prior to the start of the game, with how many players can his team begin the game? _____
    Short Answer

2. A match should not be considered valid if a team fields fewer than how many players? _____
    Short Answer

3. The use of halfway-line flags is optional.   T   F

4. Corner-flag posts that are 6 feet high should be allowed.   T   F

5. A goalkeeper must wear colors which distinguish him from the othe goalkeeper.   T   F

6.   A ball last played by a defensive player hits the corner-flag post and rebounds back into the field of play. _____

The ball goes out of bounds by knocking down a corner-flag post after having last been played by a...

7.   Defensive player. _____

8.   Offensive player. _____

9.   Time may expire when the ball is off the field and out of play.   T   F

10. At the conclusion of the first period on a very foggy day, the Referee tells the teams to change sides immediately so that the second period may begin. One team objects. The Referee must allow the half-time interval.   T   F

11. If a fullback scores with his hand against his own goal, the Referee should allow the goal.   T   F

LAW V — THE REFEREE

12. A Referee may reverse his decision...
   a. At any time.
   b. As long as the game has not been restarted.
   c. Only when the ball is in play.
   d. Never.

13. If players stop play after hearing a whistle from a spectator, the Referee is required to stop play and resume it with a drop ball.   T   F

14. Coaching from the boundary lines is permitted.   T   F

15. Only the captain has the right to address the Referee.   T   F

LAW VIII — THE START OF PLAY

16. A team kicks-off and by its combined play, manages to kick the ball into the opponents' goal without an opponent having played the ball. It is a goal.
   T   F

17. A defensive player stands with one foot on each side of the halfway-line at the kick-off. _____

18. A Goalkeeper may participate in a drop ball.   T   F

19. A player involved in a drop ball plays it twice in succession. _____

20. After a drop ball has hit the ground, a player directly kicks the ball into his own goal. _____

LAW XI — OFF-SIDE

21. The most vital element in the determination of when a player is in an off-side *position* is: _____

    Short Answer

22. The off-side position should be called (whistled) when the offender: _____

    Short Answer

23. A player can't be in an off-side position if he is in line with the ball the moment it is played.   T   F

24. A player standing with both feet partially touching the halfway line can not possibly be off-side.   T   F

25. It is off-side if a Goalkeeper within his own Penalty-area throws the ball to a teammate who is in an off-side position.   T   F

26. A player participating in a drop ball directly kicks the ball to a teammate in an off-side position. This should result in an off-side being whistled.   T   F

27. A player can not be off-side if he receives the ball directly from a clearing kick made by his own goalkeeper.   T   F

LAW XII — FOULS AND MISCONDUCT

28. An offense or attempted offense is considered to have been committed at the place where the player *initiated* the inappropriate action.   T   F

29. Spitting at an opponent can result in either a direct free-kick or a PK.   T   F

30. A player who obstructs may be fairly charged from behind.   T   F

31. If a player tries to handle the ball, the Referee should penalize the intent.   T   F

32. The Referee shall penalize the goalkeeper who catches the ball, rolls it, picks it up, takes two steps, then clears it downfield.   T   F

33. Obstruction, in order to be called, must be intentional.   T   F

34. A Goalkeeper may leave his penalty-area and play on the forward line in his goalkeeper colors.   T   F

35. If the Goalkeeper handles the ball on the penalty-area line, the Referee should award a direct free-kick to the opponents.   T   F

36. Player interference with the clearing move of the opposing Goalkeeper should be cautioned and an IFK given.   T   F

37. Steps taken by the goalkeeper to either regain balance or to bring the ball under control are not counted.   T   F

38. An attacking player within his opponents' goal area unintentionally handles the ball. It falls at his feet and he kicks it into the goal. _____

39. A player who accidentaly kicks so high that his teammate if forced to move out of the way. _____

40. A player leans on the shoulders of a teammate in order to head the ball. _____

41. Two players on the same team strike each other inside their own penalty-area. _____

42. A defensive player unintentionally handles the ball within his own penalty-area. _____

43. When the ball is in play at midfield, a player inside his own penalty-area takes a swing at an opponent, but misses. _____

44. A player spits on the Referee. _____

45. A player arriving late at the game enters the field without permission. _____

46. The ball is rolling along the touch-line when a substitute picks it up. _____

47 During play, a player receives permission to leave the field. On his way off, the ball comes to him and he shoots it into the opponents' goal. _____

48. A corner-kick is taken. While the ball is in flight, a defender pushes an offensive player within the goal-area. The Referee blows his whistle for the infraction and the ball continues into the goal. _____

49. Within his penalty-area a defender distracts an opponent by shouting at him. _____

50. A Goalkeeper inside his own penalty area with the wind at his back, throws the ball directly into his opponents' goal. _____

51. Inside his penalty-area, the goalkeeper lies down to show his contempt for the other team. _____

52. A Goalkeeper is fairly charged in his own goal-area when he is not in possession of the ball and when he is not obstructing an opponent. _____

53. A Goalkeeper lies on the ball longer than is necessary within his penalty area. _____

54. A forward stands in front of the Goalkeeper. The Goalkeeper is forced to take 3 steps just to get around the forward. He then takes 3 steps and clears the ball. _____

55. A Goalkeeper lying on the ground with his arm outstretched, has 2 fingers on a stationary ball. An attacker kicks the ball into the goal. _____

56. A practice ball rolls in front of the Goalkeeper, distracting him during play within his penalty-area. _____

57. *Attacking players may get within a defensive wall.*　　T　　F

LAW XIII — FREE-KICKS

57. Attacking players may get within a defensive wall.　　　T　　F

58. On any free-kick, one foot may be placed under the ball and the kicker may 'lift' the ball.　　　T　　F

59. An IFK may not be taken until the Referee blows his whistle.　　　T　　F

60. A player may take a free kick before waiting for the opponents to retreat the required ten yards.　　　T　　F

61. A player takes a direct free-kick from inside his own penalty-area. He kicks the ball back to his goalkeeper who misses the ball completely and it rolls into his own goal. _____

62. On an IFK, an attacker 'runs over' the ball and makes contact. A teammate then kicks the ball into the goal. _____

LAW XIV — PENALTY-KICK

63. The Referee is not allowed to signal for the taking of the kick until all players are placed correctly, as required by law.　　　T　　F

64. After the Referee signals for the penalty-kick to be taken and before the kicker plays the ball, the Goalkeeper may move along the goal-line but not forward.　　　T　　F

65. All offensive and defensive encroachment results in a caution being given to the offender(s).　　　T　　F

66. If a penalty-kick is retaken, the Goalkeeper and/or the kicker may be changed.　　　T　　F

67. An attacking player encroaches followed by the ball being fisted over the top of the goal by the Goalkeeper. _____

68. Three defenders and one attacker encroach into the penalty area. The ball enters the goal. _____

69. A penalty-kick bounces back from the cross-bar back to the kicker who then kicks it into the goal. _____

LAW XV — THE THROW-IN

70. The throw goes directly into one's own goal. _____

Fill in — FAIR... RETAKE... or FOUL

On an otherwise legal throw-in, the player:

71. Releases the ball in a downward direction at chest height. _____

72. Releases the ball from 10 feet behind the touch-line. _____

73. Has part of both feet inside the field with only the heels on the touch-line. _____

74. Throws the ball which first lands two feet outside the touch-line prior to it entering the field of play. _____

LAW XVI — GOAL-KICK   LAW XVII — CORNER KICK

75. The kick need not be made in a forward direction.   T   F

76. During the taking of a goal-kick, no opposing players may be within the kicker's penalty-area.   T   F

77. Only part of the ball need be within the quarter circle.   T   F

78. The corner-flag post may be removed when taking the kick, provided it is immediately replaced.   T   F

79. The player taking a goal-kick runs up three yards and kicks it again before anyone else can play it. _____

80. From a corner-kick the ball hits the Referee and rebounds to the kicker, who kicks it directly into his opponents' goal. _____.

MECHANICS

81. To indicate encroachment on a corner-kick, the linesman lifts his flag overhead and shades it for approximately 3 seconds.   T   F

82. The ball goes out of play and suddenly back in again. The linesman should remain stationary with an upraised flag even if the Referee is not looking at him and play has proceeded downfield.   T   F

HESITATOR

- Stands back with hands on hips and watches play.

- Whistle goes up to his mouth but he never blows it.

- Has never called a penalty kick.

- Calls players "gentlemen" even when they are maiming one another.

- Has Diarrhea before and after each game.

- Whispers "Play On."

- Refuses to caution coach for fear of low rating.

- Spends 10 minutes before the game trying to decide which Linesman should be the Senior Linesman.

- Is afraid of God.

- Hides from wife.

- Keeps *Fair or Foul* hidden inside a plain brown cover.

Assume that the Referee runs the left-wing diagonal —

Pick the appropriate letter which indicates where the linemen are in the following four situations.

	L1	L2
Goal-kick	83.	84.
Corner-kick	85.	86.
Penalty-kick	87.	88.
Kick-off	89.	90.

Direction of play

Assume that the Referee runs the left-wing diagonal.

Direction of play

Fill in the number (1-10) which represents the position of the Referee for each of the following situations.

All kicks are taken toward the goal at the top (↑).

91. Kick-off _____

92. Goal-kick _____

93. Corner-kick (left corner) _____

94. Penalty-kick _____

...NEAR THE GOAL.

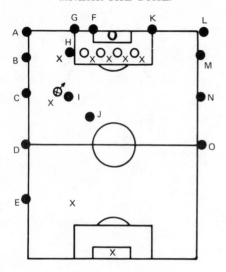

95. The Referee is at position...
    F... G... H... I... J

96. The *Trail* linesman is at...
    A... B... C... D... E

97. The *Lead* linesman is at...
    K... L... M... N... O

x = Attackers

O = Defenders

⊕ = The Ball

● = Possible positions

...NEAR MIDFIELD.

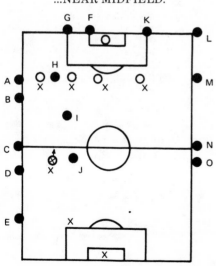

98. The Referee is at position...
    F... G... H... I... J

99. The *Trail* linesman is at...
    A... B... C... D... E

100. The *Lead* linesman is at...
    K... L... M... N... O

KEY AND CRITIQUE

1. 11

2. 7   High School must start with 11 players.

3. True

4. True   The post may not be *shorter* than 5 feet.

5. True   He must distinguish himself from *all* other players and the Referee.

6. PO   Offense or Defense. Makes no difference.

7. TI ⎫

8. GK ⎭ The Defense gets the benefit of doubt as to whether it went over the touch-line or the goal-line.

9. True   ... But you won't be too popular.

10. True

11. True   The advantage clause is implemented.

12. B

13. False   He should shout, "Play On".

14. False   It is allowed for Youth, High School, and College.

15. False   No one has the right to address the Referee. The Captain has no special privileges.

16. True

17. R/KO   This tests your knowledge of the law. You'll probably never see it.

18. True

19. PO ⎫

20. KO ⎭ The ball is in play the instant it makes contact with the ground.

21. His position in relation to the ball   Having at least two opponents between him and the opponents goal-line - merely an exception.

22. Participates in play. Takes advantage of his position

23. True

-192-

24.	True	
25.	True	A clearing throw/kick by the goalkeeper is no different from a kick made by an attacking field player.
26.	True	A player is eligible for being off-side any time after the ball has been put into play (hits the ground).
27.	False	See comment for Question 25.
28.	True	Goalkeeper throws the ball violently, hitting an opponent who is outside the penalty-area. Result: PK.
29.	True	A 1982 change to FIFA law.
30.	True	Remember, it must be non-violent.
31.	False	A stern word or two may be in order.
32.	True	
33.	True	Double possession by the Goalkeeper is not allowed.
34.	True	You'll see a lot indoors, too.
35.	False	Lines are part of the area they bound.
36.	True	Be especially firm about this one.
37.	True	Be lenient, please. Remember the spirit.
38.	KO	To be a hand ball, it must be intentional.
39.	IFK	Dangerous play is blind to uniform color.
40.	IFK	He should also be cautioned for ungentlemanly conduct.
41.	IFK	To be a DFK or PK, it must be directed toward an opponent.
42.	PO	See comment for Question 38.
43.	PK	Strike or *attempted* strike.
44.	IFK	See comment for Question 41.
45.	IFK	Also administer a caution.
46.	DB	A substitute is considered an outside agent.
47.	IFK	Also administer a caution.
48.	PK	The whistle stops play. Continuation is not allowed. Hope the PK is converted.
49.	IFK	
50.	KO	See comment for Question 25.

51. IFK   ... And don't forget to caution for ungentlemanly conduct.

52. IFK   May be charged only when in possession, in the goal area.

53. IFK   You should usually first ask him to get up.

54. IFK   If you didn't grant an IFK for the Goalkeeper who had his clearing move interferred with, then you must sanction him for taking 6 steps.

55. IFK   Possession is possession, no matter how tenuous.

56. DB

57. True   Watch closely, not too many defenders like this to occur.

58. True   A tricky move, but fair.

59. False   ... Unless the Referee has made it into a ceremonial free-kick.

60. True   ... And, once the ball is in play, you don't retake.

61. R/DFK   The ball is not yet in play.

62. GK   On an IFK the ball must first travel its circumference before it can be 'directly' kicked into the goal for a score.

63. True   Never rush the taking of a penalty kick.

64. False

65. True   Most Referees are unaware of this.

66. True

67. IFK   Don't forget the caution.

68. R/PK

69. IFK   The ball is played twice in succession by the player taking the PK.

70. CK   Think of the throw-in as being indirect.

71. Fair   Most players, coaches, spectators and far too many Referees think this is illegal.

72. Retake   Must be within 1 meter of the touch-line.

73. Fair   High School and College still operates in the Dark Ages on this one.

74. Retake   The ball must be thrown into the field of play. This one was bounced (not in-flight).

75. True

76. True

77. False

78. False

79. R/GK   The ball is not yet in play.

80. IFK   Kicker played the ball twice in succession. (Referee doesn't count).

81. False   That is the signal for a foul. The flag should be held motionless overhead. This should rarely be necessary because it should have been taken care of by the linesman.

82. True   The linesman remains in that position indefinitely if necessary.

83. B   Next to last defender.

84. I

85. B

86. J

87. E

88. H

89. F

90. H

91. I

92. 2

93. 8

94. 7

95. H

96. E   More next-to-last defender nonsense.

97. L

98. H   This required positioning makes no sense. Both Referee and lead linesman are monitoring off-side.

99. D

100. M

A TEST, IF YOU THINK YOU KNOW THE LAWS OF SOCCER . . . .

1. Describe Law V, IBD 8.

2. Translate 10 yards to meters.

3. What is a place-kick, and where is it described?

4. Name the accepted shapes of the goalposts.

5. Which Law contains information on the players' numbers on the jersey?

6. Which Law has no decisions of the International Board?

7. Under Law VI, who is responsible for supplying the Linesman's flags, the Linesman or the Referee?

8. Where is the drop-ball mentioned in the Laws?

9. In which Law does the Linesman and his duties in relation to the off-side occur?

10. Laws III and IV use the terms "sent off" and "ordered off" when mentioning players and equipment. What is the difference in these two terms?

Answers below:

1. This important decision urges the Referee to interfere as little as possible in the game, and that small and insignificant offenses shall not be penalized.
2. 9.15 meters.
3. A place-kick is a kick-off, and is described in Law VIII.
4. The goalposts may be square, rectangular, round, half-round, or elliptical.
5. There is nothing in the laws which mentions the numbers on players' jerseys.
6. Law XVII, Corner Kick.
7. Neither one. The home club is to supply the flags. We understand that somewhere in the world this may occur, but haven't found one yet.
8. The drop-ball is mentioned in Laws I, II, III, VIII, and X.
9. No law specifically refers to the Linesman and his off-side duties. Law VI indicates that the Linesman shall draw the Referee's attention to any breaches of the Laws of the Game.
10. Under Law III, a player may be "ordered off" for disciplinary reasons. He may be "sent off," under Law IV, in order to adjust to his equipment.

We're sorry about these nasty questions. We hope it accomplished the same for you that it did for us . . . a little digging through the Laws we thought we knew so well.

X

Awareness
and
Improvement

A NOTE ON PROTESTS

"Defeat requires an explanation. Victory covers a multitude of sins."

Soccer is a game of wide-open activity, and a sport where most persons feel they are experts. Although scoring is low, tie games do not often result, and a loser must come to grips with the meaning of defeat. In certain circles where soccer becomes more than recreation, the loser's ire and frustration is taken out on the Referee. This takes the form of physical or verbal abuse or threatened or active protest.

It is well-known that the Referee, with normal human limitations, is remembered for his errors. Fortunately, these errors usually do not occur with the same frequency as player errors, but they are a greater subject of discussion among coaches and players. Errors in judgment are at times not even known to the Referee, and errors in interpretation or law application are later discovered through discussions with a rule interpreter or with fellow Referees. Unfortunate as they are, Referee errors must be accepted by everyone connected with soccer.

We are happy to report that since our last edition of this book, more and more soccer organizations have indicated a refusal to consider protests that question the judgment of the Referee. Only those rulings dealing with player eligibility, disciplinary actions, or field conditions are considered, and even then seldom allowed. It is unfair that the Referee's task and performance should be constantly scrutinized, and that games are sometimes won over the bargaining table. Once the Referee is given his authority, he must be backed by the league. If the sport is to progress, league organizers must openly admit that, "The Referee must be supported, even if he is wrong."

From our files, listed below are situations where leagues have chosen not to allow a protest:

1. A twelfth player was on the field and participated in a goal against the opposition. The Referee allowed the goal and the resulting kick-off before discovering the error.

2. The Referee was wearing the patch of another organization. (We're serious, this was actually protested.)

3. The Referee felt a player had sustained an injury which was too serious for continuing the game. He was not allowed to play.

4. The Referee admitted after the game that he made a mistake in awarding a Penalty-Kick. (The goal was scored.)

5. A Referee walked off the field at halftime, leaving his partner for the second half. The partner continued the game.

6. A Referee awarded a Penalty-Kick for Dangerous Play.

7. A game was played without field markings. No protest was made in writing before the game.

8. A Referee allowed eleven players on one side after one of their teammates was ejected.

9. A player was allowed to play with an arm cast, which was against league regulations.

10. The Referee insisted that another series of five kicks from the penalty-spot would be taken, after the original series of five was tied, during a game that was to be settled by such kicks.

The number of obvious and not-so-obvious Referee errors defies the imagination. It will happen to you, and a game will be protested. Whatever your mistake, never make it twice, and if a protest is made, don't become involved in any way after you have made your written report.

"Be turned not aside by the barking of dogs."
David Livingston

If you referee and coach, remember that you have certain responsibilities.

RETALIATION IS A GAME ALL BY ITSELF

By Willy Keo

If there were but one problem in soccer the world over, from Maracana in Rio to Wembley in London, to the weekend game in town, it would be inflammatory refereeing. Of course, any decision brings only 50% acceptance. The whistle never is a 100% pleaser, but we must recognize that some referees are efficient and others are not.

Plagued with the need for "play on", referees often let fouls go uncalled. "Play on" may mean just that, but players' memories are often longer than the Referee's, and the "I'll get him!" remains as important as winning the game. The retaliation is seldom the "eye for the eye", and the "trip for the trip." It is often the vicious foul for the marginal pain, the heel-nip for the harmless push off the ball.

Looking at the fouls here might help us all to be a little more aware, and to think about these favorites before they happen.

The Bothersome, But Not Harmful

The shirt tug. The slow player who can't keep up often utilizes this one. Retaliation comes quick and sure, particularly at midfield. It seldom happens near goal, for it is too much of a risk of a Penalty Kick.

The pants grab. Hands are busy, and will grab whatever is loose in a desperate situation. This intimidation will distract and incense even the coolest competitor.

The early bump. With the hip, back, shoulder, knee, or arm, and usually on air balls, this one is an obstruction more accepted by Referees as if it were a skill and not a violation of "playing the man." Any bump will do, and referees feel its not a foul because it wasn't too hard.

The coaching move. Talking a player off the ball, out of earshot of the Referee brings frustration to the violated. How do you detect this? There's nothing better than being close to play.

The Semi-Violent

The instep or toe-step. During play, its sometimes just as easy to step on an opponent's foot as it is to go for the ball. Also, it looks just like the ball's being played. Free kicks and crowded defensive walls also bring this on.

Pre-ball and after-the-ball fouling. The ball is played away, and now's the time to get the little dig in, usually a slight, bothersome kick which says, "I'm giving a test to both you and to the ref. What are you going to do?"

The slide tackle. "But I got the ball, ref!" Bordering on the violent, it usually happens from the rear. The element of surprise adds to the indignity of the situation. Getting the ball *and* the legs is all too common.

The Violent

The foot-over-the-ball-block. The foot goes over the ball, and cracks the shin of the opponent who is in on the tackle. This is easily a shin-breaker.

The tackle from behind. You know this is building from five yards away! This extreme danger to the back and to the legs must bring on a minimum of a yellow card. Of all the fouls, this is the one you must really feel!

Head-butting. This despicable act is often seen by the crowd but is lost to the Referee. This extreme move results from total frustration when a player has lost several physical battles.

Spitting. Intimidation at its worst. Referees may not see it, for it occurs during play.

The list is by no means exhaustive, but in this list resides the birth of retaliation. Getting even takes many turns. If the whistle doesn't blow, players assume what happened is legal. Some say these are professional acts performed by amateurs. Despite being outside of the rules, they are part of the lore of the game. Stopping them will make a better game for the public.

Willy Keo is one of America's best known soccer journalists and writers. A native of St. Louis, his involvement in the game spans five decades. He has engaged in none of the above acts.

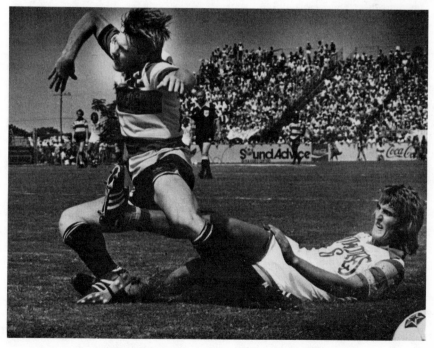

The tackle from behind. Are you ready for it?

"A PHYSICAL GAME IS NOT NECESSARILY A DIRTY ONE"

Sam Foulds

The fence you must straddle between fair or foul in a soccer game has no equal in sport. FIFA frequently reminds referees that the unintentional foul is not a soccer crime and therefore should not be penalized. This is fine in theory, but is not necessarily practiced. Your decisions and interpretations are based on judgement. Common sense must prevail. It is genuinely the intent of some players never to foul, but the foul is rightly called. It is the intent of others to foul, and they think of NOTHING ELSE five yards away as they close the gap on the opponent. The yellow card is in order. While you must be sensitive to the demands made by the law, you should also be aware of the demands of the AMERICAN scene.

Referees in America have little historical perspective where soccer is concerned. The game did not begin in the late 1960's, when youth programs introduced thousands of parents to the game, and when foreign players started looking longingly to our shores. Rather, it began 100 years ago, where legitimate safe physical contact was a part of its character. The British influence was total. Now, the modern game brings Third World, European, and South American influence, where skill, footwork, and semi-direct moves (call them indirect) to goal disdain hard physical play. American players are robust and forceful. This is a trait that is evident in the American character. This character emerges on the field, and referees must be highly sensitive to it. *The hard player, within the laws, must be allowed to see an opponent fall without fear of interruption from the referee.*

It helps if you play, or did play the game. Your question should always be, "Is the intention to play the ball or the man? He can't do both!" Players can disguise a foul, and others are called just for being hard. One key element that lends vitality to dull and docile games is the fair *shoulder* charge. This miscalled "violation" can be an application of physical contact without being dangerous. Though legitimate, it is an effective approach for obtaining the ball in a tight situation. It is a lost art in present-day soccer. The foul should result only if the player is charged, in the wrong place, at the wrong time, or violently. *Violence is a matter of degree, difficult to measure.*

More discussion in referee meetings and clinics should be directed to the fair charge and to the fair tackle. What is needed is not a new definition of violence, but an understanding of the real nature of fair play. Professional indoor soccer, a throw-back to the old days (when the laws were the same as they are today) is bringing physical contact and zest to the outdoor game. Skill and physical action exist side-by-side, just as the indoor and outdoor games can complement one another. When does a nudge become a charge, and when does a charge become violent? You decide! *The skill of a physical action is just as worthy as the skill of a non-physical one.*

Contrasted with the sly moves of players who tend to intimidate by foul means, the open, fair, physical move to play the ball is for all to see and appreciate. Referees have a responsibility to remember that "A physical game is not necessarily a dirty one."

Sam Foulds has been in soccer for almost 70 years, and has never been in trouble with referees. However, he has silently absorbed some whistles which should never have been. He is Historian of the United States Soccer Federation, and has authored "America's Soccer Heritage". He was largely responsible for the establishment of the United States Soccer Hall of Fame in Oneonta, New York.

A fair, vigorous shoulder charge during play.

SILENCE FROM THE TOUCHLINE... FOR ONCE.

One of the basic unresolved problems for referees concerns the amount of "coaching" that is allowed from the boundary lines. Even in World Cup games, with the whole soccer world watching, coaches are seen directing players from the bench.

Referees discuss and occasionally fantasize about the ideal coach, sitting on the bench, accepting decisions, setting an example that is followed by players. There are such coaches among us, and when they are spotted, they deserve recognition. Such a coach is Layton Shoemaker, soccer coach and Athletic Director at Messiah College in Grantham, Pennsylvania.

Layton Shoemaker (center, rear) watches from the sideline during a recent European tour of his Messiah College team. It is evident to even the casual observer that there is something different about a Messiah game.

Shoemaker's philosophy is basic:

1. No encroachment is allowed, at any time, for any reason.

2. Tactical fouls are not taught or allowed.

3. No intentional fouls are allowed.

4. Only captains may speak with the referee. This is done infrequently and with respect. The reason for this is clarification of a call.

5. The coach must set the example. Coaches do not yell at the referee from the sideline.

6. Players are instructed to play a clean game of 'soccer regardless of how the opponents are playing or how the officials may be officiating.

7. Players' conduct will not embarrass or humiliate an opponent.

8. Players are not to kick, throw, or hold a ball once the referee has blown a whistle to stop play.

9. Players are not to gesture in an attempt to influence the call of an official.

10. A defender may not intentionally grab a ball that is lofted over the head.

Even at Messiah, the referee must be reminded that the duty of the referee is to protect the players who obey the laws from those who do not. Players competing within the laws must always be protected, whether encroachment or a violent foul is in question. This protection must be both consistent and courageous. As for the sideline coaching, you can always enforce Law V, IBD 12.

Hints for Referees:

- Always hear what goes on from the sidelines.

- Use an agreed upon signal with Linesmen to draw your attention to problems from the bench. (see "Communication") This is to be used only if the Linesman cannot handle the problem.

- Know who represents the team *before* the game.

- In stress situations, don't look to the bench unless you wish to change someone's attitude.

- If you anticipate problems from a certain bench, assign your stronger Linesman to that side.

- Remember that college rules allow an IFK if there are problems from the bench area.

The only thing which separates humankind from savagery is Law!

"To ignore dissent is to encourage it. To deal with it is to reduce it to a minimum."

Syd Stokes, at an NASL Referee Clinic

IS THIS IN THE SPIRIT OF THE GAME? The Acrobatic Throw-In.

In the 1978 Third Edition, we stirred a hornet's nest of controversy by introducing the unorthodox throw-in of Michael Ryan of Albuquerque, New Mexico. The throw-in, begun with a running start and completed with an acrobatic flip near the touch-line, enables a "whip action" and a special advantage for longer throw-ins.

While it appears that the requirements of Law XVII have been fulfilled, some referees have felt that the acrobatic throw-in is (a) dangerous to the thrower, (b) dangerous to other players who may be standing near the touch-line, and (c) against the spirit of the laws. Others felt it should be allowed and applauded the ingenuity of the idea. NISOA has recently endorsed the move and has covered it in their approved rulings.

Voga Wallace, of the University of Virginia, under the close scrutiny of a NISOA referee. He executes his acrobatic throw-in during a college playoff game. What would you do if a defensive player stationed himself near the touchline where Voga is to land? Are you ready for the many unusual events that could happen in your game?

"OPEN YOUR EYES, REF!"

by Arthur Seiderman

Officials' eyesight is questioned in all sports. More appropriately, "Use your eyes, ref" would in some cases be a good suggestion. While your eyes are always open, there may be some areas where your visual skills may be letting you down. Your visual system provides you with almost all of the sensory data from which calls are made and action is directed. You may have 20/20 vision, but that alone is not enough. You can improve your skills by performing and by maintaining some simple exercises, and on a regular basis.

Peripheral Vision — This concept is highly important to soccer, for the Referee must constantly keep play between himself and the Linesman. The flag must be seen, yet if you are always moving your head for a direct look at the Linesman, you will miss important aspects of play. The way to maintain awareness of a broad area on the field, including that of the Linesman, is through an expanded peripheral field.

To improve peripheral awareness by stimulating the peripheral area of the retina, follow this three step exercise:

1. Sit in a comfortable chair and extend your thumb out in front of you at arm's length.
2. Focus on your thumb with both eyes.
3. Maintain this visual fixation while you move your head slowly to the left and then to the right.

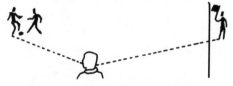

Speed of Recognition — The speed at which you make accurate decisions, whether it be a foul, out of bounds, or any other call, depends on how fast and how accurately the eyes can process information. By working with a tachistiscope, a projector which flashes numbers on a screen at varying speeds, you can speed your recognition. You can begin by having .10 of a second for calling out 5 numbers flashed, working up to as many as 9 numbers in .01 of a second. This exercise could be very popular in a referee meeting.

Visualization — How well can you see in your mind an image of an action or an event? Visualization can develop this for you, and is particularly important in training new officials. Most clinics are designed to teach the laws of the game, but few referees can visualize the fouls and other calls that are to be made in a game. Like any other skill, this requires practice and use. Simple visualizations:

1. Close you eyes and visualize a peaceful spot under a tree in a forest.

2. Close your eyes and visualize what your spouse wore to dinner last night.

3. Close your eyes and visualize a difficult call from your last game.

The development of the visual system involves more than the mere reading of a chart on the wall. Visualize yourself as the world's #1 Referee, but keep the eyes open if you visualize this on the field.

Arthur Seiderman, co-author of *The Athletic Eye*, (Hearst/Morrow) is the Director of the Sports Vision Center, Veteran's Stadium, Philadelphia, PA., 19148.

The Linesman should always be within the peripheral view of the Referee.

GAMES FOR REFEREES

A kick-about, known as a scrimmage to players and a safety valve for a coach who has run out of ideas and energy, is the too-easy way of getting together for fun and exercise. Unfortunately a kickabout only allows the skilled to show their skills and the not-so-skilled to be embarrassed. It only takes a little imagination to turn your outdoor sessions into a pleasurable, meaningful experience. The following games have been implemented in training clinics.

Out of Bounds. Setting: Played on a 20x20 yard field, with 3 players on each team. The object is for players to score goals between cones set 3 feet apart.

Referees: located around the periphery of the field, with pencil and paper. Each time the ball goes out of bounds, the Referees record which team is to be awarded the throw-in. One player quickly reports to the recorder and indicates who last touched the ball. Twenty-five decisions are to be made. At least 80 to 90% of the decisions should be accurately made by the Referees. Note: If the players can't agree who last touched the ball, either answer is correct. The game is controlled by the Referee.

With your Linesmen surrounding the 20x20 yard field, they will be judging the out-of-bounds from different angles.

Concentration. Setting: Two circles of Referees, with at least five Referees in a circle. Each set passes a ball for 60 seconds. Ball may not be passed to a player standing next to another.

Referees: One head Referee for each circle counts the number of touches, or passes, and keeps the time. Another Referee must jog, walk, or sprint (according to directions from the head Referee) around the two circles, all the while counting the number of touches for each circle. Change running Referee each minute.

Variations: Passing players can become verbally involved: (a) One player with the ball shouts "Law I." The player who receives the ball responds, "The Field of Play." (b) A player may say, "indirect free kick," and the circling Referee should raise his hand until the ball is played a second time. (c) Player shouts a foul, such as "obstruction," "tripping," or "violent charging." The circling Referee then yells out, "indirect," or "direct." These variations on the game, while the Referee is counting, present additional demands on the Referee, taxing his concentration.

REFEREE GAMES (Cont.)

Six-A-Side Kickabout. Setting: One Referee, two Linesmen, size of field variable according to skill and conditioning of players. Object is to score goals between two cones set three feet apart. No goalkeepers. Linesmen stay even with second to last defender (not easy without a goalkeeper).

Referees: Are players in game. They must play conventional soccer, and each silently counts only left (or right) footed passes by all players. Stop game each two minutes. Linesmen, who are not to signal for offside, count as well, and must report their tally. Center Referee controls game, calls fouls and other violations.

Variations: (a) Referee instructs players to call player's game before passing. If violation, IFK. (b) Players to pass only with left foot, or after first trapping the ball, or after first stopping it with the hand, or only after using the outside of the foot, etc., etc. (c) Referee can control game only with voice, or with the whistle, or after the whistle, only by using arm and hand signals.

This game has infinite variety, and the Referee should change the rules constantly to sharpen listening, concentration, and cooperation of the participants. The Referees will enjoy these games, for they are kept moving, and are thinking. Referees are taught here to be flexible, cooperative, responsive, and imaginative.

> The Referee should take total charge of this game.

Decision-Making. Setting: As above, with Six-A-Side, but force decisions by the Referee and Linesmen. Require a whistle and an "imaginary" foul if none exists every five touches, or each time a ball is played backwards, or headed, or trapped poorly (judgment), or toe-kicked, etc. Instruct the Referee to change all the rules, and see how he is able to control the group through voice and authority.

The day of a single Referee/Instructor merely talking to students on the field is past. Whatever you do, make it interesting, fast-moving, and challenging. BUT GO ON THE FIELD! Develop a Referee spirit in your group. Stress non-physical competitiveness, and create games where decisions are made. Final Hint: In each group, there will be at least one Referee who will not understand the game, and who may even be noncooperative. The "take charge" Referee will deal effectively with this problem.

The American Youth Soccer Organization (AYSO) has used referee games in the training of their young referees. The emphasis is on field work where the Referees learn to make decisions on their own.

THE PHIELD TEST

Referees, like players, are competitive. A healthy competition, and a test of Referees' speed and agility is offered in the PHield Test. It can easily be set up on any soccer field. The difference between the slowest and fastest Referee in your group should be no more than 20 seconds. Suggested passing time: 60 seconds.

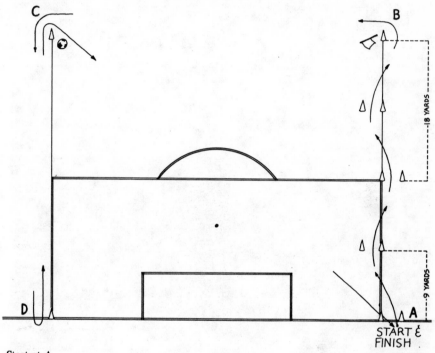

Start at A

A → B   run backward, weaving through cones (add one second for each cone hit or set of cones missed)

B   pick up linesman's flag

B → C   PROPERLY carry linesman's flag at a full sprint. . . either side acceptable (add 2 seconds for improper flag carriage)

C   drop flag, pick up ball and make a PROPER throw-in toward the goal (add 2 seconds for improper throw-in)

C → D → C   sideways run, facing penalty-area . . . do NOT cross feet (add 2 seconds for improper run)

C → A   sprint to finish . . . between cones at A

XI

The American Scene

THE FIFA REFEREE... AT THE TOP

The FIFA badge is worn by fewer than 700 Referees in the 143 FIFA member countries. These men have risen to the top of their avocation through long years of officiating at club, semi-pro, and professional levels. They are originally recommended for the FIFA list by their home countries.

FIFA is not obliged to accept referee nominations for the international list, but they usually do. Every country may nominate up to seven referees whether they have 50,000 or 50 referees in the national association. After the Referee has officiated two Class "A" international matches, he has won his badge. Therefore, some qualify but never receive full recognition.

FIFA appoints Referees and Linesmen only for World Cup and Olympic Games, both the preliminary and final rounds of games. For all other matches of an international nature, whether at the club or national level, the appointments are made by the country or Federation concerned, or by an agreement between the two countries, if a match is a friendly one. In each game of the final tournament of the World Cup and Olympic Games, the three match officials are selected from different neutral countries. In all other cases, the three officials come from the same neutral country, though an exception can be made in the preliminary matches of the Olympic Games where countries can mutually agree on Linesmen from a nearer country.

FIFA Referees receive no payment for officiating in an international match. All travel and living expenses are paid. None of these men make a living officiating, although they are probably the most professional group of sports Referees in the world. They are constantly scrutinized by Referee "Inspectors" or "Assessors," but are not subjected to written tests. Their field performance and physical fitness is the main concern of the inspector, and detailed reports on most FIFA Referees are kept in Zurich. From these reports are drawn the lists for World Cup and Olympic Games competitions.

Due to the nature of the game, its worldwide popularity, the unusual rules calling for one man maintaining complete control over the game and its timing and record-keeping, certainly the most demanding neutral position in all of sports officiating falls on the shoulders of the FIFA Referee.

The seven FIFA Referees currently on the list in the United States are:

Bellion, Edward	Arlington, Texas
Bratsis, Angelo	Holbrook, Massachusetts
D'Ippolito, Gino	Yonkers, New York
Evans, Robert	Dallas, Texas
Kibritjian, Toros	Monterey Park, California
Krollfeifer, Howard	La Jolla, California
Socha, David	Ludlow, Massachusetts

Studying to be FIFA Referees.

THE REFEREE IN THE NORTH AMERICAN SOCCER LEAGUE

Many of the 25,000 registered referees in North America longingly look at officials in the North American Soccer League (NASL) and wish they were part of the action. The average Referee in this league has more than 10 years' experience in highly competitive soccer, and has been closely watched by Assessors and other soccer organizers. Great demands are made on these officials, as they have a time committment that is not matched by game fees, and a responsiblility to the league which must be built on dedication. Recognition, of course, is there, and these officials know they are the best in professional soccer. Werner Winesmann, experienced in World Cup, Olympic, and NASL play, summed it up by saying, "I think that without a doubt NASL games are the most difficult to handle anywhere."

In most cases NASL officials are recommended by their State Association, and have had extensive experience as instructors and clinicians in local chapters. They are approved through a series of written and physical tests. Attitude, personality, physique, age, and the ability to get along with others all weigh heavily on their selection. Each league city has at least two Assessors whose detailed observations of games are carefully weighed.

All seven FIFA referees from the United States officiate in the NASL, two of them fulltime professional referees in the Major Indoor Soccer League in the winter season. The 85 officials, including one woman, are divided into stratified categories, and assignments are made accordingly. Most games are officiated by Premier Referees (the highly favored, internationally-experienced, usually over 40 in age) and Referees, just a step below. Supplementary Referees, on their way up and under close scrutiny, complete the men in the middle. Senior Linesmen, as effective as any you will find in the world, are carefully judged in this difficult role, and await their chance for a game as Referee. Linesmen are new to the league and are in the learning mode. The NASL has wanted to bring these Linesmen into the competition early, before age 30. The reduced number of teams in the NASL has worked against this process, and a Linesman must now be exceptional to enter the list.

Physical fitness is important for all officials, and all 85 are tested with the 12 minute run (Cooper test) twice during the season. The standards are as follows:

Age	Under 30	30-39	40-49	50 and over
MEN	1.75 miles	1.65 miles	1.55 miles	1.50 miles
WOMEN	1.65 miles	1.55 miles	1.45 miles	1.35 miles

Close cooperation is imperative to a team effort in the NASL. With this in mind, the countdown before a game is planned accordingly:

90 minutes before kickoff: Field inspection and part of pre-game conference.

60 minutes before kickoff: Instruct field timer, and complete field pre-game conference.

45 minutes before kickoff: Receive Lineup forms from coaches.

30 minutes before kickoff: Assessor leaves dressing room, after final instructions to Linesmen.

A Fourth Official is part of the Referee team (usually a Linesman from the list), and his duties are to control the benches, observe timer, and to monitor the handling of substitutes. Four North Americans from each team must be on the field at all times.

The attractiveness of the game is paramount to the league ownership, and Referees are required to perform certain duties that are not common in amateur soccer. Since "lost time"* is of concern to owners, Referees are instructed to conduct all restarts within 10 seconds after the ball is out of play. Kickoffs following goals are to be taken within 30 seconds, and goalkeepers must distribute the ball within 10 seconds after having the ball under control.

In an effort to increase the Referee's control in the middle, and to give status and responsibility to Linesmen, the Linesmen are to act on their own initiative in their zone of control. If the Linesman feels there is a foul or other infraction, the flag will go up.

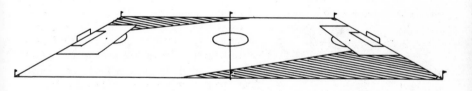

The shaded area represents the Linesman's area of responsibility.

It is felt that the standard of officiating in America is improving each year. Nowhere is this more apparent than in the North American Soccer League.

*Lost time, when the clock is running and the ball is out of play, adds up to between 23 and 30 minutes each game. This includes all stopping for fouls, goals, throw-ins, substitutions, corner-kicks, penalty kicks, injuries, and drop-balls.

THE SHOOTOUT

In 1970 FIFA adopted the "Taking of Kicks from the Penalty Mark" to determine which of two teams in a drawn match, in knockout competition, would be declared the winner. Some years later, the NASL "Shootout" to determine winners was approved, and has been widely used by other leagues as well. If a game is still tied following overtime, it is decided by the Shootout. Drama, excitement, and a greater element of fairness* are the hallmarks of the Shootout. Most organizers feel the Shootout involves more skills on the part of both kicker and goalkeeper. It can best be described as "one on one" between goalkeeper and kicker.

Procedure:

Only players on the field at the end of game may participate.

Only the goalkeeper may be substituted, but not reinstated, following substitution.

Play begins at a point on the 35 yard line, and the kicker has 5 seconds to score.

The visiting team shoots first. Alternative attempts are made thereafter until each team has had five attempts, or a team cannot possibly win.

Goalkeeper Restrictions

May not move before ball is played, and must be on the line between the goalposts.

May not touch the ball with the hands outside of the Penalty Area. Sanction: Penalty Kick.

May not foul the kicker. Sanction: Penalty Kick. May not participate as a shooter.

Shooter Restrictions

Must shoot within 5 seconds.

May not foul the goalkeeper. Sanction: no goal, if goal is scored.

May not play ball after it has made contact with the goalkeeper, goal posts, or cross bar.

Has only one attempt until all eligible players have shot.

Officials' Duties

Referee

Makes rulings on fouls and their penalties.

Final judge on all matters of timing.

Senior Linesman

Activates timing device.

Signals start of each attempt, and end of 5 seconds.

SHOOT OUT (Cont.)

Junior Linesman

Back-up timing of kicks.**

* Readers may remember the 1982 World Cup Semi-Final game between France and Germany, which was decided by Kicks from the Penalty Spot. Later, Referee Charles Corver was reprimanded for his allowing blatant moves by the German goalkeeper before the ball was kicked. These moves, allowing the goalkeeper to stop several attempts, proved the difference in this game.

** NASL uses a 4th official for record-keeping. Most non-NASL competitions will not have this luxury. *Fair or Foul* recommendation: The Junior Linesman is to be assigned as record-keeper, as well as the back-up timer.

In the shootout, you are all alone against the goalkeeper.

THE UNITED STATES SOCCER FEDERATION REFEREE

The United States Soccer Federation (USSF) is the national governing body of soccer in the United States. It is recognized by the world governing body, FIFA (Federation International de Futbol Association). One of the permanent standing committees in the USSF is the Referee Committee. This volunteer Committee has established five different grades of Referees, with standard certification criteria for each grade.

USSF REFEREE GRADES

In order to provide uniform standards for soccer referees in the United States, the USSF Referee Committee has adopted the five referee grades listed below. These grades supercede all grades which have previously been adopted by state associations and leagues so that uniform and comparative grading exists throughout the United States.

1. **USSF Associate Referee**
   a. Minimum Age: None
   b. Badge: USSF; Rocker: Associate.
   c. Competence Level: Beginning referee for youth games.

2. **USSF Referee (Class 1 and Class 2)**
   a. Minimum Age: None.
   b. Badge: USSF; Rocker: Referee.
   c. Competence Level: All youth games.

3. **USSF State Referee (Class 1 and Class 2)**
   a. Minimum Age: 19 years.
   b. Badge: USSF; Rocker: State.
   c. Competence Level: All youth games and all senior amateur games except interstate games in senior national competitions.

4. **USSF National Referee (Class 1 and Class 2)**
   a. Minimum Age: 25 years.
   b. Badge: USSF; Rocker: National; Brass Pin "USSF National Referee".
   c. Competence Level: All games except formal FIFA international matches.

5. **USSF International Referee (Class 1 and Class 2)**
   a. Minimum Age: 25 years.
   b. Badge: FIFA or USSF; Rocker: National; FIFA Pin.
   c. Competence Level: All games.
   d. Citizenship: U.S. Citizenship required (USSF Rule 1209).

The vast majority of Referee registrations are for Class 2 (Referee). Of the 25,000 Referees currently registered, almost 18,000 are in this category. Seven FIFA (International) and less than 100 National Referees are registered. 2500 State Referees are current, and the remainder are Associate Referees. A Referee must spend at least a year (12 months) in one grade before moving on to another.

The FIFA Laws guide all competitions involving USSF affiliated teams.

AGITATOR

- Makes mountains out of mole hills.

- Does his best to **aggravate** players, coaches, and fans.

- Insults **goalkeeper** about his gloves during the coin toss.

- Tells linesman that he has a cheap looking uniform.

- When he is in the stands, yells at the Referee.

- Tells the coach that this is the poorest field he has ever reffed on.

- Tells his Linesmen at half time that they stink.

- Argues with God.

- Is divorced.

- Shows everyone a 'typro' he found in *Fair or Foul.*

THE AMERICAN YOUTH SOCCER ORGANIZATION...
YOUTH SOCCER RULES

The American Youth Soccer Organization began in September 1964 in California, and began competition in January 1965 with nine teams. Recent figures indicate 250,000 players in 32 states, Washington, D.C., and Guam. The philosophy of AYSO includes full participation, with each player playing a minimum of one-half a game, regardless of ability. Teams are selected on a regional (community) basis, with a full attempt made for team balancing. The rules of the game and conduct as mentioned below are highly recommended for youth soccer organizations.

The Referee in AYSO

The 1,000,000 games that are played under the AYSO banner each year are officiated by more than 15,000 unpaid referees. Regional organizers organize and train, and assign referees and Linesmen. With the exception of AYSO's National Training Camps for Instructors, all of the training is done locally. Uniformity is achieved through national publications and training aids, overseen by the National Director of Officiating and his National Referee Commission.

AYSO soccer is recreational, as opposed to "club", or "travelling" teams found in many communities. The vast majority of games involve boys or girls under age 12. The Referee in these games is usually a parent, and sometimes a teenage player who seeks a new challenge. AYSO strongly recommends the Diagonal System of control for all of its regions, and has endorsed this system in its camps and clinics.

Referee classifications in AYSO include Junior Referee (referees in teenage years), Referee (red badge), a Regional designation, Area Referee (white badge), for Area playoffs, and National Referee (black badge), the highest designation. The white and black badges require testing and field evaluation, and the black badge also requires the passing of the phield Test.

The coin toss is performed about 1,000,000 times a year in AYSO.

REGISTRATION, DURATION, OVERTIME, SIZE OF BALL

Division	Age Player Must be Under As of 31 Dec.	Law VII. Duration of The Game	Playoff Game Overtime Periods	Law II. The Ball
I	19	80 min.	10 min.	No. 5
II	17	70 min.	9 min.	26.5—28 inch circum. 14—16 oz.
III	15	60 min.		
IV	13	50 min.	8 min.	No. 4 25—26.5 inch circum. 12—14 oz.
V	11			
VI	9	40 min.	7 min.	No. 3 23.5-25 inch circum. 9—12 oz.

Half-time is 5-10 min.

SUBSTITUTION

All registered players in attendance at League and AYSO playoff games must participate and play at least half of the game, *excluding overtime*.

Such participation is controlled as follows:

1. Halfway through the first half, and halfway through the second half, the Referee halts the game,* stops his watch and notes on lineup sheets those players substituting. Stoppage is made when the ball is out of play, such as during a throw-in, corner-kick, following a goal, or before a free-kick is to be taken. Additionally, subsititutions may be made at halftime.

2. Respective coaches of each team may substitute any players or none during such interruptions, as long as, at game's end, all players have been substituted.

CHARGING THE GOALKEEPER

Charging the goalkeeper shall not be permitted in the penalty-area, nor shall the goalkeeper be harrassed or interfered with while attemping to put the ball into play.

DROP-BALLS

In the event that play has been stopped with the ball in the penalty-area, and the FIFA rules call for play to be resumed with a drop-ball, the game shall be restarted with a drop-ball being taken at the closest point outside the penalty-area.

* FF recommendation: If the ball does not go out of play in one or two minutes following the mid-point in the half, the Referee may stop the game when the ball is in a neutral area, and resume with a drop ball following substitutions.

HIGH SCHOOL DIFFERENCES FROM FIFA

1. *FIELD OF PLAY*

Length — 100 yards to 120 yards.

Width — 55 yards to 75 yards.

Penalty-Kick Line — 2 feet long.

Corner-Flags — may not be removed.

Nets should extend backward approximately 24 inches level with the cross-bar.

Spectator Area — Marked with a dashed line and a minimum of 10 yards behind the touchline and goal line.

Other Special Areas — Marked with a solid line and 5 yards back of the touchline (minimum).

- Team Area—20 yards long. It begins 10 yards from the halfway line. Coaches and team members are restricted to this area. When teams are placed on opposite sides of the field, the coaching areas shall extend 10 yards on either side of the halfway-line.

- Official Area—Extends 5 yards on each side of the halfway-line (total 10 yds.)

2. *THE BALL*

Leather or similar material which is *weather resistant.*

The home team provides 3 or more game balls of similar quality. If not, the Referee chooses game balls from those offered by both teams.

Inflated to manufacturer's recommended pressure.

3. *THE PLAYERS*

A game may not be started with less than 11 players, one of whom shall be the goalkeeper.

The captain may address an official on matters of interpretation or to obtain essential information.

An injured player who is attended to on the field must be replaced.

Substitutes report to the scorer.

There is no limit to the amount of substitutes from off the field. They may be made during stoppage from:

Goal-Kick
Corner-Kick (only if possession and player is at scorer's table).
Disqualification
Caution
Between periods
After a goal
Injury (the injured player shall be replaced)
Throw-In (only if possession and player at scorer's table)

A substitute may not be made for the taking of a Penalty Kick.

Repeated substitutions to consume time—Referee may order the clock stopped. If repeat, IFK from where the ball was.

4. PLAYERS' EQUIPMENT

It is recommended that the home team wear a light-colored shirt and socks and the visitors wear dark-colored shirts and socks.

Numbers must be different, worn on the back, and at least 6 inches in height.

Numbers on front must be at least 4 inches high.

Casts (even if padded) are not allowed.

Jewelry may not be worn unless religious or medical. It must be taped down.

Studs on shoes may not project more than ½ inch and shall not be made of aluminum.

Head wear may not be worn with the exception of headbands or hair control devices made of soft material.

5. REFEREE, UMPIRE AND LINE JUDGES

The officials shall be a referee and an umpire assisted by a timer, scorer and two ball holders (one referee and two qualified line judges may be used).

The officials shall dress alike.

Shall inform the captains that intentionally fouling of the G/C results in disqualification.

Notification of timekeeper of all called time-outs.

The whistle shall be sounded each time the ball crosses a touch-line or goal-line.

Signals must be given and the infraction called out. Signals are the same as those contained within fair-or-foul except:

Goal — the right arm moves down 90°.
Trip — touch your heel.

Any disqualification must be reported in writing to the proper high school authorities.

6. BALL HOLDERS, TIMER AND SCORER

The home team provides at least 2 ball holders.

Timekeepers:

The official timer is the one from the home school.
Time may be kept by the Referee by mutual agreement of the coaches.
The last 10 seconds of each period shall be audibly called out.
Signal 2 minutes before the end of the half and the game.

Scorer:

The home team provides the official scorer.
Must have teams line up at least 5 minutes prior to game time.
Records all cautioned and disqualified players.

7. DURATION OF THE GAME/LENGTH OF PERIODS

Two equal periods of 40 minutes each (or four 20-minute quarters if approved by the state high school association). Overtime—two periods of 5 minutes *may* be played as per league directive.

Interval between quarters:

1st and 2nd, 3rd and 4th, 1st and 2nd overtime periods—Maximum of 2 minutes for changing ends.
2nd half and overtime—5 minutes
Halftime—10 minutes (unless opposing coaches agree to a different length)

Time-out:

For the taking of a penalty-kick
Following the scoring of a goal
For a caution or disqualification

Suspended game due to unforeseen conditions:

If ½ or more of the game has been played—It is a complete game.
If less than ½ of the game has been played—Reschedule.

9. IN AND OUT OF PLAY

The Referee will whistle whenever the ball is out of play.

A second whistle is given after a substitution, penalty-kick, caution, ejection, injury or encroachment.

Temporary suspension—Injury or unusual situation.

If one team clearly is in possession—IFK.
If neither team has possession—DROP-BALL.

Drop-Ball

Dropped at waist level.
Must be done between two opposing players.
Can't be taken within the penalty area—Go to nearest point outside the PA.
A drop-ball resulting from going out of bounds is taken 5 yards from the boundary line.

10. SCORING

The Referee shall terminate the game if:

A team refuses to play after being instructed to do so.
A team has fewer than 11 players at the start of the game.

A forfeit is 1-0 unless the offending team is behind, then the actual score stands.

12. FOULS AND MISCONDUCT

It is dangerous play when the tackler's cleats are displayed in a hazardous manner.

The act of moving the hands or arms to protect oneself and making contact with the ball is *intentional* handling.

A player with both feet off the ground can't be charged.

Goalkeeper:

Any charge of the GK other than when he obstructs (non-intentional)—DIRECT.

Intentionally charging the GK in possession of the ball—DIRECT and DISQUALIFY.

He is considered to be in possession and no one can attempt to play the ball when he:

Bounces the ball; or
Is in the act of drop-kicking.

Team CAUTION can be issued for:

Encroachment on free-kicks.
Intentional handballs by the defense.
Unnecessary delay of the game.

14. PENALTY-KICK

Encroachment and other infringements do not result in an automatic CAUTION.

15. THROW-IN

The feet must be totally behind and not in contact with the touch-line.

COLLEGE DIFFERENCES FROM FIFA

1. THE FIELD AND EQUIPMENT

The field of play

Length: 110 to 120 yards

Width: 65 to 75 yards

Penalty-Kick Line = 2 feet long. Kicks may be taken from any position on the line.

Corner-flags may not be removed. Football style corner-flags or pylons may be used for artificial surfaces.

Nets should extend backward 2 feet level with the cross-bar.

Goal posts and cross-bars are to be between 4 to 5 inches and must be painted white.

Team benches and timers' tables—shall be on the same side of the field and at least 10 feet from the touch-lines.

The ball

There must be 3 balls and all must be of the same make.

When dropped from 100 inches onto a cement floor, it should rebound from 60 to 65 inches.

Players' equipment

Home team must wear white or light-colored jersey—Visiting team wears dark-colored jersey.

Numbers on back are mandatory—Minimum height is 6 inches.

Numbers at least 4 inches in height must be worn on the front.

Any player wearing a non-conforming uniform receives a CAUTION.

2. PLAYERS AND SUBSTITUTES

Substitutes

Seven substitutes are permitted. (More are allowed only by special league arrangements.)

Unlimited resubstitution is allowed.

Must first report to the scoring table.

If violation of the substitution rule—IFK where the ball was.

Substitutions on . . .

- — Goal-kick and corner-kick
- — After a goal
- — Between periods
- — Injury—only the injured player can be replaced
- — Cautions—only the cautioned player(s)

Whenever there is a substitution for an injury or caution, the opponents can replace a like number.

3.   OFFICIALS AND THEIR DUTIES

Referee

A second whistle is required for a kick-off and a PK (Rule 7).

Timekeeper is notified for all time-outs and the players to be credited with goals and assists are confirmed.

All fouls must be signaled. Signals are the same as those contained within Fair or Foul, except that the heel is touched to indicate a trip.

Red and yellow cards must be used for cautions and disqualifications.

Forfeit if a team is not prepared to play within 15 minutes after the contracted time.

Forfeit if a coach prolongs a discussion with an official or refuses to leave the field. If assigned Referee does not appear, the Senior Referee is assigned.

Linesman assumes the role of Referee.

Ball Persons

Home team provides two who will carry an extra ball and will act as ball retrievers.

They are to be instructed by and are under the direct supervision of the game officials.

Timekeeper

The official timer is designated by the home team.

Referee instructs timer of duties.

He stops the clock after a goal, when a player is carded, and for a penalty kick.

He signals Referee when a substitution is to be made.

He notifies the nearest official audibly of a countdown of the last 10 seconds of playing time of any period.

He notifies the Referee and teams 2 minutes in advance of the start of the second half.

4.   TIME FACTORS, PLAY AND SCORING

Time factors

Half-time interval—Maximum of 10 minutes (no minimum) unless consent by Referee and both coaches.

If the game is tied, two extra periods of 10 minutes each are to be played. The coin is retossed.

Interval between end of regulation play and overtime is a maximum of 5 minutes.

Interval between overtime periods is a maximum of 2 minutes.

Ball in and out of play

No drop-balls in the Penalty Area (nearest point outside the PA).

The drop-ball is administered from waist level.

Scoring

A forfeit game is 1-0.

6.   VIOLATIONS AND MISCONDUCT

Goalkeeper privileges and violations

Goalkeeper is considered to be in possession (ball can't be played) when he is bouncing the ball with his hand and also when he drops the ball for a kick.

It is not considered possession when the goalkeeper rolls the ball along the ground with his hand. The goalkeeper may have double possession.

Misconduct

Caution of a non-participant results in an IFK where the ball was.

Team caution for deliberate hand-ball and time wasting.

Coaching must be *verbal*, directed toward one's own team, done without aids, and confined to the immediate bench area. A repetition results in IFK where the ball was.

Dangerous play

No penalty is committed against a teammate.

7.   AWARDED KICKS AND THE THROW-IN

Free-kicks

IFK:

- A substitution made at an improper time—where the ball was.
- Unauthorized field entry—where the ball was.
- Illegal coaching—the second time—where the ball was.

Penalty-kick

Encroachments and other infringements do not result in automatic cautions.

Throw-in

The feet must be totally behind and not in touch with the touch-line (NISOA rule interpretation).

XII

The Indoor Game

THE INDOOR GAME

Arguments abound regarding the origin of outdoor soccer. When the game moved indoors in 1974, few argued that the fact that a new American game was born. With the coming of the Major Indoor Soccer League (MISL) in 1979, fans, players, and coaches alike witnessed an American phenomena that could surpass interest in the outdoor game. A tackle every three seconds, an average of 5 penalties in a game, fast action followed by multiple shots on goal, and free and unlimited subsitution provide new challenges and opportunities for Referees.

Innovation is the hallmark of the indoor game. With little historical precedent, even the method of controlling games is under constant surveillance and change. Through the Technical Committee of the USSF, several changes are made to the laws each year. Another change is the enlistment of America's first fulltime soccer officials. On a seven months' contract, these Referees have provided full professionalism and consistency in the league.

Indoor soccer has its own set of laws, with some slight changes for MISL play. Youth, college, and other amateur leagues have amended these laws for local play. Referees will no doubt encounter a variety of rule differences for local play.

A Summary of Major Differences in the Indoor Game

Law I - Field of Play. (see illustration) A confined area and perimeter walls make the game quick and non-stop. Walls and two red lines are the only major differences.

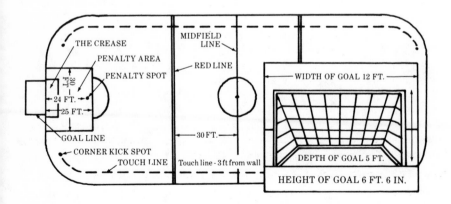

INDOOR SOCCER (Cont.)

Law VII - Duration of the Game. The game is four 15 minute quarters, with halftime not less than 5 minutes. At the end of the 1st and 3rd periods, the interval is at least 2 minutes.

Law IX - Ball In and Out of Play. Ball is out of play when it has crossed the perimeter wall or touched a building structure above the field of play.

Law XI - Three Line Violation. The ball may not be played across three lines (two red lines and the center line) in the air and towards the opponent's goal line without touching another player. This does not apply to a team short-handed by two players.

Law XII - Fouls and Misconduct. The nine direct penal fouls may apply, plus charging an opponent into the perimeter wall (boarding). If a foul is called and the Referee feels it was serious, the offender may be asses a two minute time penalty, and possibly cautioned. A caution must accompany the second time penalty. A further cautionalbe offense brings a 5 minute time penalty and an ejection from the game.

Indoor soccer can get very rough near the perimeter wall.

Goalkeeper Restrictions:
Must release the ball in five seconds.
Penalties against the goalkeeper must be served by another player.
Intentional hand balls by the goalkeeper outside of the Penalty Area are considered serious. They are usually subject to a two minute penalty.

Delay of Game Penalty. A player who deliberately plays the ball over the perimeter wall shall be guilty of delay of game and shall be assessed a 2 minute time penalty.

Time Penalties
When a player is sent to the penalty box, the other team has a "Man Advantage", and usually employes a "Power Play" to score.
One penalized palyer may return to paly if the opponent scores a goal unless the opponent also has a penalized player.
If a player is penalized while two teammates are serving penalties, the third penalty time shall not begin until the first has expired.

Law XIII - Free Kick. Opponents must remain 10 feet from the ball on free kicks. The ball must be put into play within 5 seconds following the signal from the Referee. Punishment: 2 minutes for ungentlemanly conduct.

Law XIV - Penalty Kick. The kick is taken at a spot 24 feet from the goal line.

Law XV - Kick In. (Indoor Soccer's answer to the throw-in.) The ball is put into play by a kick in at the point where it passed over the perimeter wall at the touchline.

INDOOR SOCCER (Cont.)

Law III - Number of Players. Five players and a goalkeeper comprise the team, with no less than four on the field at a time. Unlimited substitution is allowed without stopping play. Substituting players can enter only if the leaving player is within the touchline in his own bench area.

When a player is penalized (sent to the penalty box), the opponents have the 'Man Advantage'. Here one team has outnumbered the opponents, and is using the 'Power Play'. Often, the Goalkeeper will participate in the attack.

Law IV - Players' Equipment. No footwear with less than 10 molded studs. Most players wear flat-soled shoes or sneakers.

Law V - Referees. One Referee controls the game. MISL uses two, with equal authority.

Law VI - Assistant Referee and Other Game Officials. The Assistant Referee, off the field, observes substitutions, signals 3-Line violations, supervises timekeepers, and keeps a record of the game, as well as controlling the bench and penalty box areas.

The close proximity of reserve players can create special problems for the Referee.

INDOOR SOCCER (Cont.)

The Referee's Two Minute card must be used for deliberate fouls or delay of game.

Hints for Referees:

The action is almost too quick for the planned, premeditated foul.

Be careful with advantage. It is not often clear or immediate.

Due to the small goal, free kicks are seldom directly scored. Look for the pass or the play off the board.

Don't get caught in corners. Look for escape routes, and stay away from the area near the goal.

Counterattacks come quickly.

This unusual photo was taken during a youth game. A game became very much out of control, and the coach attacked the Referee. Fortunately these incidents are few. (From 'Futbol Means Soccer' by Larry Harris)

XIII

You and the Youth

WHEN YOU REFEREE YOUTH GAMES

Just as most players enjoy their first soccer experience through youth competition, Referees learn by involvement in games of young players. It is here that games are most available and organizers most anxious to "fill the ranks."

At the same time, there is a great need in youth soccer for quality officiating, of a kind that will greatly increase the education and enjoyment of all. Most young players, coaches, and parents have a limited knowledge of the game, and the burden of instruction may fall on the Referee.

Few youth organizations have written charters defining the role of the Referee, and these words seldom mention more than vague ideas such as "interpreter of the laws," "sole authority," or "official league representative." Youngsters and their needs, however, provide many interesting and challenging possibilities for the Referee.

THE REFEREE SHOULD ENCOURAGE PLAYERS WHENEVER POSSIBLE

Examples:

(a) A player makes a mistake, and teammates react negatively. Referee: "That's all right. I once saw Pele miss a shot like that." To the culprit: "Isn't that your teammate? He'll never get better unless you help him."

(b) A goalie makes a good save, giving away a corner kick. There's a lull in play. Referee: (Walking by the goalie): "Good save. I thought that one was going in."

(c) After a goal (the scoring team cannot hear): "That was a good goal, no one's fault.

The game provides many opportunities for this kind of banter. Come alive in the game, always preparing players for the inevitable decision they won't particularly like!

THE REFEREE CAN COACH PLAYERS

Examples:

(a) A youngster is playing dangerously by kicking high or "going over" the ball. Referee: "Keep your feet down and go through the ball, and you won't hurt anyone." You could even make the motion, so everyone knows you're doing your best to prevent a repetition.

(b) A player places the ball in the hole in the corner of the goal area for a goal kick. Referee: "You'll never get it out of that hole. Did you know you could place it anywhere in this side of the area? *Hint*: If you tell the player not to put it in the hole before it is placed, no one will ever guess what you've said, for the ball will not be moved from one place to another.

In most cases, the Referee is to be seen and heard in his instructing, and the instructing must not be such as to directly affect the score.

THE REFEREE SHOULD ADMIT CERTAIN MISTAKES

Examples:

(a) An offside is called, and play is stopped. A second defensive player is seen standing on the goal line. (Don't be smug. It happens to all of us.) Referee: "Oh, no!" I sure missed him over there. Thanks for pointing him out, but the whistle has already blown. We'll have a drop ball." (Note: Some Referees will allow the free kick, even though they know they are in error. This compounds the mistake.)

(b) The foul is called, but the advantage immediately materializes. Referee: (shaking head) "You had the advantage. My mistake. Take the kick."

FURTHER HINTS

1. Almost every injury in youth soccer is genuine and unrehearsed. Unless unusual circumstances prevail, (the ball headed for the net), stop the game immediately when each opponent injury occurs.

2. Many of the nine penal offenses (and obstruction) are committed in innocence, and should therefore not be called.

3. Pushing and dangerous play are the two most common fouls with youth players. You will see a lot of "simultaneous" pushing by two players, where neither gains an advantage. Don't call it, but give some words of advice without stopping play. Dangerous play is more serious, obviously. An experienced youth Referee has said that "the only real job of the youth Referee is to prevent players from hurting themselves."

    Example: Most young players, when late approaching a rolling ball will jump and turn their backs on the kicker (self-preservation). They may land on the opponent's legs, feet, or back (if the opponent also turns!) This habit is not easily stopped by the coach. You may have better luck as a Referee, by calling for dangerous play, or jumping at an opponent."

4. Youngsters become experts on very minor and inconsequential aspects of the laws, such as throw-ins or other out of bounds situations. When you see something that should not be called, such as a player lifting the foot just after the throw-in, say loudly, "That throw-in is OK." Tiny criticism from players is therefore stopped before it starts. You might remember this one for all of your games.

5. Learn the names of at least five players on each team during the first five minutes of play. This will aid your concentration and may help you when you want to address a certain player. "He really knows what he's doing. He even knows my name," the player will think, when spoken to.

6. Unless some player has been placed in some physical danger, most "borderline" calls in youth games should not be made. There is nothing more disconcerting than the Referee who calls "goalkeeper steps" perfectly, while disregarding the myriad of fouls that can result when players decide to test the Referee and each other. Most children quickly forget, have little knowledge of what really is allowed, and are innocent in their enthusiasm for the game.

7. Always give the appearance of enjoying yourself. Many youth games are not particularly well-played, and you may suddenly have an urge to be elsewhere. Be seen smiling at least once each game, and try to make a poor game an acceptable experience.

The youth Referee who views himself as a full, firm, authority with a textbook knowledge of the laws may be missing the real joy of the official's soccer experience: that of being a consistent "facilitator" of play and of being a sensitive and sensible adult.

Sometimes players will give you a hint on what they 'think' they did.

Seven year old Ken Laitin reports his first goal to the Referee. Ken has played in 750 games since, and is now a registered Referee. He also co-authored a book for young players.

EVERY PLAYER IS DIFFERENT

Each game is different, and dependent on the age group of the participants. Go into each contest with a full understanding of the players. Can you add to this list?

Under 9 *"Age of Innocence"*
- Obedient to all decisions of Referee and coach
- Pressure from parents, most of whom are new to game
- Fear of opponent, and often the ball
- Awkwardness
- No concept whatever of offside.

Under 11 *"The Emerging Skills"*
- Openly, intensively competitive, without intention in fouls
- No dissent
- Parents becoming aware of fair/foul throw-ins, goalkeeper steps, injustices in play
- Game moves more quickly. Less predictable than any other group. Outstanding players cannot dominate.

Under 13 *"The Differences in Skills"*
- Intolerance of teammates' incompetence
- Call Referee's attention to minor infractions (throw-ins, etc.)
- Will question "hand balls"
- Team cooperation emerges — Players encourage one another.

Under 15 *"Aggressiveness Toward Opponents and Teammates"*
- Sense injustices, but don't yet know what to do about it
- Widespread difference in abilities
- Game control essential
- Player safety is more important.

Under 17 *"Has More Experience and Dangerous Familiarity with the Laws"*
- Question authority of Referee, coach and parent
- Will retaliate, openly, on intentional foul
- Great frustration with own faults
- Limited parental interest.

Under 19 *"Watch Out"*

- Coach-Referee understanding and cooperation essential
- Everyone thinks he is an expert on all aspects of the game
- Will test Referees very soon in match
- Retaliation common
- Obstruction very common
- Will encroach
- Much "banter" between and among players

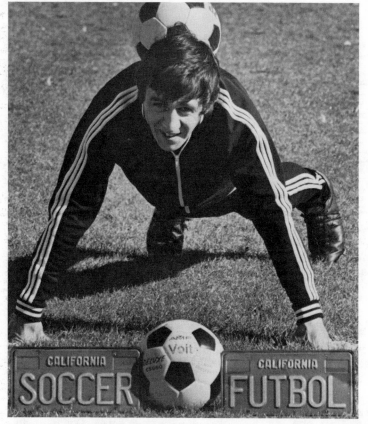

Larry Harris, coauthor of FAIR OR FOUL, has written a book called FUTBOL MEANS SOCCER, and Adrian Walsh agrees. Adrian is the Guinness World Recordholder in Ball Control, and has an array of 50 tricks. Referees must be aware of players' tricks, and should possess a few of their own. (From You Can Control the Soccer Ball, by Adrian Walsh.)

THE INTERNATIONAL BOARD . . .
HOW SOCCER'S LAWS ARE CHANGED

The laws of the game are quite static, and few people connected with the game expect changes from year to year. The Off-Side law was brought to its present form in 1925. The Penalty-Arc was added in 1935. It is apparent that there is almost a sacrosanctity about the laws governing play.

The International Board consists of representatives from the four British Associations and one from FIFA. The countries — England, Ireland, Scotland, and Wales — each have one vote. FIFA, representing 142 countries, has four. No change takes place without a clear 75% majority. Therefore, no law or wording in the law may be changed without the approval of FIFA, and vice versa.

Any country may propose a change. If the National Association in Brazil, for instance, wanted to suggest a rule change eliminating the center circle, it would first be sent to the FIFA Referees' Committee, a group of seven, which screens all requests. The Committee may either reject the request, or submit it as a FIFA proposal (4 votes). The remaining four votes (countries) are advised of the proposal and the reasons ("because the circle serves only one function, one that is easily administered by the Referee) and the Board will then meet on the change.

The Board, of course, carries a great responsibility. The Referees' Committee naturally performs much of their work by dispensing with proposals that have already failed, and which would have no chance of passing.

An Editorial Board also exists, one which aids in the precise phrasing of law changes. Ken Aston of England, noted Referee authority and former long-time FIFA representative on the International Board, feels that the Board functions well, though the British dominance may seem unfair to some individuals and countries. "The conservatism of the British toward the laws of soccer keep these laws from constantly changing. Wide-sweeping changes in the laws would bring confusion to those who write, those who teach, and to those who must abide by and enforce the laws," he declares.

It should be noted that FIFA does give permission to National Associations from time to time where an experiment in the laws is desired. For example, the North American Soccer League has been given permission to experiment with Law 11 (Off-Side). A line, 35 yards from, and parallel to each goal-line, defines an area in which players may be judged off-side, as opposed to a player's own half of the field.

Experiments with the laws of the game are authorized by FIFA only if first authorized by the International Board. Presently, FIFA has granted permission for experiments in the following areas: (1) the short, or mini-corner (taken at the intersection of the penalty-area line and goal-line); (2) kick-in instead of a throw-in (used in America in college play in the 1950's; and (3) temporary expulsion for certain misdemeanors which are normally punished with a caution.

XIV

The Laws of the Game

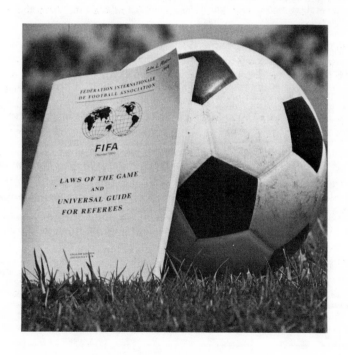

LAWS OF THE GAME

Laws of the Game	*Decisions of the International Board*

LAW I *(continued)*

(1) **Dimensions.** The field of play shall be rectangular, its length being not more than 130 yards nor less than 100 yards and its breadth not more than 100 yards nor less than 50 yards. (In International Matches the length shall be not more than 120 yards nor less than 110 yards and the breadth not more than 80 yards nor less than 70 yards.) The length shall in all cases exceed the breadth.

(2) **Marking.** The field of play shall be marked with distinctive lines, not more than 5 inches in width, not by a V-shaped rut, in accordance with the plan, the longer boundary lines being called the touch-lines and the shorter the goal-lines. A flag on a post not less than 5 ft. high and having a non-pointed top, shall be placed at each corner; a similar flag-post may be placed opposite the half-way line on each side of the field of play, not less than 1 yard outside the touch-line. A halfway-line shall be marked out across the field of play. The centre of the field of play shall be indicated by a suitable mark and a circle with a 10 yards radius shall be marked round it.

(3) **The Goal-Area.** At each end of the field of play two lines shall be drawn at right-angles to the goal-line, 6 yards from each goal-post. These shall extend into the field of play for a distance of 6 yards and shall be joined by a line drawn parallel with the goal-line. Each of the spaces enclosed by these lines and the goal-line shall be called a goal-area.

(4) **The Penalty-Area.** At each end of the field of play two lines shall be drawn at right-angles to the goal-line, 18 yards from each goal-post. These shall extend into the field of play for a distance of 18 yards and shall be joined by a line drawn parallel with the goal-line. Each of the spaces enclosed by these lines and the goal-line shall be called a penalty-area. A suitable mark shall be made within each penalty-area, 12 yards from the mid-point of the goal-line, measured along an undrawn line at right-angles thereto. These shall be the penalty-kick marks. From each penalty-kick mark an arc of a circle, having a radius of 10 yards, shall be drawn outside the penalty-area.

(1) In International matches the dimensions of the field of play shall be: maximum 110 x 75 metres; minimum 100 x 64 metres.

(2) National Associations must adhere strictly to these dimensions. Each National Association organising an International Match must advise the visiting Association, before the match, of the place and the dimensions of the field of play.

(3) The Board has approved this table of measurements for the Laws of the Game:

130 yards	.....	120 Metres
120 yards	.....	110
110 yards	.....	100
100 yards	.....	90
80 yards	.....	75
70 yards	.....	64
50 yards	.....	45
18 yards	.....	16.50
12 yards	.....	11
10 yards	.....	9.15
8 yards	.....	7.32
6 yards	.....	5.50
1 yard	.....	1
8 feet	.....	2.44
5 feet	.....	1.50
28 inches	.....	0.71
27 inches	.....	0.68
9 inches	.....	0.22
5 inches	.....	0.12
3/4 inch	.....	0.019
1/2 inch	.....	0.0127
3/8 inch	.....	0.010
14 ounces	.....	396 grams
16 ounces	.....	453 grams
15 lb./sq.in.	.....	1 kg/cm^2

(4) The goal-line shall be marked the same width as the depth of the goal-posts and the cross-bar, so that the goal-line and goal-posts will conform to the same interior and exterior edges.

(5) The 6 yards (for the outline of the goal-area) and the 18 yards (for the outline of the penalty-area) which have to be measured along the goal-line, must start from the inner sides of the goal-posts.

(6) The space within the inside areas of the field of play includes the width of the lines marking these areas.

(7) All Associations shall provide standard equipment, particularly in International Matches, when the Laws of the Game must be complied with in every respect and especially with regard to the size of the ball and other equipment which must conform to the regu-

-248-

— prohibit photographers from passing over these lines,

— forbid the use of artificial lighting in the form of "flashlights".

(1) The ball used in any match shall be considered the property of the Association or Club on whose ground the match is played, and at the close of play it must be returned to the Referee.

(2) The International Board, from time to time, shall decide what constitutes approved materials. Any approved material shall be certified as such by the International Board.

(3) The Board has approved these equivalents of the weights specified in the Law: 14 to 16 ounces = 396 to 453 grammes.

(4) If the ball bursts or becomes deflated during the course of a match, the game shall be stopped and restarted by dropping the new ball at the place where the first ball became defective.

(5) If this happens during a stoppage of the game (place-kick, goal-kick, corner-kick, free-kick, penalty-kick or throw-in) the game shall be restarted accordingly.

LAW II. – THE BALL

The ball shall be spherical; the outer casing shall be of leather or other approved materials. No material shall be used in its construction which might prove dangerous to the players.

The circumference of the ball shall not be more than 28 in. and not less than 27 in. The weight of the ball at the start of the game shall not be more than 16 oz. nor less than 14 oz. The pressure shall be equal to 0.6-0.7 atmosphere, which equals 9.0-10.5 lb./sq.in. (= 600-700 gr/cm^2) at sea level. The ball shall not be changed during the game unless authorised by the Referee.

LAW III. – NUMBER OF PLAYERS

(1) A match shall be played by two teams, each consisting of not more than eleven players, one of whom shall be the goalkeeper.

(2) Substitutes may be used in any match played under the rules of an official competition at FIFA, Confederation or National Association level, subject to the following conditions:

(a) that the authority of the international association(s) or national association(s) concerned, has been obtained,

(b) that, subject to the restriction contained in the following paragraph (c) the rules of a competition shall state how many, if any, substitutes may be used, and

(c) that a team shall not be permitted to use more than two substitutes in any match.

(3) Substitutes may be used in any other match, provided that the two teams concerned reach agreement on a maximum number, not exceeding five, and that the terms of such agreement are intimated to the Referee, before the match. If the Referee is not informed, or if the teams fail to

(1) The minimum number of players in a team is left to the discretion of National Associations.

(2) The Board is of the opinion that a match should not be considered valid if there are fewer than seven players in either of the teams.

(3) A competition may require that the referee shall be informed, before the start of the match, of the names of not more than five players, from whom the substitutes (if any) must be chosen.

(4) A player who has been ordered off before play begins may only be replaced by one of the named substitutes. The kick-off must not be delayed to allow the substitute to join his team.

A player who has been ordered off after play has started may not be replaced.

A named substitute who has been ordered off, either before or after play has started, may not be replaced (this decision only relates to players who are ordered off under Law XII. It does not apply to players who have infringed Law IV.)

reach agreement, no more than two substitutes shall be permitted.

(4) Any of the other players may change places with the goalkeeper, provided that the Referee is informed before the change is made, and provided also, that the change is made during a stoppage of the game.

(5) When a goalkeeper or any other player is to be replaced by a substitute, the following conditions shall be observed:

(a) the Referee shall be informed of the proposed substitution, before it is made,

(b) the substitute shall not enter the field of play until the player he is replacing has left, and then only after having received a signal from the Referee,

(c) he shall enter the field during a stoppage in the game, and at the half-way line.

(d) A player who has been replaced shall not take any further part in the game.

(e) A substitute shall be subject to the authority and jurisdiction of the Referee whether called upon to play or not.

Punishment:

(a) Play shall not be stopped for an infringement of paragraph 4. The players concerned shall be cautioned immediately the ball goes out of play.

(b) If a substitute enters the field of play without the authority of the Referee, play shall be stopped. The substitute shall be cautioned and removed from the field or sent off according to the circumstances. The game shall be restarted by the Referee dropping the ball at the place where it was when play was stopped.

(c) For any other infringement of this law, the player concerned shall be cautioned, and if the game is stopped by the Referee, to administer the caution, it shall be re-started by an indirect free-kick, to be taken by a player of the opposing team, from the place where the ball was, when play was stopped. If the free-kick is awarded to a team within its own goal area, it may be taken from any point within that half of the goal area in which the ball was when play was stopped.

Laws of the Game

LAW IV. – PLAYERS' EQUIPMENT

(1) A player shall not wear anything which is dangerous to another player.

(2) Footwear (boots or shoes) must conform to the following standard:

(a) Bars shall be made of leather or rubber and shall be transverse and flat, not less than half an inch in width and shall extend the total width of the sole and be rounded at the corners.

(b) Studs which are independently mounted on the sole and are replaceable shall be made of leather, rubber, aluminium, plastic or similar material and shall be solid. With the exception of that part of the stud forming the base, which shall not protrude from the sole more than one quarter of an inch, studs shall be round in plan and not less than half an inch in diameter. Where studs are tapered, the minimum diameter of any section of the stud must not be less than half an inch. Where metal seating for the screw type is used, this seating must be embedded in the sole of the footwear and any atachment screw shall be part of the stud. Other than the metal seating for the screw type of stud, no metal plates even though covered with leather or rubber shall be worn, neither studs which are threaded to allow them to be screwed on to a base screw that is fixed by nails or otherwise to the soles of footwear, nor studs which, apart from the base, have any form of protruding edge rim or relief marking or ornament, should be allowed.

(c) Studs which are moulded as an integral part of the sole and are not replaceable shall be made of rubber, plastic, polyurethene or similar soft materials. Provided that there are no fewer than ten studs on the sole, they shall have a minimum diameter of three eights of an inch (10 mm.). Additional supporting material to stabilise studs of soft materials, and ridges which shall not protrude more than 5 mm. from the sole and moulded to strengthen it, shall be permitted provided that they are in no way dangerous to other players. In all other respects they shall conform to the general requirements of this Law.

(d) Combined bars and studs may be worn, provided the whole conforms to the general requirements of this Law. Neither bars nor studs on the soles shall project more

Decisions of the International Board

(1) The usual equipment of a player is a jersey or shirt, shorts, stockings and footwear. In a match played under the rules of a competition, players need not wear boots or shoes, but shall wear jersey or shirt, shorts, or track suit or similar trousers, and stockings.

(2) The Law does not insist that boots or shoes must be worn. However, in competition matches Referees should not allow one or a few players to play without footwear when all the other players are so equipped.

(3) In International Matches, International Competitions, International Club Competitions and friendly matches between clubs of different National Associations, the Referee, prior to the start of the game, shall inspect the players' footwear, and prevent any player whose footwear does not conform to the requirements of this Law from playing until such time as it does comply.

The rules of any competition may include a similar provision.

(4) If the Referee finds that a player is wearing articles not permitted by the Laws and which may constitute a danger to other players, he shall order him to take them off. If he fails to carry out the Referee's instruction, the player shall not take part in the match.

(5) A player who has been prevented from taking part in the game or a player who has been sent off the field for infringing Law IV must report to the Referee during a stoppage of the game and may not enter or re-enter the field of play unless and until the Referee has satisfied himself that the player is no longer infringing Law IV.

(6) A player who has been prevented from taking part in a game or who has been sent off because of an infringement of Law IV, and who enters or re-enters the field of play to join or re-join his team, in breach of the conditions of Law XII, shall be cautioned. If the Referee stops the game to administer the caution, the game shall be restarted by an indirect free-kick, taken by a player of the opposing side, from the place where the ball was when the Referee stopped the game. If the free-kick is awarded to a team within its own goal area, it may be taken from any point within that half of the goal area in which the ball was when play was stopped.

LAW IV *(continued)*

than three-quarters of an inch. If nails are used they shall be driven in flush with the surface.

(3) The goalkeeper shall wear colours which distinguish him from the other players and from the referee.

Punishment: For any infringement of this Law, the player at fault shall be sent off the field of play to adjust his equipment and he shall not return without first reporting to the Referee, who shall satisfy himself that the player's equipment is in order; the player shall only re-enter the game at a moment when the ball has ceased to be in play.

LAW V. – REFEREES

A Referee shall be appointed to officiate in each game. His authority and the exercise of the powers granted to him by the Laws of the Game commence as soon as he enters the field of play.

His power of penalising shall extend to offences committed when play has been temporarily suspended, or when the ball is out of play. His decision on points of fact connected with the play shall be final, so far as the result of the game is concerned. He shall:

(a) Enforce the Laws.

(b) Refrain from penalising in cases where he is satisfied that, by doing so, he would be giving an advantage to the offending team.

(c) Keep a record of the game; act as timekeeper and allow the full or agreed time, adding thereto all time lost through accident or other cause.

(d) Have discretionary power to stop the game for any infringement of the Laws and to suspend or terminate the game whenever, by reason of the elements, interference by spectators, or other cause, he deems such stoppage necessary. In such a case he shall submit a detailed report to the competent authority, within the stipulated time, and in accordance with the provisions set up by the National Association under whose jurisdiction the match was played. Reports will be deemed to be made when received in the ordinary course of post.

(1) Referees in International Matches shall wear a blazer or blouse the colour of which is distinct from the colours worn by the contesting teams.

(2) Referees for International Matches will be selected from a neutral country unless the countries concerned agree to appoint their own officials.

(3) The Referee must be chosen from the official list of International Referees. This need not apply to Amateur and Youth International Matches.

(4) The Referee shall report to the appropriate authority misconduct or any misdemeanour on the part of spectators, officials, players, named substitutes or other persons which take place either on the field of play or in its vicinity at any time prior to, during, or after the match in question so that appropriate action can be taken by the Authority concerned.

(5) Linesmen are assistants of the Referee. In no case shall the Referee consider the intervention of a Linesman if he himself has seen the incident and from his position on the field, is better able to judge. With this reserve, and the Linesman neutral, the Referee can consider the intervention and if the information of the Linesman applies to that phase of the game immediately before the scoring of a goal, the Referee may act thereon and cancel the goal.

(6) The Referee, however, can only reverse his first decision so long as the game has not been restarted.

(e) From the time he enters the field of play, caution any player guilty of misconduct or ungentlemanly behaviour and, if he persists, suspend him from further participation in the game. In such cases the Referee shall send the name of the offender to the competent authority, within the stipulated time, and in accordance with the provisions set up by the National Association under whose jurisdiction the match was played. Reports will be deemed to be made when received in the ordinary course of post.

(f) Allow no person other than the players and linesmen to enter the field of play without his permission.

(g) Stop the game if, in his opinion, a player has been seriously injured; have the player removed as soon as possible from the field of play, and immediately resume the game. If a player is slightly injured, the game shall not be stopped until the ball has ceased to be in play. A player who is able to go to the touch or goal-line for attention of any kind, shall not be treated on the field of play.

(h) Send off the field of play, any player who, in his opinion, is guilty of violent conduct, serious foul play, or the use of foul or abusive language.

(i) Signal for recommencement of the game after all stoppages.

(j) Decide that the ball provided for a match meets with the requirements of Law II.

LAW VI. – LINESMEN

Two Linesmen shall be appointed, whose duty (subject to the decision of the Referee) shall be to indicate:

(a) when the ball is out of play,

(b) which side is entitled to a corner-kick, goal-kick or throw-in,

(c) when a substitution is desired.

They shall also assist the Referee to control the game in accordance with the Laws. In the event of undue interference or improper conduct by a Linesman, the Referee shall dispense with his services and arrange for a substitute to be appointed. (The matter shall be reported by the Referee to the competent authority.) The Linesmen should be equipped with flags by the Club on whose ground the match is played.

(7) If the Referee has decided to apply the advantage clause and to let the game proceed, he cannot revoke his decision if the presumed advantage has not been realised, even though he has not, by any gesture, indicated his decision. This does not exempt the offending player from being dealt with by the Referee.

(8) The Laws of the Game are intended to provide that games should be played with as little interference as possible, and in this view it is the duty of Referees to penalise only deliberate breaches of the Law. Constant whistling for trifling and doubtful breaches produces bad feeling and loss of temper on the part of the players and spoils the pleasure of spectators.

(9) By para. (d) of Law V the Referee is empowered to terminate a match in the event of grave disorder, but he has no power or right to decide, in such event, that either team is disqualified and thereby the loser of the match. He must send a detailed report to the proper authority who alone has power to deal further with this matter.

(10) If a player commits two infringements of a different nature at the same time, the Referee shall punish the more serious offence.

(11) It is the duty of the Referee to act upon the information of neutral Linesmen with regard to incidents that do not come under the personal notice of the Referee.

(12) The Referee shall not allow any person to enter the field until play has stopped, and only then, if he has given him a signal to do so, nor shall he allow coaching from the boundary lines.

(1) Linesmen, where neutral, shall draw the Referee's attention to any breach of the Laws of the Game of which they become aware if they consider that the Referee may not have seen it, but the Referee shall always be the judge of the decision to be taken.

(2) National Associations are advised to appoint official Referees of neutral nationality to act as Linesmen in International Matches.

(3) In International Matches Linesmen's flags shall be of a vivid colour, bright reds and yellows. Such flags are recommended for use in all other matches.

LAW VII. – DURATION OF THE GAME

The duration of the game shall be two equal periods of 45 minutes, unless otherwise mutually agreed upon, subject to the following: (a) Allowance shall be made in either period for all time lost through accident or other cause, the amount of which shall be a matter for the discretion of the Referee; (b) Time shall be extended to permit a penalty-kick being taken at or after the expiration of the normal period in either half.

At half-time the interval shall not exceed five minutes except by consent of the Referee.

(1) If a match has been stopped by the Referee, before the completion of the time specified in the rules, for any reason stated in Law V it must be replayed in full unless the rules of the competition concerned provide for the result of the match at the time of such stoppage to stand.

(2) Players have a right to an interval at half-time.

LAW VIII. – THE START OF PLAY

(a) **At the beginning of the game,** choice of ends and the kick-off shall be decided by the toss of a coin. The team winning the toss shall have the option of choice of ends or the kick-off. The Referee having given a signal, the game shall be started by a player taking a place-kick (i.e., a kick at the ball while it is stationary on the ground in the centre of the field of play) into his opponents' half of the field of play. Every player shall be in his own half of the field and every player of the team opposing that of the kicker shall remain not less than 10 yards from the ball until it is kicked-off; it shall not be deemed in play until it has travelled the distance of its own circumference. The kicker shall not play the ball a second time until it has been touched or played by another player.

(b) **After a goal has scored,** the game shall be restarted in like manner by a player of the team losing the goal.

(c) **After half-time;** when restarting after half-time, ends shall be changed and the kick-off shall be taken by a player of the opposite team to that of the player who started the game.

(1) If, when the Referee drops the ball, a player infringes any of the Laws before the ball has touched the ground, the player concerned shall be cautioned or sent off the field according to the seriousness of the offence, but a free-kick cannot be awarded to the opposing team because the ball was not in play at the time of the offence. The ball shall therefore be again dropped by the Referee.

(2) Kicking-off by persons other than the players competing in a match is prohibited.

Punishment. For any infringement of this Law, the kick-off shall be retaken, except in the case of the kicker playing the ball again before it has been touched or played by another player; for this offence, an indirect free-kick shall be taken by a player of the opposing team from the place where the infringement occurred, unless the offence is committed by a player in his opponents' goal area, in which case, the free-kick shall be taken from a point anywhere within that half of the goal area in which the offence occurred.

A goal shall not be scored direct from a kick-off.

(d) **After any other temporary suspension;** when restarting the game after a temporary suspension of play from any cause not mentioned elsewhere in these Laws, provided that immediately prior to the suspension the ball has not passed over the touch or goal-lines, the Referee shall drop the ball at the place where it was when play was suspended and it shall be deemed in play when it has touched the ground; if, however, it goes over the touch or goal-lines after it has been dropped by the Referee, but before it is touched by a player, the Referee shall again drop it. A player shall not play the ball until it has touched the ground. If this section of the Law is not complied with the Referee shall again drop the ball.

LAW IX. – BALL IN AND OUT OF PLAY

The ball is out of play:

(a) When it has wholly crossed the goal-line or touch-line, whether on the ground or in the air.

(b) When the game has been stopped by the Referee.

The ball is in play at all other times from the start of the match to the finish including:

(a) If it rebounds from a goal-post, cross-bar or corner-flag post into the field of play.

(b) If it rebounds off either the Referee or Linesmen when they are in the field of play.

(c) In the event of a supposed infringement of the Laws, until a decision is given.

(1) The lines belong to the areas of which they are the boundaries. In consequence, the touch-lines and the goal-lines belong to the field of play.

LAW X. – METHOD OF SCORING

Except as otherwise provided by these Laws, a goal is scored when the whole of the ball has passed over the goal-line, between the goal-posts and under the cross-bar, provided it has not been thrown, carried or intentionally propelled by hand or arm, by a player of the attacking side, except in the case of a goalkeeper, who is within his own penalty-area.

The team scoring the greater number of goals during a game shall be the winner; if no goals, or an equal number of goals are scored, the game shall be termed a "draw".

LAW XI. – OFF-SIDE

1. A player is in an off-side position if he is nearer to his opponents' goal-line than the ball, unless:
   (a) he is in his own half of the field of play, or
   (b) there are at least two of his opponents nearer their own goal-line than he is.
2. A player shall only be declared off-side and penalised for being in an off-side position, if, at the moment the ball touches, or is played by, one of his team, he is, in the opinion of the Referee
   (a) interfering with play or with an opponent, or
   (b) seeking to gain an advantage by being in that position.
3. A player shall not be declared off-side by the Referee
   (a) merely because of his being in an off-side position, or
   (b) if he receives the ball, direct, from a goal-kick, a corner-kick, a throw-in, or when it has been dropped by the Referee.
4. If a player is declared off-side, the Referee shall award an indirect free-kick, which shall be taken by a player of the opposing team from the place where the infringement occurred, unless the offence is committed by a player in his opponents' goal area, in which case, the free-kick shall be taken from a point anywhere within that half of the goal area in which the offence occurred.

(1) Law X defines the only method according to which a match is won or drawn; no variation whatsoever can be authorised.

(2) A goal cannot in any case be allowed if the ball has been prevented by some outside agent from passing over the goal-line. If this happens in the normal course of play, other than at the taking of a penalty-kick: the game must be stopped and restarted by the Referee dropping the ball at the place where the ball came into contact with the interference.

(3) If, when the ball is going into goal, a spectator enters the field before it passes wholly over the goal-line, and tries to prevent a score, a goal shall be allowed if the ball goes into goal unless the spectator has made contact with the ball or has interfered with play, in which case the Referee shall stop the game and restart it by dropping the ball at the place where the contact or interference occurred.

(1) Off-side shall not be judged at the moment the player in question receives the ball, but at the moment when the ball is passed to him by one of his own side. A player who is not in an off-side position when one of his colleagues passes the ball to him or takes a free-kick, does not therefore become off-side if he goes forward during the flight of the ball.

LAW XII. – FOULS AND MISCONDUCT

A player who intentionally commits any of the following nine offences:

(a) Kicks or attempts to kick an opponent;

(b) Trips an opponent, i.e., throwing or attempting to throw him by the use of the legs or by stooping in front of or behind him;

(c) Jumps at an opponent;

(d) Charges an opponent in a violent or dangerous manner;

(e) Charges an opponent from behind unless the latter is obstructing;

(f) Strikes or attempts to strike an opponent or spits at him;

(g) Holds an opponent;

(h) Pushes an opponent;

(i) Handles the ball, i.e., carries, strikes or propels the ball with his hand or arm. (This does not apply to the goalkeeper within his own penalty-area);

shall be penalised by the award of a **direct free-kick** to be taken by the opposing team from the place where the offence occurred, unless the offence is committed by a player in his opponents' goal area, in which case, the free-kick shall be taken from a point anywhere within that half of the goal area in which the offence occurred.

Should a player of the defending team intentionally commit one of the above nine offences within the penalty-area he shall be penalised by a **penalty-kick.**

A penalty-kick can be awarded irrespective of the position of the ball, if in play, at the time an offence within the penalty-area is committed.

A player committing any of the five following offences:

1. Playing in a manner considered by the Referee to be dangerous, e.g., attempting to kick the ball while held by the goalkeeper;

2. Charging fairly, i.e., with the shoulder, when the ball is not within playing distance of the players concerned and they are definitely not trying to play it;

3. When not playing the ball, intentionally obstructing an opponent, i.e., running between the opponent and the ball, or interposing the body so as to form an obstacle to an opponent;

(1) If the goalkeeper either intentionally strikes an opponent by throwing the ball vigorously at him or pushes him with the ball while holding it, the Referee shall award a penalty-kick, if the offence took place within the penalty-area.

(2) If a player deliberately turns his back to an opponent when he is about to be tackled, he may be charged but not in a dangerous manner.

(3) In case of body-contact in the goal-area between an attacking player and the opposing goalkeeper not in possession of the ball, the Referee, as sole judge of intention, shall stop the game if, in his opinion, the action of the attacking player was intentional, and award an indirect free-kick.

(4) If a player leans on the shoulders of another player of his own team in order to head the ball, the Referee shall stop the game, caution the player for ungentlemanly conduct and award an indirect free-kick to the opposing side.

(5) A player's obligation when joining or rejoining his team after the start of the match to 'report to the Referee' must be interpreted as meaning 'to draw the attention of the Referee from the touch-line'. The signal from the Referee shall be made by a definite gesture which makes the player understand that he may come into the field of play; it is not necessary for the Referee to wait until the game is stopped (this does not apply in respect of an infringement of Law IV), but the Referee is the sole judge of the moment in which he gives his signal of acknowledgement.

(6) The letter and spirit of Law XII do not oblige the Referee to stop a game to administer a caution. He may, if he chooses, apply the advantage. If he does apply the advantage, he shall caution the player when play stops.

(7) If a player covers up the ball without touching it in an endeavour not to have it played by an opponent, he obstructs but does not infringe Law XII para. 3 because he is already in possession of the ball and covers it for tactical reasons whilst the ball remains within playing distance. In fact, he is actually playing the ball and does not commit an infringement; in this case, the

LAW XII *(continued)*

4. Charging the goalkeeper except when he
   (a) is holding the ball;
   (b) is obstructing an opponent;
   (c) has passed outside his goal-area.
5. When playing as a goalkeeper and within his own penalty-area:
   (a) from the moment the ball comes under his control, he takes more than 4 steps without releasing the ball into play and having released it – he touches the ball again before it has been touched or played by another player, or
   (b) indulges in tactics which, in the opinion of the Referee, are designed merely to hold up the game and thus waste time and so give an unfair advantage to his own team

shall be penalised by the award of an **indirect free-kick** to be taken by the opposing team from the place where the infringement occurred, unless the offence is committed by a player in his opponents' goal area, in which case, the free-kick shall be taken from a point anywhere within that half of the goal area in which the offence occurred.

A player shall be **cautioned** if:

(j) he enters or re-enters the field of play to join or rejoin his team after the game has commenced, or leaves the field of play during the progress of the game (except through accident) without, in either case, first having received a signal from the Referee showing him that he may do so. If the Referee stops the game to administer the caution the game shall be restarted by an indirect free-kick taken by a player of the opposing team from the place where the ball was when the Referee stopped the game. If the free-kick is awarded to a team within its own goal area it may be taken from any point within the half of the goal area in which the ball was when play was stopped. If, however, the offending player has committed a more serious offence he shall be penalised according to that section of the law he infringed;

(k) he persistently infringes the Laws of the Game;

player may be charged because he is in fact playing the ball.

(8) If a player intentionally stretches his arms to obstruct an opponent and steps from one side to the other, moving his arms up and down to delay his opponent, forcing him to change course, but does not make "bodily contact" the Referee shall caution the player for ungentlemanly conduct and award an indirect free-kick.

(9) If a player intentionally obstructs the opposing goalkeeper, in an attempt to prevent him from putting the ball into play in accordance with Law XII, 5(a), the referee shall award an indirect free-kick.

(10) If after a Referee has awarded a free-kick a player protests violently by using abusive or foul language and is sent off the field, the free-kick should not be taken until the player has left the field.

(11) Any player, whether he is within or outside the field of play, whose conduct is ungentlemanly or violent, whether or not it is directed towards an opponent, a colleague, the Referee, a linesman or other person, or who uses foul or abusive language, is guilty of an offence, and shall be dealt with according to the nature of the offence committed.

(12) If, in the opinion of the Referee a goalkeeper intentionally lies on the ball longer than is necessary, he shall be penalised for ungentlemanly conduct and
(a) be cautioned and an indirect free-kick awarded to the opposing team;
(b) in case of repetition of the offence, be sent off the field.

(13) The offence of spitting at officials and other persons, or similar unseemly behaviour shall be considered as violent conduct within the meaning of section (n) of Law XII.

(14) If, when a Referee is about to caution a player, and before he has done so, the player commits another offence which merits a caution, the player shall be sent off the field of play.

LAW XII *(continued)*

(l) he shows by word or action, dissent from any decision given by the Referee;

(m) he is guilty of ungentlemanly conduct.

For any of these last three offences, in addition to the caution, an **indirect free-kick** shall also be awarded to the opposing team from the place where the offence occurred unless a more serious infringement of the Laws of the Game was committed. If the offence is committed by a player in his opponents' goal area, a free-kick shall be taken from a point anywhere within that half of the goal area in which the offence occurred.

A player shall be **sent off** the field of play, if, in the opinion of the Referee, he:—

(n) is guilty of **violent conduct** or serious foul play;

(o) uses foul or abusive language;

(p) persists in misconduct after having received a caution.

If play be stopped by reason of a player being ordered from the field for an offence without a separate breach of the Law having been committed, the game shall be resumed by an **indirect free-kick** awarded to the opposing team from the place where the infringement occurred, unless the offence is committed by a player in his opponents' goal area, in which case, the free-kick shall be taken from a point anywhere within that half of the goal area in which the offence occurred.

LAW XIII. – FREE-KICK

Free-kicks shall be classified under two headings: "Direct" (from which a goal can be scored direct against the offending side), and "Indirect" (from which a goal cannot be scored unless the ball has been played or touched by a player other than the kicker before passing through the goal).

When a player is taking a direct or an indirect free-kick inside his own penalty-area, all of the opposing players shall be at least ten yards (9.15 m) from the ball and shall remain outside the penalty-area until the ball has been kicked out of the area. The ball shall be in play immediately it has travelled the distance of its own circumference and is beyond the penalty-area. The goalkeeper shall not

receive the ball into his hands, in order that he may thereafter kick it into play. If the ball is not kicked direct into play, beyond the penalty-area, the kick shall be retaken.

When a player is taking a direct or an indirect free-kick outside his own penalty-area, all of the opposing players shall be at least ten yards from the ball, until it is in play, unless they are standing on their own goal-line, between the goal-posts. The ball shall be in play when it has travelled the distance of its own circumference.

If a player of the opposing side encroaches into the penalty-area, or within ten yards of the ball, as the case may be, before a free-kick is taken, the Referee shall delay the taking of the kick, until the Law is complied with.

The ball must be stationary when a free-kick is taken, and the kicker shall not play the ball a second time, until it has been touched or played by another player.

Notwithstanding any other reference in these Laws to the point from which a free-kick is to be taken, any free-kick awarded to the defending team, within its own goal area, may be taken from any point within that half of the goal area in which the free-kick has been awarded.

Punishment: If the kicker, after taking the free-kick, plays the ball a second time before it has been touched or played by another player an indirect free-kick shall be taken by a player of the opposing team from the spot where the infringement occurred, unless the offence is committed by a player in his opponents' goal area, in which case, the free-kick shall be taken from a point anywhere within that half of the goal area in which the offence occurred.

LAW XIV. – PENALTY-KICK

A penalty-kick shall be taken from the penalty-mark and, when it is being taken, all players with the exception of the player taking the kick, and the opposing goal-keeper, shall be within the field of play but outside the penalty-area, and at least 10 yards from the penalty-mark. The opposing goalkeeper must stand (without moving his feet) on his own goal-line, between the goal-posts, until the ball is kicked. The player taking the kick must kick the ball forward; he shall not play the ball a second time until it has been touched or played by another player. The ball shall be deemed in play directly it is kicked, i.e., when it has travelled the distance of its circumference, and a goal may be scored direct from such a penalty-kick. If the ball touches the goalkeeper before passing between the posts, when a penalty-kick is being taken at or after the expiration of half-time or full-time, it does not nullify a goal. If necessary, time of play shall be extended at half-time or full-time to allow a penalty-kick to be taken.

Punishment:

For any infringement of this Law:

(a) by the defending team, the kick shall be retaken if a goal has not resulted.

(1) In order to distinguish between a direct and an indirect free-kick, the Referee, when he awards an indirect free-kick, shall indicate accordingly by raising an arm above his head. He shall keep his arm in that position until the kick has been taken and retain the signal until the ball has been played or touched by another player or goes out of play.

(2) Players who do not retire to the proper distance when a free-kick is taken must be cautioned and on any repetition be ordered off. It is particularly requested of Referees that attempts to delay the taking of a free-kick by encroaching should be treated as serious misconduct.

(3) If, when a free-kick is being taken, any of the players dance about or gesticulate in a way calculated to distract their opponents, it shall be deemed ungentlemanly conduct for which the offender(s) shall be cautioned.

(1) When the Referee has awarded a penalty-kick, he shall not signal for it to be taken, until the players have taken up position in accordance with the Law.

(2) (a) If, after the kick has been taken, the ball is stopped in its course towards goal, by an outside agent, the kick shall be retaken.

(b) If, after the kick has been taken, the ball rebounds into play, from the goalkeeper, the cross-bar or a goal-post, and is then stopped in its course by an outside agent, the Referee shall stop play and restart it by dropping the ball at the place where it came into contact with the outside agent.

(3) (a) If, after having given the signal for a penalty-kick to be taken, the Referee sees that the goalkeeper is not in his right place on the goal-line, he shall, nevertheless, allow the kick to proceed. It shall be retaken, if a goal is not scored.

(b) If, after the Referee has given the signal for a penalty-kick to be taken, and before the ball has been kicked, the goal-keeper moves his feet, the Referee shall, nevertheless, allow the kick to proceed. It shall be retaken, if a goal is not scored.

Laws of the Game

(b) by the attacking team other than by the player taking the kick, if a goal is scored it shall be disallowed and the kick retaken.

(c) by the player taking the penalty-kick, committed after the ball is in play, a player of the opposing team shall take an indirect free-kick from the spot where the infringement occurred.

If, in the case of paragraph (c), the offence is committed by the player in his opponents' goal area, the free-kick shall be taken from a point anywhere within that half of the goal area in which the offence occurred.

Decisions of the International Board

(c) If, after the Referee has given the signal for a penalty-kick to be taken, and before the ball is in play, a player of the defending team encroaches into the penalty-area, or within ten yards of the penalty-mark, the Referee shall, nevertheless, allow the kick to proceed. It shall be retaken, if a goal is not scored.

The player concerned shall be cautioned.

(4) (a) If, when a penalty-kick is being taken, the player taking the kick is guilty of ungentlemanly conduct, the kick, if already taken, shall be retaken, if a goal is scored.

The player concerned shall be cautioned.

(b) If, after the referee has given the signal for a penalty-kick to be taken, and before the ball is in play, a colleague of the player taking the kick encroaches into the penalty-area or within ten yards of the penalty-mark, the Referee shall, nevertheless, allow the kick to proceed. If a goal is scored, it shall be disallowed, and the kick retaken.

The player concerned shall be cautioned.

(c) If, in the circumstances described in the foregoing paragraph, the ball rebounds into play from the goalkeeper, the crossbar or a goal-post, the Referee shall stop

the game, caution the player and award an indirect free-kick to the opposing team from the place where the infringement occurred.

Decisions of the International Board

(5) (a) If, after the referee has given the signal for a penalty-kick to be taken, and before the ball is in play, the goalkeeper moves from his position on the goal-line, or moves his feet, and a colleague of the kicker encroaches into the penalty-area or within 10 yards of the penalty-mark, the kick, if taken, shall be retaken.

The colleague of the kicker shall be cautioned.

(b) If, after the Referee has given the signal for a penalty-kick to be taken, and before the ball is in play, a player of each team encroaches into the penalty-area, or within 10 yards of the penalty-mark, the kick, if taken, shall be retaken.

The players concerned shall be cautioned.

(6) When a match is extended, at half-time or full-time, to allow a penalty-kick to be taken or retaken, the extension shall last until the moment that the penalty-kick has been completed, i.e. until the Referee has decided whether or not a goal is scored.

A goal is scored when the ball passes wholly over the goal-line.

(a) direct from the penalty-kick,

(b) having rebounded from either goalpost or the cross-bar, or

(c) having touched or been played by the goalkeeper.

The game shall terminate immediately the Referee has made his decision.

(7) When a penalty-kick is being taken in extended time:

(a) the provisions of all of the foregoing paragraphs, except paragraphs (2) (b) and (4) (c) shall apply in the usual way, and

(b) in the circumstances described in paragraphs (2) (b) and (4) (c) the game shall terminate immediately the ball rebounds from the goalkeeper, the cross-bar or the goalpost.

LAW XV. – THROW-IN

When the whole of the ball passes over a touch-line, either on the ground or in the air, it shall be thrown in from the point where it crossed the line, in any direction, by a player of the team opposite to that of the player who last touched it. The thrower at the moment of delivering the ball must face the field of play and part of each foot shall be either on the touch-line or on the ground outside the touch-line. The thrower shall use both hands and shall deliver the ball from behind and over his head. The ball shall be in play immediately it enters the field of play, but the thrower shall not again play the ball until it has been touched or played by another player. A goal shall not be scored direct from a throw-in.

Punishment:

(a) If the ball is improperly thrown in the throw-in shall be taken by a player of the opposing team.

(b) If the thrower plays the ball a second time before it has been touched or played by another player, an indirect free-kick shall be taken by a player of the opposing team from the place where the infringement occurred, unless the offence is committed by a player in his opponents' goal area, in which case, the free-kick shall be taken from a point anywhere within that half of the goal area in which the offence occurred.

LAW XVI. – GOAL-KICK

When the whole of the ball passes over the goal-line excluding that portion between the goal-posts, either in the air or on the ground, having last been played by one of the attacking team, it shall be kicked direct into play beyond the penalty-area from a point within that half of the goal-area nearest to where it crossed the line, by a player of the defending team. A goalkeeper shall not receive the ball into his hands from a goal-kick in order that he may thereafter kick it into play. If the ball is not kicked beyond the penalty-area, i.e., direct into play, the kick shall be retaken. The kicker shall not play the ball a second time until it has touched – or been played by – another player. A goal shall not be scored direct from such a kick. Players of the team opposing that of the player taking the goal-kick

(1) If a player taking a throw-in, plays the ball a second time by handling it within the field of play before it has been touched or played by another player, the Referee shall award a direct free-kick.

(2) A player taking a throw-in must face the field of play with some part of his body.

(3) If, when a throw-in is being taken, any of the opposing players dance about or gesticulate in a way calculated to distract or impede the thrower, it shall be deemed ungentlemanly conduct, for which the offender(s) shall be cautioned.

(1) When a goal-kick has been taken and the player who has kicked the ball touches it again before it has left the penalty-area, the kick has not been taken in accordance with the Law and must be retaken.

shall remain outside the penalty-area until the ball has been kicked out of the penalty-area.

Punishment: If a player taking a goal-kick plays the ball a second time after it has passed beyond the penalty-area, but before it has touched or been played by another player, an indirect free-kick shall be awarded to the opposing team, to be taken from the place where the infringement occurred, unless the offence is committed by a player in his opponents' goal area, in which case, the free-kick shall be taken from a point anywhere within that half of the goal area in which the offence occurred.

LAW XVII. – CORNER-KICK

When the whole of the ball passes over the goal-line, excluding that portion between the goal-posts, either in the air or on the ground, having last been played by one of the defending team, a member of the attacking team shall take a corner-kick, i.e., the whole of the ball shall be placed within the quarter circle at the nearest corner-flag-post, which must not be moved, and it shall be kicked from that position. A goal may be scored direct from such a kick. Players of the team opposing that of the player taking the corner-kick shall not approach within 10 yards of the ball until it is in play, i.e., it has travelled the distance of its own circumference, nor shall the kicker play the ball a second time until it has been touched or played by another player.

Punishment:

(a) If the player who takes the kick plays the ball a second time before it has been touched or played by another player, the Referee shall award an indirect free-kick to the opposing team, to be taken from the place where the infringement occurred, unless the offence is committed by a player in his opponents' goal area, in which case, the free-kick shall be taken from a point anywhere within that half of the goal area in which the offence occurred.

(b) For any other infringement the kick shall be retaken.

"I've got a pain in my appendices."

XV

Appendices

GLOSSARY, DEFINITIONS, AND TERMS

AYSO – The AmericanYouth Soccer Organization.

Bicycle-kick – See scissor-kick.

Bridging – Stooping in front or behind an opponent in an effort to gain an advantage, usually on a high ball.

Caution – An official disciplinary action by the Referee to a player who (a) persistently infringes on the Laws of the Game, (b) shows dissent by word or action from any decision given by the Referee, (c) is guilty of ungentlemanly conduct and (d) enters or leaves the field without the permission of the Referee.

Charging – Bodily contact, usually consisting of one shoulder against another shoulder. A charge may be fair or foul. See Section X, The Rules Almanac, Charging.

Club Linesman – A Linesman with a flag who has been appointed by the Referee to indicate out of bounds balls. He is usually a club official or supporter.

Continental Federations – There are six Continental Federations under the direction of FIFA. They are: (1) CONCACAF (Confereracion Norte-Centroamericana y del Caribe de Futbol); (2) Confederacion Sudamericana de Futbol (CONMEBOL) (SOUTH AMERICA); (3) Asian Footbal Confederation (ASIA); (4) Union of European Football Associations (UEFA) (Europe); (5) Oceania Football Confederation (OFC) (Oceania); (6) The African Football Confederation (AFRICA).

Dead Ball – The ball is dead whenever it is not in play. This occurs when the ball is outside of the field of play or due to any temporary suspension of the game due to an infringement of the rules or when the game is otherwise stopped by the Referee.

Deliberate foul (see intentional foul) – These two terms are often confused, and should not be carelessly bandied about by the Referee. A deliberate foul is more extreme, and more purposely planned, than an intentional foul. Deliberate handling of the ball (catching it as a defensive measure) for instance, is planned, against the spirit of the game, and should be dealt with by a caution for the first offense. Intentional handling (where the hand moves with intent toward, and has contact with the ball) should be called, but the player penalized without the caution.

Diagonal System – The internationally recognized system of game control, involving a Referee and two neutral Linesmen.

Direct Free-Kick – A free-kick awarded for an opponent's infraction. A goal may be scored directly into an opponent's goal.

Double-Kick – See Scissor-Kick.

Drop-Ball – A ball which is dropped on the field by the Referee after he has stopped the game due to an injury, foreign object on the field, or due to a similar circumstance when no breach of the laws has occurred.

Dual System of Control — The Two Referee System of Control, where two Referees with equal authority are on the field.

End-line — The entire goal-line from touch-line to touch-line.

FIFA — The Federation Internationale de Football Association, which is the international governing body of soccer. Address: FIFA, 11 Hitzigweg, 8032 Zurich, Switzerland.

Formations — The lining up of players into certain prescribed locations on the field, according to style of play and team objectives. The GK is not mentioned in formation discussions, for his is the only fixed position on the field. Players located immediately in front of the GK are listed first. The most common formations are 2-3-5, 4-2-4, and 4-3-3. Sometimes it helps if the Referee knows a team's basic formation, particularly with regard to judging the off-side.

Forwards — The front line of a team, usually consisting of an outside left and right (wings), inside left and right, and center forward.

Free-Kick — An unchallenged kick in any direction. It is awarded for an infringement by the opposing side.

Indirect . . . A goal may not be scored directly.

Direct . . . A goal may be scored directly into an opponent's goal.

Fullback — One of two players (normally) who are positioned in front of the goalkeeper.

GK — The goalkeeper.

Goal — (a) That area between the upright posts and under the cross-bar, (b) the two posts and the cross-bar themselves, (c) the unit of scoring. A ball passing completely over the goal-line and in the area termed "goal" is a "goal."

Goal-Kick — The kick that puts the ball in motion after it has gone behind the goal-line of the defense and was last touched by a member of the offensive team. A goal-kick is not in play until it has passed out of the penalty-area.

Goalkeeper (goalie) — Sometimes called "goaldie" by seven year olds just beginning soccer. The player who guards the goal. He may use his hands within his own penalty-area. He has all the privileges of every other player on the field, plus a few of his own.

Goal-Line — The end-lines (width of the field) which extend from touch-line to touch-line, passing directly under the cross-bars of the two goals.

Goal-Mouth — That area immediately in front of the goal.

Going Over the Ball — The practice of raising one's foot above and over the ball in such a manner that when the opponent attempts to kick the ball, he is likely to be cleated in the shin. This is dangerous play, and players should be cautioned.

Halfbacks — The middle line of a team. The first line of defense, or the second line of offense.

Halfway-Line — The line in the center of the field extending from touch-line to touch-line and dividing the field into two equal parts.

Hand-Ball — A ball touching the hand or arm of any player on any part of the field, with the exception of the goalkeeper within his own penalty-area. The player must have intentionally moved the hand toward the ball, or must have been carrying the hand or arm in an unnatural position in order for the "hands" to be called. (See section on women's soccer for exception.)

Hidden fouls — Those fouls that usually go undetected by the Referee, and are therefore unpunished. They are usually committed by experienced players and can cause unpleasant incidents in a game.

Hitch-kick — (See scissor-kick)

Holding — Grasping an opponent with any part of the hand or arm.

Hungarian Off-side — Fullbacks deliberately moving forward to put an opposing forward in an off-side position. This is legal.

IFK — Indirect Free-Kick.

Indirect Free-Kick — A free-kick awarded for an opponent's infraction. A goal may not be scored directly.

Inswinger — A term used in conjunction with a corner-kick which hooks in toward the goal. (See outswinger)

Intentional foul (see deliberate foul) — Intentional fouls are not always deliberate. In officiating a game, the Referee must judge the premeditation of the player. If a player willfully and repeatedly tries to gain an advantage by unfair means, then his acts are deliberate. However, if his violations are sporadic and generally non-disruptive to the continuance of the game without incident, his acts are to be judged intentional, and penalized, but not subject to disciplinary action.

'Keeper — The goalkeeper.

Kick-off — A kick at the center of the field at the start of each period and after each score.

Laws of Soccer — The rules of the game, as set down by FIFA, broken down into 17 laws.

Law 18 — An unwritten law sometimes used rather blatantly by Referees to justify any type of decision which deviates from the laws of soccer, international board rulings, or common interpretations. It should be viewed as a common sense law pertaining only to those aspects and situations of the game not previously documented.

Modified Diagonal System — A new system of game control which has won favor with many Referees, coaches, and players. It places three Referees on the field, each with a whistle. It is generally acknowledged that fewer fouls result from this system.

Neutral Linesman — A fully qualified Referee who is assigned to act as Linesman on the diagonal system of control.

Obstruction — The deliberate action of one player as he prevents another's movement on the field. It is sanctioned by an indirect free-kick. When the ball is within playing distance of the player who obstructs, the obstruction is legal.

Off-side — Being illegally in advance of the ball. The off-side law has remained unaltered since 1925 (except in the North American Soccer League).

Off-side Position — Being illegally in advance of the ball, but not sanctioned by the Referee. Usually, this is due to a player's not taking advantage of this off-side position.

Outswinger — A term used in conjunction with a corner-kick which hooks out and away from the goal toward the center of the field. (See also inswinger.)

Pass — To kick, head, or otherwise advance the ball deliberately to a teammate.

Penalty-Area — That 18 x 44 yard rectangular area in front of each goal, in which the goalkeeper may touch the ball. Any defensive action committed in this area which would have resulted in a direct free-kick if committed elsewhere results in a penalty-kick.

Penalty-Kick — An unchallenged kick taken by the offense from a spot or line 12 yards from the goal-line. The goalkeeper is the only defensive player allowed in the penalty-area until the ball has been put in play (traveled its circumference) by the kicker.

Pitch — The field of play.

Periods — The quarters or halves of a game.

Place-Kick — A kick at the ball while it is stationary and on the ground. All free-kicks, corner-kicks, goal-kicks, and kick-offs must be place-kicks.

Playing Distance — That distance between the player and the ball that would allow the player to reach out with a part of his body (usually his foot) and play the ball.

Pushing — Use of the hands to move an opponent. Resting a hand on an opponent is pushing.

Quarter Circle — The corner-area, from which corner-kicks are taken.

Referee — The appointed official in charge of a game. Notice that throughout this book the Referee begins with a capital "R." The capital "R" stands for Respect by players and Respect for players.

Reference System — An experimental system of officiating used in Russia with two Linesmen on one side of the field and the Referee on the other. (We're told it hasn't worked out!)

Sanctioned — Penalized.

Sandwiching — Two teammates converging on an opponent simultaneously. This type of "boxing in" is penalized with a direct free-kick, as it is regarded as holding.

Save — A move by the goalkeeper that prevents a score.

Scissor-Kick — A move whereby the kicker's feet leave the ground, causing his body to be parallel with the ground with his feet at a higher elevation than his head. The intent is to kick the ball over his head in a single motion. If the ball is within playing distance of an opponent, this attempt is dangerous play, and results in an indirect free-kick. This is true even if no contact was made with this opponent, even though the intent was to kick the ball. Also known as a bicycle-kick, hitch-kick, reverse-kick, and double-kick.

Senior Linesman — Designated by the Referee, the Linesman who will take over for the Referee if needed.

Senior Referee — The Referee in charge when the Dual (Two Referee System) is being employed. The identity of the Senior Referee should be known only to the two Referees, and this should be determined before game time.

Short Corner — Making a quick pass instead of a long cross toward the goal when taking a corner-kick.

Strikers — The two inside forwards in a 3-3/4 offense/defense.

Touch — That space outside of the field of play, separated from it by the touch-lines.

Touch-line — The side-lines traveling the length of the field on both sides of the field which extend from goal-line to goal-line.

Tripping — Intentionally throwing, or attempting to throw an opponent by use of the legs.

USSF — The United States Soccer Federation. The USSF, the governing body of soccer in the United States, is located at 350 Fifth Avenue, Room 4010, New York, N.Y. 10001.

Violent Conduct — Intentional rough play which should carry both technical and disciplinary sanctions at the same time.

Volley — To kick a ball before it bounces, as one does in tennis after having double-faulted.

Warning — A "soft caution" given by the Referee to a player who is guilty of some infringement of the laws. If the infringement is repeated, a caution usually results (yellow card).

Wings — The two outside players of the forward line.

Worrying the Goalkeeper — Interfering with the goalkeeper's progress by word or action, usually while he has possession of the ball. This is sanctioned by an indirect free-kick and a caution.

BIBLIOGRAPHY

1. Conklin, Hale. *Basic Referee Instruction Course (BRIC)*. A self-contained pre-recorded slide program designed for instructing the novice referee. 280 slides, 6 half-hour audio tapes, and printed script. Available only to American Youth Soccer Organization referees through AYSO.

2. Federation Internationale de Football Association. *Laws of the Game and Universal Guide for Referees*. Published annually, with up-to-date decisions of the International Board. Also available in French, Spanish, and German. The United States Soccer Federation now publishes its own version for the United States.

3. FIFA. *Signals by the Referee and Linesman*. 26 pp. Write for their latest price list.

4. Football Association, 22 Lancaster Gate, London W2. *F. A. Guide for Referees and Linesmen*. 75 pp. Covers many areas of Referee conduct and signaling, with many questions on the laws of the game, with diagrams. Published annually.

5. Gennrich, James. *Referee's Handbook for Youth Soccer*. 62 pp. Covers all aspects of how a referee is to do the job. Very thorough. Contact: 509 Laurel Drive, Thiensville, Wisconsin 53092.

6. *Handbook for Referee Instructors*, available through FIFA. Approved and recommended by the FIFA Referee's Committee. An excellent guide for referee instructors.

7. Harris, Larry. *FÚTBOL MEANS SOCCER, Easy Steps to Understanding the Game*. 160 pp. heavily illustrated. Teaches the laws painlessly and effectively, with some humor. An excellent device to bring you up to snuff. Soccer for Americans, Box 836, Manhattan Beach, California 90266.

8. Harris, Paul. *THE LITTLE BOOK OF SOCCER, Everyone's Illustrated Guide to the Laws of the Game*. 48 pp., 78 illustrations. The complete summary of what is important about the laws of the game. Very popular with newcomers and coaches. Available through Soccer for Americans, Box 836, Manhattan Beach, California 90266.

9. Jahn, Tom, and Arthur Mackenzie. *The Referee in Soccer*. A total referee instruction program, with instructor's manual, 127 slides, and student guide. Available through TOMAC Enterprises, Box 5108, Downey, California 90242.

10. Lover, Stanley. *Association Football Laws Illustrated*. Pelham Books, London, 1970. 128 pp. The excellent illustrations provide the graphic emphasis that is absent in so many books. Deals particularly well with Laws XI and XII, the most discussed laws in the game.

11. Maisner, Larry, and Bill Mason. *The Rules of Soccer: Simplified*. 12 pp. The essentials of the rules are summarized and made simple. An excellent handy companion for what is important. Available from Premart Sports, 1948 S. La Cienega Boulevard, Los Angeles, California 90034.

12. Mason, Bill. *Flip Charts for Referee Instruction*. Useful charts for classroom or small group discussion. Restarts, off-side, fouls and misconduct, and other major areas covered in all beginning courses. Available through the American Youth Soccer Organization.

13. National Collegiate Athletic Association *SOCCER GUIDE* (The Official Rulebook and Guide). Published annually by College Athletics Publishing Service, 349 East Thomas Road, Phoenix, Arizona.

14. National Federation of State High School Associations, 400 Leslie Street, Elgin, Illinois 60120. *Soccer Rules Book.* National Federation Edition. Complete rules, comments, interpretations, and suggestions for tournament progression. Published annually.

15. Paine, Reg. *The Referee's Quiz Book.* 93 pp. 1976 Pan Books, London. Many questions and answers on the laws of the game, presented in an interesting fashion.

16. *Referee Magazine.* Box 161, Franksville, Wisconsin 53126. Published monthly. If you study officiating in other sports, you'll do better at soccer.

17. Ridden, Ken. "Refereeing." A series of four instructional films, 25 minutes each. Available in film or cassette form (color). Write for information: Transatlantic Sports, 7112 Whetstone Road, Alexandria, Virginia 22306.

18. Rous, Sir Stanley, and Donald Ford. *A History of the Laws of Association Football.* Published by FIFA, 1974. Contains all you ever wanted to know about the history of the laws of the game but were afraid to ask.

19. Sellin, Eric. *The Inner Game of Soccer.* 1976, 343 pp. A conversational, incisive treatment of all aspects of refereeing including numerous comments on the laws. The serious referee should have a copy, as Sellin leaves no stone unturned. Available through the author, at 312 Kent Road, Bala-Cynwyd, Pennsylvania 19004.

20. United States of America Minisoccer Federation. *Laws of the game.* 5671 Oakgrove Avenue, Oakland, California 94618. Complete rules of the indoor game which is normally played on a basketball court-size area.

21. United States Soccer Federation. *Official Indoor Soccer Rules.* Published annually.

22. United States Soccer Federation. *Official Rule Book.* Available through USSF at 350 Fifth Avenue, Suite 4010, New York, NY 10001. Published annually for USSF affiliated competitions.

Now that you've been through it all, are you ready for this in your games?